WAR AND INTERNATIONAL JUSTICE
A KANTIAN PERSPECTIVE

BRIAN OREND

Wilfrid Laurier University Press

This book has been published with the help of a grant from the Social Sciences and Humanities Research Council of Canada. We acknowledge the financial support of the Government of Canada through the Book Publishing Industry Development Program for our publishing activities.

Canadian Cataloguing in Publication Data

Orend, Brian, 1971-
    War and international justice : a Kantian perspective

Includes bibliographical references and index.
ISBN 0-88920-337-7 (bound)

1. War—Moral and ethical aspects. 2. Just war doctrine. 3. Kant, Immanuel, 1724-1804—Contributions in just war doctrine. I. Title.

U22.O73 2000   172'.42   C99-931118-2

Copyright © 2000
Wilfrid Laurier University Press
Waterloo, Ontario, Canada   N2L 3C5

Cover design by Leslie Macredie. Cover photo by Kurt Lange.

The author and publisher wish to acknowledge the following journals in which material from this book, in revised format, has appeared or is forthcoming: *Canadian Journal of Law and Jurisprudence* for "Kant on International Law and Armed Conflict" (July 1998) and "Terminating War and Establishing Global Governance" (July 1999); *Dialogue* for "Evaluating Pacifism" (forthcoming, 2001); *Journal of the History of Philosophy* for "Kant's Just War Theory" (April 1999); *Journal of Philosophical Research* for "A Just War Critique of Realism and Pacifism" (forthcoming, winter 2000); *Journal of Social Philosophy* for "Jus Post Bellum" (forthcoming, spring 2000).

To the three women in my life:
 my mother, Mary Lou;
 my sister, Krista; and
 my fiancé, Jane

"The concept of freedom...is the keystone of the whole architecture of the system of practical reason..."
Immanuel Kant
Critique of Practical Reason

"Rich or poor, I shall be free. I shall not be free in this or that land, in this or that region. I shall be free everywhere on earth."
Jean Jacques Rousseau
Emile

Table of Contents

Acknowledgements

I owe many people many thanks with regard to this work. First, to all those at WLU Press, especially Sandra Woolfrey and Carroll Klein, for making it a reality. Thanks also to the Aid to Scholarly Publications Program of the Humanities and Social Sciences Federation of Canada for a subvention and for some very helpful anonymous reviews.

This work has its origins in my doctoral dissertation, defended one stressful morning in December 1997 at Columbia University in New York City. I would like to thank Columbia's Philosophy Department for the fantastic fellowship offer to study in that magical city, as well as the Social Sciences and Humanities Research Council of Canada for additional fellowship funding.

Particular thanks is due to the brilliant yet merciless members of my dissertation committee: Thomas Pogge; Bonnie Kent; Frances Kamm; David C. Johnston; and Jeremy Waldron. Special thanks to David for the "C.C." experience; to Bonnie for pushing me; and to Thomas, not only for showing me what political philosophy can be but for being the best of all possible mentors, and a friend.

A warm thank you must also be given to all my colleagues at the University of Waterloo. Not only have they provided me a friendly work atmosphere, many of them were formerly my professors: Bill Abbott; Jenny Ashworth; Andrew Cooper; Terry Downey; Rolf George; Geoffrey Hayes; Brian Hendley; Richard Holmes; Karin MacHardy; Jan Narveson; Joe Novak; Jim Van Evra; and Judy Wubnig. I must single out John English and thank him so much for all the friendship and opportunity he has given me over the years. Thanks also to Kurt Lange for permission to use the cover photograph.

Many people have read this work prior to publication. Their comments have always been provocative and critical, yet generous and constructive. I am indebted to them all; no writer gets anywhere without being scrutinized in this way. Most gratifying, perhaps, was their shared conviction of the importance and relevance of the subject matter, and thus on the need for serious reflection on the latest problems concerning warfare and the pursuit of international justice.

List of Abbreviations

In this work, I use a number of abbreviations in order to avoid repeating cumbersome phrases. They are defined thoroughly within the body of the text.

CI = Categorical Imperative
CP = Consequentialist form of Pacifism
DDE = Doctrine of Double Effect
DP = Deontological form of Pacifism
DR = Descriptive Realism
FPJ = Formal Principle of Justice (part of UPJ)
GA = General Assembly (of the UN)
ICJ = International Court of Justice (of the UN)
JAB = *Jus ad Bellum* (the justice of resorting to war)
JIB = *Jus in Bello* (the justice of conduct in war)
JPB = *Jus post Bellum* (justice after war)
JWT = Just War Theory
KI = Kantian Internationalism
KJWT = Kant's Just War Theory
MJ = Minimal Justice (criteria states must meet)
MPJ = Material Principle of Justice (part of UPJ)
MPR = Moral Prescriptive Realism (a kind of PR)
NP = Normative Principle regarding aggression
PMF = Permanent Military Force
PPR = Prudential Prescriptive Realism (a kind of PR)
PR = Prescriptive Realism
SC = Security Council (of the UN)
SD = State Duty
SDR = Strong Descriptive Realism (a kind of DR)
SFPJ = State-level Formal Principle of Justice (part of SUPJ)
SMPJ = State-level Material Principle of Justice (part of   SUPJ)
SMPR = Strong Moral Prescriptive Realism (a kind of MPR)
SPPR = Strong Prudential Prescriptive Realism (a kind of PPR)
SR = State Right
SUPJ = State-level Universal Principle of Justice
UDHR = Universal Declaration of Human Rights
UN = United Nations
UPJ = Universal Principle of Justice
WDR = Weak Descriptive Realism (a kind of DR)
WMPR = Weak Moral Prescriptive Realism (a kind of MPR)
WPPR = Weak Prudential Prescriptive Realism (a kind of PPR)

Introduction

Image: Through a lens that casts an eerie blue glow, one can make out a nondescript building. Simultaneously, it is in the middle of two things: a desert and the cross hairs of a jet pilot's scope. Seconds later, a streak from the side of the screen slams into the building, which erupts in an explosive cloud of dust.

Image: An enclosed marketplace on a Saturday morning in an atmospheric Central European town. People haggle over the price of vegetables. Seconds later, the camera gets slammed into the ground, causing the picture to cut out, and then reappear. The scene shifts: the missile has hit the market dead-on. Instead of haggling, there is screaming. Bright red blood drenches everything. Bodies have been blown apart. Survivors reach up in shocked desperation towards the camera.

Image: A central African village, surrounded by heat and lush foliage. A crowd of agitated villagers is chasing after something: it must be that handful of people at the bottom of the screen. Soon, the smaller group is surrounded by the villagers. The smaller group huddles together, backs touching, facing outwards, saying something very rapidly. Hands raise up. Knives, meat cleavers and machetes come down, hacking into forearms raised up in defence. Such shields are too soft; the small group is quickly and brutally butchered.

On front pages and nightly newscasts, war's ugly face seems ever present. Since the global Cold War between the superpowers collapsed in 1989-90, numerous regional "hot" wars have erupted and commanded public attention. These wars have seared into our collective consciousness some of the shattering images described above. The images themselves, respectively, depict recent television coverage of the Persian Gulf War, Bosnia and Rwanda.

Even a partial listing of recent wars is distressingly large: the Persian Gulf War (1991); the Bosnian civil war (1992-95); the Somalian intervention (1993); Russia's Chechnya campaign (1993-95, 1999-2000); the Rwandan civil war (1994-95); wars in the heart

---

Notes to the Introduction are on p. 11.

1

of Africa, like Zaire/Congo and Sierra Leone (1996-99); and the conflict over the Kosovo region in Serbia (1998-99).

The recent surge of armed conflict, accompanied by an onslaught of disturbing images, has revived great interest in questioning the ethics of war and peace. Can a thing as dark and dangerous as warfare ever be justified? Can the violence war unleashes ever be effectively contained? Can the horrors war produces ever be worth it? Why do we put people on trial for war crimes? Is war itself a crime? Are we fools to hope that, one day, we might live in a world without war?

This book seeks to offer coherent, substantive answers to many of these questions. It addresses the ethics of war and peace from the perspective of Kantianism. Not just any old "-ism," Kantianism is rooted in the comprehensive worldview articulated by the German philosopher Immanuel Kant (1724-1804). A foremost figure of the Enlightenment, Kant developed theories on the nature of human understanding and of moral obligation that have since propelled him, and his legacy, into the pantheon of world-historical intellectual achievement. More importantly, Kant was one of the first of the great philosophers to pay attention to the complex, and increasingly relevant, questions of international justice.

This book has two modest aims in connection with Kant and the ethics of war and peace. The first is to show that Kant has a compelling just war theory and to reveal its general structure and content. A just war theory, in general, is a system of ideas explaining when and how a state can behave morally when it comes to the beginning, middle and end of warfare. The second aim of this work is to show that a contemporary Kantian approach to the ethics of war and peace can build on the best of what Kant has to say without following him with regard to his deficiencies. The result, it will be argued, is a reasonable, principled and fresh perspective on the serious moral problems surrounding armed conflict in our time.

In part 1 of the work, the three chapters deal with the first task of interpreting Kant. The opening chapter offers a condensed characterization of Kant's basic moral and political presuppositions, both domestic and international. Such a characterization is the essential context within which his just war theory is developed. The second chapter will contend, against the traditional understanding of this matter, that Kant has a just war theory. Furthermore, it will show that this theory is comprehensive and suggestive, revealing a number of gaps in the theory offered by what we might call the Just War Tradition, composed of such thinkers as Augustine, Aquinas and Grotius.

The substance of chapters 1 and 2, therefore, will be that Kant has made an invaluable contribution to just war theory, a contribution that ought to be recognized in a way that has yet to gain widespread attention. His insights ought to be incorporated into any cogent contemporary account of the matter. But, in spite of the magnitude of Kant's achievement in this regard, admission must be made that his account suffers from a number of ambiguities, flaws and implausibilities. The task of chapter 3 will be to diagnose and evaluate such weaknesses and to suggest which errors a contemporary reconstruction, based on Kantian principles, ought to avoid. The chapter will close by enunciating ten general principles of Kant's which should constitute the foundation of contemporary Kantian internationalism. It will be argued that this contemporary Kantian internationalism is a deep and distinctive perspective on foreign affairs—one worthy of detailed study and attention.

Part 2 of the book contains four chapters. The first chapter, which is chapter 4 of the book, accomplishes two things: 1) it offers an understanding of the nature of human rights, upon which contemporary Kantian internationalism is based; and 2) it offers a condensed yet substantive conception of international justice in general, from a contemporary Kantian point of view. This conception builds on the account of the human rights of persons and extends to the international arena, in which the rights and duties of states are prominently in play. These offerings set the firm framework within which a contemporary Kantian just war theory can be fashioned.

Before any just war theory can be constructed, prominent alternatives to the theory must be explored and overturned. Chapter 5 focuses on this very important issue, undertaking a refutation of the theory's main rivals: realism, on the one hand, and pacifism on the other.

Having completed the negative task of refuting the alternatives, attention will be turned at last to the positive task of developing a contemporary Kantian just war theory. Chapter 6 begins this work by constructing particular norms of *jus ad bellum*, which concerns the justice of resorting to war in the first place. The principles will be carefully elucidated and applied to two real-world cases, namely, World War II and to a posited armed intervention in the Rwanda of 1994-95.

It must be noted that, following Kant himself, the main focus of this work is on *jus ad bellum* and *jus post bellum*. One of the great deficiencies of Kant's account is his relative neglect of *jus in bello*, which concerns the justice of conduct within war. Here he is vastly outdone by the efforts of the Just War Tradition and, indeed, such contemporary international laws of armed conflict as the Hague and Geneva Conventions. The Kantian tradition seems to have comparatively little to contribute in this regard.

The discernment of appropriate principles of *jus post bellum*, which concerns justice after war, will be the task of chapter 7. There is a division between short-term principles of *jus post bellum* (those with regard to the cessation of hostilities of a particular war) and long-term principles (those with regard to the progressive elimination of war in general). Kant deals with both, and so will this chapter. Emphasis will, however, be placed on the first, as it constitutes one of Kant's most original and important contributions to just war theory. Indeed, the principles discovered in conjunction with this first topic will be applied to the case of the 1991 Persian Gulf War. The second topic will not be ignored, however; particular consideration will be given to Kant's storied proposal of a cosmopolitan federation between nations.

A subsidiary task of this book is to show how the norms of contemporary Kantian just war theory, as structured above, stand vis-à-vis those of the positive laws of armed conflict. In terms of *jus ad bellum*, we will witness a fundamental convergence between the two, with contemporary Kantianism perhaps offering a wider and deeper account of the core concepts of human rights protection, self- and other-defence from aggression and pro-rights armed intervention in a non-aggressive country. But the story changes when we consider *jus post bellum*. Here the laws of armed conflict appear considerably outperformed by the Kantian tradition; and the argument will be made that they should be reformed in light of its normative power.

But why should attention be paid at all to what the positive laws of armed conflict include or omit? After all, is it not sufficient if states actually behave in accordance with the moral principles elucidated by the Kantian tradition, regardless of what the current law happens to suggest they do? The answer is at least two-fold. The first aspect is to point out that, even if the actual behaviour is the most important thing, we nevertheless still have law in this regard. And it seems compelling to contend that this law, if it is to have point and relevance, ought to reflect the best current moral understanding of these phenomena. This is especially clear when we note that states frequently consult international law when considering their options for action, and especially after the fact to justify their choices. The second aspect, by way of response, is that showing at least some concern for international law appears called for in light of Kant's oft-noted legal rigorism. Since the man himself was so utterly concerned with laws, rules and imperatives, it follows that some regard for evaluating what the laws of war are, and ought to be, is at least congenial as a subsidiary aspect of the main work.

What does this work, thusly organized, contribute to the state of the art on international justice and the ethics of war and peace?

Recent works by Kant scholars have tended to downplay Kant's *prescriptions* for international justice, and to focus instead on Kant's *descriptive* philosophy of history, in which perpetual peace is somehow seen as the inevitable end of the historical process. Michael Doyle's work has been especially influential with regard to this trend.[1] This work's emphasis is explicitly the other way around, seeking to return attention to some of the most controversial, and relevant, of Kant's thoughts on foreign affairs.

The consensus view of the relatively small number of scholars who *do* study Kant's prescriptions for international justice is an adamant denial that Kant has a just war theory. One of the main goals of this book is to show that this traditional view is wrong and can only be sustained by a selective reading of the relevant texts. Admittedly, there are a few scholars who *are* open to the notion that Kant has a just war theory.[2] But their work does not develop in detail Kant's wartime principles, much less compare them to those of the Just War Tradition. This work seeks to fill that glaring gap.

In terms of a contemporary Kantian understanding of just war theory, the work breaks new ground by offering a rigorous conception of what it means to be a Kantian with regard to international justice, and thus does not rely on the hand-waving so often present in such cases. The contemporary Kantian account is explicitly grounded in a substantive understanding of human rights and the need to protect them. This distinguishes it from rival contemporary just war doctrines, where only passing reference is made to human rights. Even Michael Walzer, arguably the greatest living just war theorist, admits that his account, though heavily reliant on human rights, does not offer a deep or substantive conception, much less a justification, of this crucially important notion.[3]

The work also seeks to add weight to the debate between just war theory and the rival doctrines of realism and pacifism by: 1) offering a much more complex and variegated conception of realism than is usual in the current just war literature; and 2) paying sustained attention to the claims of pacifism, and not simply relying on one or two well-worn arguments against it, such as that it constitutes an indefensible "clean hands" policy.

In terms of the development of norms of *jus ad bellum* and *jus post bellum*, a number of innovations in the principles are recommended and they are applied, in a fresh fashion, to such recent real-world cases as the Persian Gulf War and Rwanda. Thought-experiment cases are also employed. The aim here is thus not merely to formulate an abstract set of imperatives but also to see how such imperatives might have concrete relevance in our world.

In terms of recommendations for the reform of the positive international laws of armed conflict, the account of short-term *jus post bellum* principles constitutes an important source for reflection on the current law of the cessation of hostilities. This law is almost entirely formal and procedural, centring on processes of surrender and on proclaiming and enforcing peace treaties. Almost no substantive legal constraints are currently placed upon the victor(s), and the contemporary Kantian account suggests that such a state of affairs ought to be revised.

Perhaps three broad aspects of this work require mention before proceeding into its body. The first point, a qualification, is that this book relies mostly on the relevant English literature, though it does draw nourishment from some important German and French sources. This emphasis arises from the fact that most of the recent relevant works on this issue of Kant and warfare have been offered by English-speaking scholars, or by German scholars writing in English. This work thus seeks to contribute to the continuing renaissance of interest, in English-speaking circles, in Kant's political philosophy.

The second point, a clarification, concerns the identity conditions of this work's main subject matter: war. One often hears, in debates about the ethics of war and peace, the forceful pronouncement that: "War is war!" People who say such things clearly believe they are making an important and powerful argument whereas other people wonder what such a redundant statement is supposed to be conveying. In order to avoid such awkwardness, war here requires something of a working definition.

Unless otherwise stated, war is to be understood in this work as actual, intentional and widespread armed conflict between political communities. Thus, fisticuffs between individual persons do not count as a war, nor does a gang fight, nor does a feud on the order of the Hatfields versus the McCoys. War is a phenomenon that occurs only between political communities, defined as those entities which either are states or intend to become states (in order to allow for civil war). Similarly, the mere threat of war and the presence of mutual disdain between these communities do not suffice as indicators of war. The conflict of arms must be actual and not merely latent. Further, the actual armed conflict must be both intentional and widespread: isolated clashes between rogue officers, or border patrols, do not count as actions of war. The onset of war requires a conscious commitment, and a significant mobilization, on the part of the belligerents in question.

Perhaps it would be apposite at this point to cite, by way of support, the views of the one and only (so-called) "philosopher of war," Carl von Clausewitz. Clausewitz famously suggested that war is the continuation of policy by other means. And surely, as a description, this conception is both powerful and plausible. It fits in nicely with his own general definition of war as "an act of violence intended to compel our opponent to fulfil our will." War, he says, is like a duel, but on "an extensive scale."[4]

As Michael Gelven has written recently, in an elegant monograph on how we ought to conceive of the essence of war, war is intrinsically vast, communal (or political) and violent.[5] It is a widespread and deliberate armed conflict between political communities. It is the entity or phenomenon falling under such a description that is the primary focus of this contribution to just war theory.

The third and final point, a disclaimer, concerns a number of clichés about just war theory. Many theorists are inclined to refer to such a theory either while holding their noses or while looking down them with regal disdain. For example, I recently heard a respected moral philosopher refer to just war theory as "the last refuge of scoundrels." There is, so to speak, a certain smell about just war theory that any defender of it must deal with, even prior to enunciating anything substantive. Three of the most commonly held beliefs of these skeptics, in this regard, are: 1) that just war theory is irredeemably tainted by its origins in Catholic doctrine; 2) that just war theory is dated and irrelevant; and 3) that just war theory is so liable to abuse as to be nothing more than a cloak with which to hide, or even justify, the commission of great evils, and by no less dubious an institution than the modern nation-state.

This work will show that none of these common criticisms of just war theory hold in the Kantian case. With regard to the first cliché, for instance, Kantian just war theory is explicitly secular in its normative moorings and thus does not fall prey to objections with regard to its source being excessively exclusionary and implausible.

With regard to the second cliché, it is thought that just war theory is irrelevant in two senses: 1) because of the onset of the nuclear era; and 2) because it is said to be applicable only to interstate wars, which are increasingly infrequent. For example, it is sometimes claimed that most future wars will be either civil wars within states or guerilla wars between established states and nomadic terrorist organizations.

Just war theory, however, remains highly relevant and applicable to anyone concerned about the momentous moral issues raised by the problem of war. The onset of the nuclear era, for one, did not alter this: indeed, the use of nuclear weapons can itself be critically evaluated according to just war norms. Besides, the radical bipolarity and nuclear brinkmanship of the Cold War increasingly seem to have been very artificial exceptions, and not the norm, when it comes to the history of hostility between nations. Since the Cold War's end in 1989-90, the most recent wars—many of them listed previously—have been fought with conventional weapons and tactics. And these are precisely the kinds of conflict that just war theory was first constructed to deal with.

With regard to the terrorist objection, it should be noted that interstate armed conflict has hardly gone the way of the dinosaur. Consider the Persian Gulf War of 1991 and the multistate war raging in the heart of Africa—Zaire/Congo—in 1998/99. Second, terrorists are not literally nomads: they enjoy the protection (either tacit or explicit) of many of the states they inhabit. Libya, Afghanistan and Iran, for example, are thought to sponsor many radical terrorist groups. As well, intrastate civil wars are still fought in what we might call a state-laden context: they are fought either over which group gets to control the existing state or over which group gets to have a new state. Thus, there are always state-to-state issues involved in contemporary armed conflict, even civil wars and terrorism. Finally, the norms of just war theory—as we will see—are sufficiently flexible to apply in a meaningful way whenever political violence is employed. Just war theory's relevance is by no means confined to a dated, Eurocentric model of states struggling, in "the concert of nations," to maintain the balance of power.

In terms of responding to the third just war cliché, Kantian just war theory is emphatically public and universal with regard to its permissions and prohibitions. States are not simply entitled to assert that they have just war theory on their side and expect to have such claims accepted at face value; rather, all such assertions are open to critical scrutiny in light of accessible evidence and a common order of moral reasoning and discourse. Just war theory, as such, cloaks nothing; to the contrary, its main purpose is to facilitate a more insightful and targeted reflection upon the justice of the resort to war, conduct within it and its process of termination.

That being said, it needs to be admitted that just war theory remains, if not smelly, then at least slippery, business. The manifold theoretical complications will quickly become evident: so many concepts and variables, so many events and entities, so many facts and values, come together under its auspices. Just war theory is a crucible in which a great number of diverse objects boil and bubble, combine and conflict. It is difficult to keep track of all things relevant, much less offer a comprehensive and coherent normative theory about them. And yet the issues dealt with in this heated and puzzling mixture are clearly of enormous practical import in our world, at least for the foreseeable future.

The brutal truth is that there is no imminent solution to the problem of war: wars are being fought and will continue to be fought for some time, leaving death and destruction in their wake. So we need just war theory to evaluate war, but the theory itself is pulled in two directions: on the one hand, towards greater theoretical substance, depth, sophistication, consistency and completion; and, on the other, towards messy, manifold, real-world cases where its pronouncements, if adhered to, will make all the difference to vulnerable human beings caught amidst the gruesome dangers of war.

My own view is that, in light of such tension between the desires for theoretical satisfaction and practical application, we have not even begun to glimpse what a complete just war theory might entail. Even Walzer's efforts, and those of the Tradition itself, fall short. We cannot rest content with the state of the art; it is, at the very least, incomplete. Complacency, which has reared its ugly head too often in the course of the theory's history, is indefensible. Perfunctory explanations of the same old just war categories simply will not suffice. Struggle must be made to improve and move the discussion forward. But perhaps the best that can be hoped for during such struggle, at least in the near future, is a "minimally adequate theory" that can be of some practical service and application.[6]

Such a minimally adequate theory will need to make some simplifying assumptions, will not be able to defend all its claims down to their deepest levels and can only be applied to a select set of cases, conveniently tailored. The account offered in this work can promise no more than to make a serious and sustained attempt at devising one version, Kantian in nature, of such a more modestly conceived approach to international justice and the ethics of war and peace.

The ultimate goal, then, is to come up with a reasonable reconstruction of a Kantian understanding of just war theory. Its culmination will occur with the development of a comprehensive set of general rules of conduct to guide states and peoples when they face the momentous problem of war. Its function will be to help control and limit warfare so that the brutal images of total war, such as those which began our account, will happen less and less frequently. Its point will be to defend those principles of justice required for a more peaceful world.

Notes

1. M. Doyle, "Kant, Liberal Legacies and Foreign Affairs," Parts 1 and 2, *Philosophy and Public Affairs* (1984): 204-35 and 323-53, respectively.
2. These would include Georg Cavallar, Pierre Laberge, Leslie Mulholland and Thomas Mertens. Their works will be referred to in chapter 2.
3. M. Walzer, *Just and Unjust Wars* (New York: Basic Books, 2nd ed., 1991), xxx.
4. Carl von Clausewitz, *On War,* trans. by A. Rapoport (Harmondsworth, England: Penguin, 1995), 100-102.
5. M. Gelven, *War and Existence* (Philadelphia, PA: Penn State University Press, 1994), passim.
6. I owe this phrase to Bonnie Kent of Columbia University's Philosophy Department.

PART ONE

Kant's Just War Theory

CHAPTER 1

Kant's Context

Introduction

In recent years, there has been tremendous interest in the contributions of Immanuel Kant to ongoing debates about the appropriate nature of international justice and law. The end of the Cold War, for example, seemed to bring with it promises of greater international cooperation of the kind envisaged by Kant. Furthermore, those interested in the more explicitly moral aspects and potentialities of international law, such as those regarding human rights protection, have looked to Kant for comfort and inspiration in the face of strong pressures from doctrines dismissive of such aspects, such as the statist strictures of realpolitik.[1]

There has, however, been widespread scholarly disagreement over Kant's precise legacy in this regard: some, for instance, have found in Kant's international writings a harbinger of world government while others have criticized Kant for failing to specify any concrete powers for his fabled cosmopolitan federation; some have accused Kant of sacrificing his exalted moral principles

Notes to chapter 1 are on pp. 34–40

on the dubious altar of state-centred expediency while others dismiss Kant as one of the most naively optimistic, and hopelessly moralistic, international thinkers ever; and, finally, some have accused Kant of glorifying the resort to warfare while others insist that Kant actually advocated "an extreme pacifism."[2] There is, in short, a ferocious and complex debate regarding which set of ideas can properly be called the "Kantian" view of these foremost issues of international law and moral theory and what, if any, value can be attached to it.

This first part of the book will offer a consistent, thorough and well-grounded interpretation of Kant's views on international justice and law in general, and of armed conflict in particular, by way of resolving these manifold scholarly controversies. The main contributions of this first part will be: 1) a succinct yet comprehensive and accurate reconstruction of the basic principles of Kant's practical philosophy, in both its domestic and international contexts; 2) proof that Kant has a just war theory—and a compelling one, at that—to guide the construction of the laws of war; 3) a rigorous conception of what counts as a Kantian perspective on these matters; and 4) a demonstration of the manifest relevance, to contemporary issues, that Kant's theory has to offer.

Groundwork to Kant's Internationalism: The Core Principles of Kant's Practical Philosophy

Kant's Theory of Morality

All of Kant's writings about morality and justice are grounded in a conception of human nature as being split between "free rationality and animal instinctuality," with rationality taking pride of place as our most deep and distinctive sense of identity and interest. Kant stipulates that, regardless of the base inclinations of our animal natures, we are to adhere to the dictates of reason itself. We must, above all, remain true to our most profound identity as rational agents.[3]

Reason, as Kant conceives it, is intrinsically normative of our speculations, of our understanding, and of our will. Its central function is to provide us with orientation and direction in our lives. Kant proclaims that reason provides us with ends proper to our deepest nature as rational beings and it also provides us with an ordered and coherent set of directives to employ as means to those ends. The most general of the ends of reason are: 1) formally, to enhance its own internal coherence and unity; and 2) materially, to promote its own realization in the external world.[4]

It is crucial to note that, for Kant, reason is a unified totality—as just described—organized into a hierarchy of parts. In particular, it is essential to note that, for Kant, practical reason is foremost in priority, ranking over both the theoretical and speculative uses of reason. Practical reason is that aspect of our reason normative of our will, i.e., of how we ought to act, and intend to act, vis-à-vis ourselves and others. The notion that practical reason has priority claim on our attention and effort reflects Kant's foundational conviction that moral progress is our most fundamental charge and duty. Here he echoes Jean Jacques Rousseau's dictum that scientific and technological achievement is idle without the development of a more humane and just set of relations between human beings. Kant even contends that the growth and spread of morality not only gives meaning to our lives but, moreover, serves as the very purpose of existence itself. It follows from the above that the foremost material end of reason is the progressive development of morality and justice.[5]

The means we are to employ in pursuit of this end are the formulations of the categorical imperative, the foremost norm of practical reason. Adherence to the dictates of the categorical imperative, in both intention and action, is constitutive of progress towards morality and justice in our world. But what is this categorical imperative? The categorical imperative is a command of reason that is not hypothetical. A hypothetical imperative stipulates the adoption of certain intentions and actions in order to meet ends that are already desired. A hypothetical imperative is thus conditional on the agent's desiring the end in question. The categorical imperative, by contrast, is thought to be unconditional: it stipulates the adoption of certain intentions and actions, regardless of whether or not the agent desires to conform to them. It is the purest expression of our deepest rational selves and must thus be followed, even if it is at odds with what our desires incline us to do. The categorical imperative thus constitutes the moral law to which all free and rational beings are duty-bound, as a command of their own deepest natures.[6]

Kant offers five formulations of the categorical imperative, stipulating controversially that "they are all at bottom ... precisely the same law."[7] When one views these five formulations as a unified whole, the categorical imperative mandates that one's actions: 1) be universally permissible; and 2) be respectful of the dignity of the human person. Thus, when agent A contemplates the taking of action T, A must consider: 1) whether the principle or maxim behind T is such that every rational agent could also endorse it without contradiction; and 2) whether T and its maxim respect the dignity and humanity of all rational persons. Only if both 1 and 2 are satisfied is it morally permissible for A to do T.

Leading Kant scholars—like Onora O'Neill, Christine Korsgaard and Thomas Pogge—concur that the categorical imperative, above all, is designed to secure universal respect for rational agency, which refers to each person's free capacity to choose between different ends of action and to be held responsible for the calibre of those choices. Our most pressing moral duty for Kant is to uphold and enhance, wherever possible, the autonomous capacity of each person to make rational choices between competing ends of action. Kant believes that when persons actualize that capacity, and act freely on their own rational choices, they thereby confer value on the world. Kant himself pronounces that freedom is the very "keystone" of the architecture of his practical philosophy.[8]

Why does Kant focus on rational agency, on the autonomy of individual choice and self-direction? The answer is that rational agency is a necessary condition for the moral progress Kant sees as the ultimate purpose of our lives and our world. For Kant, only a free and rational will can become one that is morally good. We cannot prescribe that a will be morally good; rather, that prescription, if it is to have genuine value, must come from nowhere else than that will itself. A morally good will is one that makes a free rational choice to adhere to the categorical imperative of practical reason; a good person is one who, even in the face of countervailing pressures and temptations, deliberately decides to stay true to his own deepest self. A good person acts from his own motivation on his own deepest rational principles.[9] So the foremost duty of morality (indeed, of reason itself) is to preserve, protect and enhance each free and rational agent—because it is only through free rational agency that our lives, and the world itself, come to have any value at all. As Kant declares grandly: "[T]he duration of the world has worth only insofar as the ultimate ends of the existence of rational beings can be met within it."[10]

Kant's general conception of morality, thusly construed, is often characterized as being deontological or non-consequential-ist. This attitude is clearly displayed in such lines as: "What is essentially good in the action consists in the mental disposition, let the consequences be what they may."[11] But what exactly does Kant mean in this regard? Kant seems to mean that, fundamentally, moral goodness is not a matter of maximizing best conse-quences in the world; rather, it is a matter of: 1) having the proper intention for action, namely, respect for the categorical imperative legislated by one's own practical reason; and 2) conscientiously making serious efforts to realize this intention through action.

It must be admitted and stressed, however, that sharp distinc-tions between deontology and consequentialism are notoriously difficult to sustain. Recent Kant revisionists have even spoken of a "Kantian consequentialism."[12] There can, indeed, be no doubt that Kant, despite his more extreme protestations, does pay some moral attention to consequences. He is, for example, greatly concerned about the growth, development and flourishing of morally good will. He is anxious for the spread of rational enlight-enment and emancipation, and even measures the value of human existence based on its presence. We shall see similar allu-sions to consequentialist modes of thought further on in the development of Kant's political philosophy.

At the same time, it is clear that the standard reading of Kant as a deontologist retains considerable plausibility. Kant's general moral vision is deontological in at least four senses. The first is that duty *(deon)* is the central concept in Kant's moral philosophy. We all must do our duty for its own sake—i.e., we all must adhere to the categorical imperative for no other reason than respect for its status as the foremost command of our rational natures. The second sense is that Kant deems it at least permissible (perhaps even obligatory) for an agent *not* to intend, and/or to act so as, to maximize overall best consequences. The third sense in which

Kant is a deontologist is that he understands a world in which duty is done as one in which rational agents are worth more— have more dignity and status—than in an alternative world in which rational agents are used as mere tools to produce best consequences overall. Finally, Kant is a deontologist because he stipulates firm limits, or side-constraints, on the promotion of ends, such as maximizing overall best consequences.[13]

It seems that this last criterion is one of the clearest distinguishing marks, if such there be, between deontology and consequentialism. Consequentialism, of course, is end-focused; in the case of utilitarianism, the focus is on maximizing the greatest happiness for the greatest number. The only constraints on action that consequentialism acknowledges are those that themselves contribute to the desired end in question. If the constraints interfere with the achievement of the ends, they are to be disregarded. Deontology, by contrast, stipulates the existence of side-constraints on action that need not themselves contribute in any way to the desired end in question, such as maximizing happiness. Kant, for example, stipulates as a side-constraint the principle that persons be treated as ends-in-themselves and not as means to some further end, such as political expediency. The rule of respecting and protecting rational agency looms large as *the* Kantian side-constraint with regard to how we may treat others and what ends we ourselves may pursue. May such a side-constraint plausibly be redescribed as a contributor to some further consequence? Perhaps—but here such a redescription seems much harder to make, at least in the case of Kant. For he stipulates that we are to respect free rational agency, even if such agency fails to be exercised in such a way as to further the growth and spread of morally good will, which is (so to speak) his preferred consequence. This is to say that the constraint on action exists regardless of whether or not it contributes materially to the desired end in question. The constraint exists simply because our deepest selves demand it. The conclusion seems to be that the side-constraints on action proposed by Kant appear to have a different and much firmer ground than those which may be postulated by overt forms of consequentialism. The grounding of the Kantian rules in a conception of rational duty, in short, imbues them with a much greater degree of inviolability than those norms acknowledged only for the sake of how well they contribute to best overall consequences. Our duty centrally involves respecting everyone's free rational agency, even if in doing so the world does not come to be as well off, good or happy as it might otherwise be.[14]

Kant's Theory of Domestic Justice

Kant's theory of justice is a subset of this general conception of morality. The sphere of justice, for Kant, is the sphere of "external" action, as opposed to "internal" intention: it has to do with how rational persons ought to interact with and treat each other. We saw above that the foremost norm of morality in general is to respect, preserve and enhance each rational agent. Kant points out that such respect and preservation, when it comes to creatures like us, involves more than merely having the proper internal intention towards human dignity and rational agency. This is the case because the free exercise of rational agency, in our world, can be seriously threatened and endangered, for instance through fraud, intimidation, coercion and violence. Thus, in the external sphere of interpersonal interaction, rational agency requires protection. But how to protect agency from such force and fraud in an effective and broadly based manner? Kant's answer is a public, universal system of positive law and order which can employ coercion on behalf of rational agency against those rogue parties that threaten it. Justice is thus, for Kant, the authorization to use coercion in defence of anyone's, indeed everyone's, free rational agency. Kant's universal principle of *Recht*, or justice (UPJ), is thus: "Act externally in such a way that the free use of your will is compatible with the freedom of everyone according to a universal law."[15]

Everyone, in other words, is to be free *from* force and fraud and to be free *to* order their personal conduct as they best see fit within a protected space that is equal to, and consistent with, such a space for all others. A just society's system of law and order must be based on this UPJ, which we might think of as an "externalized" version of the categorical imperative itself: i.e., *as* the categorical imperative, applied to the external sphere of interpersonal interaction involving the use of force. The UPJ is to be our guide, our foremost source of orientation and direction, when it comes to devising, and/or reforming, a system of positive laws that aims to regulate through force our external relations.

We might, in seeking greater specificity, follow the lead of Pogge and break down the UPJ into the following component principles: 1) the Formal Principle of Justice (FPJ): all rational beings ought to co-exist under a coherent, ordered and determinate system of positive laws; 2) the first Material Principle of Justice (MPJ 1): the content of such a system of laws must be aimed, first and foremost, at protecting and enhancing the agency of every rational being; and 3) the second Material Principle of Justice (MPJ 2): above and beyond MPJ 1, the system of positive laws is to promote the advance of practical reason and morally good will.[16]

It is of the utmost importance to note that, in terms of FPJ-MPJ 2, there is a tension between priority and justification. Kant explicitly stipulates that FPJ has priority claim on our attention over MPJ 1 and MPJ 2. This is to say, in Kant's words, that it is "the foremost duty of justice" to found a determinate system of law and order for all.[17] However, FPJ is justified only to the extent to which it contributes to MPJ 1 and 2, namely, to the protection of rational agency and the flourishing of enlightenment and emancipation. The point of a just legal system for Kant is to make the world safe for the growth of morality and good will. This tension between priority and justification within the UPJ produces a marked political tension between what we might call, following Allan Rosen, Kant's "conservatism" (i.e., his support for law and order) and his "liberalism" (i.e., his support for human rights and ever-larger personal freedoms).[18]

So the sphere of justice, for Kant, is a sphere of coercion. Even though coercion seems at first to be at odds with the freedom that resides at the core of Kant's practical philosophy, he contends in a famous phrase that it is consistent with such a value when it is used to "hinder a hindrance to freedom."[19] Coercion is morally justified when used to protect persons from standard threats to the exercise of their free rational agency. Such standard threats include the unlawful use of force and fraud by unscrupulous others. It follows from these principles that we may employ coercion in any manner consistent with the UPJ.

The deepest import of the UPJ is that, for Kant, we are to order, and/or reform, our external conduct and our basic social institutions so that they conform to its requirements. Three crucial imperatives are derived from this general contention. The first is that we are to move from the "wild, lawless freedom" of the pre-political state of nature—if we happen to find ourselves in that condition—to a lawful state of positive freedom, wherein citizens are simultaneously co-legislators and subjects. Indeed, Kant emphasizes that the UPJ entitles people to coerce any and all recalcitrant parties in the state of nature to join a civil society structured to secure everyone's rational agency.[20] This lawful state, or "juridical condition," must fulfil three requirements R in order for it to be a state worthy of the name: R1) it must effectively preclude the resort to violence by private citizens in the resolution of conflicts over rights claims; R2) it must include a coherent, unified and public system of determinate positive laws which will preclude interpretive conflict over the meaning of both the natural law of the UPJ and, indeed, the positive laws themselves; and R3) it may allow as peremptory or final only those universal rights consistent with the UPJ.[21]

The second crucial imperative implied by the UPJ is that, once we have established a civil society that fulfils requirements R1-3, we are to structure it so that it respects human rights, which are those fundamental liberties and entitlements expressive and protective of rational agency and how it ought always to be treated. After all, Kant declares that: "The foremost issue is that rights are thereby secured for everyone, which is the supreme principle, limited by no other, from which all maxims concerning the commonwealth must be derived." Human rights, he proclaims, "immediately command rational respect." Such rights constitute "a sacred institution"; they can even be said to be "the apple of God's eye."[22]

Which human rights does Kant believe we have? While he claims that the right to freedom—i.e., freedom from force and fraud, and freedom to be self-directing within a protected space of personal liberty—is "the one innate right," he also stipulates that other rights flow from this contention, notably to equality (before the law and of opportunity) and to private property.[23]

The third imperative flowing from the UPJ is the most ambiguous and indeterminate: above and beyond the baseline requirements of law and order and universal human rights protection, we are to structure civil society so that, in general, enlightenment and good will are fostered. Kant is largely silent on specifics in this regard, though he does refer obliquely to certain requirements of free trade and public education systems. The point here, and the reason for his reticence, is that political structures can only set up a general framework within which salutary moral character can develop: they cannot and may not themselves mandate, or enforce, such ethical development. If they attempted to do so, such would constitute "paternalistic" government, which Kant labels "the worst despotism imaginable." Against such anti-autonomy intrusiveness, Kant proclaims, in a fashion that seems to anticipate John Stuart Mill: "[N]o one can compel me... to be happy after his fashion; instead, every person may seek happiness in the way that seems best to him, if only he does not violate the freedom of others to strive towards such similar ends." Thus, Kant reaffirms that the core function of a just polity is to secure law and order and enforce respect for everyone's human rights, leaving the public to seek its own general welfare and happiness as it best sees fit.[24]

Kant stipulates that all of these three imperatives of a just society can only be fulfilled when there is a "republican constitution," defined as one wherein there is a legislative body, an effective executive to enforce its laws, and a competent judiciary to decide particular cases and thereby shape the one consistent and universal system of just laws ordering the polity.[25]

It is important to note that Kant views all of these aspects of FPJ-MPJ 2 as the dictates of (practical) reason itself and, as such, they must all be shared and consented to by all of us as rational agents. So Kant is a kind of social contract theorist: in our deepest rational selves, we all affirm the UPJ and its FPJ-MPJ 2 components and thereby form a "general will" to establish a republic in line with their specifications. The broad outline of such an ideal Kantian republic seems clear: namely, a kind of classical liberalism, calling only for that exact amount of government necessary to provide for the rule of law and order, and to secure all our human rights. The watchwords of Kantian governance are: law and order; equal human rights to freedom and property; socio-economic opportunity; trade, development and commerce; and self-driven effort, industry and enlightenment. If all these criteria are fulfilled, Kant—influenced by the French Revolution then underway—proclaims that the result will be a "patriotic state" of free and equal citizens.[26]

Kant's General Conception of International Justice

The Incompleteness of a Domestic Theory of Justice

Kant thinks that any purely domestic theory of justice, such as that sketched above, is radically incomplete. Why? Because recognition of the fact that there are other states in the world leads to two potent considerations:

1) Reason's mandate for a universal, complete and coherent system of directives demands consideration of all political realms, both domestic and international. The categorical imperative and the UPJ are not thought to be parochial in nature or provincial in scope: Kant is unswervingly universalist regarding their domain. As the imperatives of practical reason itself, they have normative purchase on, and application to, all rational beings, whether on this side of the border or beyond.

2) No matter how peaceful and just a domestic society is, such can be shattered by an external attack. This is to say that domestic justice, to some extent, *depends upon* (Kant even says it is "subordinate to")[27] international justice.

So Kant believes firmly that one cannot isolate questions of domestic justice from those of international justice. Many commentators credit this insistence on the close causal, conceptual and normative links between the domestic and the international case as being Kant's greatest and most original contribution to the history of political thought. He has been called, as a result, the first truly internationalist political philosopher.[28]

Given that we must consider international justice, how are we to conceive of it? What, in Kant's view, are its original premises, and what are its substantive conclusions? In short: what are the essential problems and what seem to be the proper solutions?

The Nature of the State: Its Rights and Duties

The starting point of Kant's international theory of justice is the premise that the state is itself a moral person.[29] A moral person for Kant is one who is a free rational agent, capable of making rational choices between alternative courses of action, and of being held responsible for the character of those choices. Moral persons, while composites of both animal instinctuality and free rationality, nevertheless find their deepest sense of identity and selfhood in their rational-moral nature and are, accordingly, to look to reason for direction in their lives. What would it mean to ascribe these or similar properties to states—and why?

There are at least two important senses in which the state exists as a moral person for Kant. The first sense is that, to the extent to which a state fulfils its function of securing justice for its member citizens, it must itself have moral value. The having of a state is a necessary condition for securing human rights and for providing the kind of secure, ordered and lawful context that permits the development of good will and virtuous character.

The second sense in which the state exists as a moral person for Kant makes essential reference to the international context. Kant contends that, for the purposes of thinking clearly and incisively about international relations, we must think of states vis-à-vis each other *as if they were* full-blown moral persons or "individuals" interacting with each other.[30] This is to say that Kant's assertion of the moral personhood of states in this second sense is, essentially, his way of employing what is now called "the domestic analogy." To employ the domestic analogy is precisely to conceive of international relations along the lines of relations between individuals within nations, and thus to ascribe to states certain powers and properties that belong to individual human beings, such as rationality and responsiveness to moral demands. Kant's implicit contention, in vintage Critical style, is that we cannot make sense of international relations unless we employ the domestic analogy.[31]

For these two reasons, it follows that we are to conceive of states as rational actors in the Kantian sense: they are free to make rational choices between alternative courses of action and they can and should be held responsible for these choices by other rational actors. The actions of rational agents are always intentional, and these intentions are discernible in the form of maxims or policies of action, just as in the individual case. Furthermore, as moral persons and rational choosers, states must find their deepest sense of identity and interest in obeying the dictates of (practical) rationality itself, of which the categorical imperative (CI) and the universal principle of justice (UPJ) are the principal imperatives. This is to say, very importantly, *that we can, and we ought, to judge morally the actions of states vis-à-vis the CI, and especially the UPJ.* States as moral persons are to obey the moral law and be subjected to judgment and criticism where found wanting.

To say that states, as moral persons, are duty bound to obey the UPJ is, for Kant, to say that states are duty bound to follow a principle analogous to the UPJ in their mutual relations, call it SUPJ (for "States' UPJ"): "Act externally in such a way that the free use of one's will—i.e., the set of one's policies and actions—is compatible with the external freedom of every other state in accord with a universal law." And, since we saw previously how the UPJ was composed of principles FPJ-MPJ 2, it must follow that SUPJ is itself composed of analogous principles SFPJ-SMPJ 2:

SFPJ: all states ought to co-exist under a coherent, ordered and determinate system of positive international laws.

SMPJ 1: the content of such a system of international laws must be aimed, first and foremost, at respecting and realizing the rights of every state equally.

SMPJ 2: above and beyond SMPJ 1, the system of international laws is to provide the framework within which practical reason and good will can be promoted and mature to their fullest development.

It is crucial to note that, as in the case of the UPJ, there is a fundamental tension between priority and justification within the SUPJ. SFPJ gets priority claim on our attention and efforts, Kant asserts, whereas the system of positive international law and order mandated by SFPJ is morally justified only to the extent to which it contributes to the SMPJ 1 securing of state rights (and ultimately human rights) and the SMPJ 2 growth of human enlightenment and good will. Here, as in the domestic case, there is a central tension, or dialectic, between Kant's conservative focus on saving us from the state of nature and imposing law and order, on the one hand, and, on the other, his liberal inclinations towards the securing of human rights.

The deepest import of the SUPJ is that we are, through our state mechanisms, to order our foreign policy conduct and to design global institutions and practices such that they satisfy SFPJ-SMPJ 2. This means, notably, that: 1) we are to move from the anarchy of the international state of nature (should we happen to find ourselves in that condition) to some kind of cosmopolitan civil society; and 2) we are to structure the global juridical condition so that it satisfies the rights of states.[32]

Why do states have rights vis-à-vis one another? States have rights because: 1) their citizens, as individuals, have human rights; and 2) in order to secure the objects of these human rights from possible violation by outsiders, a collective agent like the state needs to be authorized, or entitled, to certain objects and actions in its own right, vis-à-vis non-members and the collective agents that act on their behalf. And what rights do states have vis-à-vis one another? There is extensive textual evidence[33] that Kant affirms the following state rights (SR) and correlative state duties (SD):

State Rights

SR 1. The right of negative freedom from force and fraud in the international state of nature.

SR 2. The right of positive freedom to self-governance within a global juridical condition. This is the right of political sovereignty.

SR 3. The right to employ and dispose of one's natural resources as one sees fit, provided such use does not violate the rights of other states.

SR 4. The right of property in one's territory. This is the right of territorial integrity.

SR 5. The right to enter into lawful contractual relations with other states at one's will.

State Duties

SD 1. Do not employ force and fraud in one's relations with other states.

SD 2. Do not interfere in the internal matters, or self-governance, of another state.

SD 3. Do not invade or capture the rightful property or territory of another state.

SD 4. Do not break lawful contractual agreements one has freely made with other states.

SD 5. Allow for basic contact and relations (Kant calls it "hospitality")[34] between citizens of another nation and one's own.

State rights and duties, much like individual rights and duties, essentially map out a set of firm commands and prohibitions, or deontological side-constraints, on how the state in question should be treated by other states. We are to treat rational and moral persons (whether they are individuals or states) in particular ways that respect their dignity, and to avoid treating them in other ways that injure them as moral persons. These rights and duties are designed to secure the rational agency of the actors in question, and may not be overridden for the sake of such other social goals as public welfare or human happiness in general.

Perhaps two aspects of this issue require further comment. The first is that, in the final analysis, SRs 1-5 do not seem to contain substantially more than is contained in the two most traditional and widely acknowledged rights of states: political sovereignty and territorial integrity. The second is that this system of state rights and duties, SRs 1-5 and SDs 1-5, essentially constitutes Kant's ideal conception of international law and order. An international system wherein SRs 1-5 were respected, and SDs 1-5 adhered to, would constitute a fundamentally just and lawful global order.

The State of Nature: International Version

For Kant, the fundamental problem of justice regarding international relations is the exact same problem of justice faced in the domestic case: moving out of the force and fraud inherent in the state of nature and into some kind of secure and ordered context of civil society, wherein both SRs 1-5 and SDs 1-5 are fulfilled.

There is no doubt that, for Kant, the current international situation constitutes a state of nature. He puts the matter most bluntly when he says that "states, like lawless savages, exist in a condition devoid of right" and that "this condition is one of war

(the right of the stronger), even if there is no actual war or contin-
uous fighting" [his italics]. Moreover, this *condition* "is in the highest degree unjust in itself." "No where," Kant concludes, "does
human nature appear less admirable than in relationships which
exist between peoples."[35]

The international state of nature is characterized by a
number of properties: 1) there is no overarching political authority to rule effectively over states; 2) states rely solely on their own
subjective interpretation of their rights claims; and 3) states are
prone to violence when their rights claims conflict with those of
other states. So, Kant's picture of what actors in the international
state of nature are like is very close to the Hobbesian picture on
the domestic plane: free, rational, self-interested, subjective, fearful of others and prone to violence. The result is that no state, in
the current global context, can enjoy reasonably secure possession of the objects of its state rights, SRs 1-5. And this has the
important, and damning, consequence that individual persons
must themselves lack secure possession of the objects of their
human rights, which form the entire material focus of Kant's
conception of justice. Since persons require secure states for their
rights, and since states require a secure global condition for their
rights, it follows that the international state of nature is at odds
with our human rights. This situation, Kant insists, amounts to
being governed by might rather than right and, as such, violates
all the requirements of justice. But what exactly is the nature of
the global civil society towards which states are to orientate themselves? What is the civil society solution to the state of nature
problem?

Civil Society: International Version

One of, if not the, most problematic and ambiguous aspects of
Kant's international theory of justice and law is determining his
views on the exact nature of what international civil society
should be. In fact, it is not even clear whether there is a determinate and consistent answer to be found; as Pogge contends: "His
[i.e., Kant's] position on this matter is extraordinarily unsettled,
sometimes leading to inconsistencies even within a single
passage."[36] This section shall endeavour, however, to put together
a charitable, persuasive and relatively consistent reading.

While some scholars contend that Kant must really be in favour of a full-blown world government—as the only logical and complete solution to the international state of nature problem[37]— it is clear that, in the end, he rejects this option. His two most forceful arguments against world government are as follows:

1. Drawing on the rather well-documented history of imperial overreach and subsequent decline and collapse, Kant contends that a world state simply would not be able to govern the entire globe with the effectiveness required by the SFPJ component of the SUPJ. In fact, he says, such a state would have to become despotic (and thus rights-violative, conflicting with SMPJ 1) to make even a serious attempt at effective global governance. But even that would not suffice, and in the end it would collapse back into the anarchy of the state of nature.[38]

2. Kant contends that states simply do not, and will not, agree to cede their sovereignty to a full-blown world state. "[E]ach state," Kant observes, "sees its own majesty...precisely in not having to submit to any external legal constraint." Furthermore, he says that nature itself has divided peoples through (amongst other things) language and religion, and this division seems to constitute yet another serious constraint on the feasibility of an overarching world state. So, the substance of this argument is that the formation of a world state cannot be a duty of ours because it is not actually possible to fulfil it: neither peoples nor the states they have established will agree to it. So world government violates Kant's "ought implies can" dictum.[39]

Given that the status quo of international relations is unacceptable for Kant, and given that a world state is not his preferred improvement on the status quo, what exactly are we mandated by practical reason to do with regard to the ends of international justice? It is clear that, for Kant, we must move towards something like, but not quite, a full-blown world state. We must get as close to a world state as is practically and morally feasible. As Kant puts it: "[T]he positive idea of a world republic cannot be realized. If all is not to be lost, this can at best find a negative substitute in the shape of an enduring and gradually expanding *federation* likely to prevent war" [his italics].[40] International federalism, and not a world republic, is Kant's solution to the problem of war and the guarantor of perpetual peace.

What exactly is the nature of this posited federation? Kant speaks of it as a "league," a "pacific federation," a "free federation," a "permanent congress of states," a "partnership or confederation," which would "end all wars for good." "This federation," he says clearly, "does not aim to acquire any power like that of a state, but merely to preserve and secure the *freedom* of each state in itself, along with that of the other confederated states, although this does not mean that they need to submit to public laws and to a coercive power which enforces them, as do men in a state of nature."[41] He speaks of a group of like-minded states voluntarily agreeing to form such a pacific federation, renouncing war as a means of conflict resolution between themselves; in doing so this federation "will provide a focal point for federal association among other states...and the whole will spread further and further by a series of alliances of this kind." In fact, Kant confidently predicts that such a federation will extend "gradually to encompass all states, thus leading to perpetual peace."[42]

So, the idea is of a voluntary and renewable social contract among states to renounce war, to perform their state duties SD 1-5 and to respect each other's state rights SR 1-5. The "federalism" part is not readily apparent—at least if we think of federalism as implying some kind of actual division of power between state and sub-state levels, with the sub-state levels enjoying considerable autonomy over a certain specified list of issues. The federation, Kant explicitly stipulates, "does *not* aim to acquire *any* power like that of a state"(my emphases).[43] The idea is more in the vein of a very familiar Kantian move: states are to act *as if there were* a real, effective federal system operative at the global level. They are, voluntarily, to constrain their own behaviour in such a way that the result—namely, perpetual peace and the secure enjoyment of rights, both state and human—is the same as if there were an actual federal system between states, based on an actual division of power and authority between the global regime and the nation-state sub-units. The result will be the same as if there really were an effective governing structure at the global level, namely, peace-with-rights, the ultimate end of the international theory of justice. Indeed, Kant intones that perpetual peace is "the entire ultimate purpose of the theory of right." Perpetual peace is "the highest political good," truly "the ultimate purpose of law within the bounds of pure reason."[44]

We might wonder why, even if only an international federation—and not a full-blown world state—is the proper end of international justice, the move towards it should be purely voluntary on the part of states. Would it not be permissible to employ force to found a world federation, just as it was permissible to employ force to found a domestic civil society? Kant's response is a firm denial. He states clearly that force may not be employed to forge a global juridical condition. He says, for example, that "[w]e might offer arguments for the use of violence on the grounds that it is in the best interests of the world as a whole." "But," he cautions, "all these supposedly good intentions cannot wash away the stain of injustice from the means which are used to implement them."[45] Here we see again a clear and forceful statement of Kant's deontological inclinations: the end does not justify the means; there are principled side-constraints on the way in which we can treat rational actors (whether individuals or states), even if it is clearly for their own—indeed, the world's own—benefit.

Kant believes that states may not employ violence to coerce other states to join his cosmopolitan federation because of the raw fact that these states have legal constitutions. As Kant says quite clearly: "For any *legal* constitution, even if it is only in small measure *lawful*, is better than none at all, and the fate of premature reform would be anarchy"(his italics).[46] Justice is so precious a thing, so to speak, that we ought not to risk its demise by invading or coercing a domestic society that is already doing a fairly decent job fulfilling its requirements. If the means (e.g., force) involve seriously risking the stability of a lawful domestic society, then we ought not to employ them in the belief that doing so will result in greater justice overall in the future.

This proposition is illustrative of Kant's conservative predilections in favour of law and order. He mandates that we are not to employ violent means which may run the risk of destroying whatever juridical condition we might have and of returning all of us to the state of nature and war. So once there exists some law and order within a state, we are not to employ violence against it in our mandated move towards a more just global order; rather, we are to employ the means of gradual political reform towards a greater and more just peace. The order of the day for Kant is piecemeal, top-down reform. Heads of state, enlightened by the public use of reason deployed by such thinkers as Kant, are to employ peaceful and voluntary means in moving from the status quo to a more secure global order. They should join together with like-minded states into a voluntary league of just countries which, leading through example, can serve as a model for the future progress of the entire international system towards perpetual peace.[47]

Conclusion

The goal of this chapter was to provide a focused and comprehensive summary of Kant's basic principles of morality and justice, especially as applied to the international arena. For without knowledge of these, we miss the essential theoretical context within which Kant locates his theory of just war. Discerning the structure of that theory, and its historical contribution to the ethics of war and peace, is the task of the following chapter.

Notes

1. See W.M. Reisman, "International Law after the Cold War," *American Journal of International Law* (1990), 859-76. There has also been enormous interest recently in Kant's descriptive philosophy of history, wherein the attainment of perpetual peace is somehow seen as the inevitable end of the historical process. This interest was launched by Michael Doyle. Doyle has argued that Kant, more than any other person or doctrine, correctly predicted the course of international relations—especially the "peace among liberal democratic states"—in the Western world during the last 200 years and counting. This book will not engage these descriptive issues or empirical claims; the focus, rather, is entirely on the normative side of Kant's internationalism. For more information about the empirical debate, consult the following sources: M. Doyle, "Kant, Liberal Legacies and Foreign Affairs," Parts 1 and 2, *Philosophy and Public Affairs* (1984), 204-35 and 323-53, respectively; M. Brown, et al., eds. *Debating the Democratic Peace* (Cambridge, MA: MIT Press, 1996); J. Rawls, "The Law of Peoples," in S. Shute and S. Hurley, eds. *On Human Rights* (New York: Basic, 1993), 40-80; C. Lynch, "Kant, the Republican Peace, and Moral Guidance in International Law," *Ethics and International Affairs* (1994), 39-58; W.L. Huntley, "Kant's Third Image: Systemic Sources of the Liberal Peace," *International Studies Quarterly* (1996), 45-76; and J. Gowa,

Ballots and Bullets: The Elusive Democratic Peace (Princeton, NJ: Princeton University Press, 1999).

2. For a list of those who think that Kant's writings mark a harbinger of world government, see W.B. Gallie, *Philosophers of War and Peace* (Cambridge: Cambridge University Press, 1979), 9, in the note. Examples of those who criticize Kant for failing to specify needed powers for his federation would be T. Carson, "Perpetual Peace: What Kant Should Have Said," *Social Theory and Practice* (1988), 173-214 and J. Bourke, "Kant's Doctrine of 'Perpetual Peace'," *Philosophy* (1942), 324-33. D. Meyers accuses Kant of being a realist in "Kant's Liberal Alliance: A Permanent Peace?" in K. Kipnis and D. Meyers, eds. *Political Realism and International Morality* (Boulder, CO: Westview Press, 1987), 212-19. For those who think Kant a naive moralist, see any work by a prominent realist, or neo-realist, such as Hans Morgenthau, George Kennan or Kenneth Waltz. Kant's cryptic remarks about war being needed to advance culture are referred to in J. Chanteur, *From War to Peace*, trans. S. Weisz (Boulder, CO: Westview, 1992), 180-215. Finally, Kant is labelled an "extreme pacifist" by F. Teson in his "The Kantian Theory of International Law," *Columbia Law Review* (1992): 90.

3. I. Kant, *Groundwork for the Metaphysics of Morals*, trans. J. Ellington, in *Kant's Ethical Philosophy* (Indianapolis, IN: Hackett, 1983), 20 (P 408). When citing Kant in this book, the following will be provided: 1) the page number from the English translation being used; and 2) the page (P) number from the standard Prussian academy edition of the works of Kant.

4. Kant, *Groundwork*, passim; I. Kant, *Critique of Pure Reason*, trans. N. Kemp-Smith (New York: St. Martin's Press, 1963), passim; I. Kant, *Prolegomena to Any Future Metaphysics*, trans. J. Ellington (Indianapolis, IN: Hackett, 1977), passim; I. Kant, *Critique of Practical Reason*, trans. Lewis White Beck (New York: Macmillan, 1993), passim; and I. Kant, *The Metaphysics of Morals*, trans. and ed. Mary Gregor (Cambridge: Cambridge University Press, 1996), passim. See also T. Pogge, "Kant's Theory of Justice," *Kant-Studien* (1988): 408; and J. Rawls, "Themes in Kant's Moral Philosophy," 291-319, in R. Beiner and W.J. Booth, eds. *Kant and Political Philosophy: The Contemporary Legacy* (New Haven, CT: Yale University Press, 1993).

5. Beiner and Booth, *Kant* note 4. See also E. Weinrib, "Law as a Kantian Idea of Reason," *Columbia Law Review* (1987): 472-508.

6. Kant, *Groundwork*, 28-40 (P 420-32); Rawls, "Themes," 291-319; and T. Pogge, "The Categorical Imperative," in O. Hoffe, ed. *Grundlegung zur Metaphysik der Sitten* (Vittori Klostermann: Frankfurt/Main, 1989), 172-93.

7. The "at bottom" quote is at Kant, *Groundwork*, 41 (P 436).
   The five formulations of the CI, with their textual locations, are as follows:
   1) The Formula of Universal Law: "Act only according to that maxim whereby you can at the same time will that it should become a universal law" *(Groundwork*, 30 [P 421]).

2) The Formula of the Law of Nature: "Act as if the maxim of your action were to become through your will a universal law of nature" *(Groundwork,* 30 [P 421]).

3) The Formula of the End-in-Itself: "Act in such a way that you treat humanity, whether in your own person or in the person of another, always at the same time as an end and never simply as a means" *(Groundwork,* 36 [P 429]).

4) The Formula of Autonomy: "Act under the idea of the will of every rational being as a will that legislates universal law" *(Groundwork,* 38 [P 431]).

5) The Formula of the Kingdom of Ends: The kingdom of ends refers to Kant's postulate of an ideal ethical commonwealth wherein all beings legislate for themselves in harmony with all others, in accordance with the ideal of treating all as ends and not as mere means. We are also to act in accord with such a conception *(Groundwork,* 36-41 [P 429-36]).

For insightful scholarship on how to interpret the "at bottom" comment, see: Pogge, "Imperative," 172-93; O.O'Neill, *Constructions of Reason: An Exploration of Kant's Practical Philosophy* (Cambridge: Cambridge University Press, 1989), passim; C. Korgaard, *Creating the Kingdom of Ends* (Cambridge, MA: Harvard University Press, 1996), passim; C. Korsgaard, "Kant's Formula of Universal Law," *Pacific Philosophical Quarterly* (1985): 24-47; C. Korsgaard, "Kant's Formula of Humanity," *Kant-Studien* (1986): 183-202; H.J. Paton, *The Categorical Imperative* (Philadelphia, PA: University of Pennsylvania Press, 1971) and L.W. Beck, "Kant's Two Conceptions of the Will in Their Political Context," in Beiner and Booth, eds., *Legacy,* 38-49.

8. Pogge, "Imperative," 172-93; O'Neill, *Constructions,* passim; Korgaard, "Universal," 24-47; and Korgaard, "Humanity," 183-202.

9. In Kant's technical terms, this would be to say that the executive faculty of the will, *Willkur,* must of its own accord act consistently with the commands of the legislative faculty of the will, *Wille,* for a will to count as being morally good. For more, see Beck, "Two," 38.

10. Kant, "The End of All Things," trans. by T. Humphrey in his ed. *Perpetual Peace and Other Essays* (Indianapolis, IN: Hackett, 1983), 96 (P 331).

11. Kant, *Groundwork,* 26 (P 416).

12. D. Cummiskey, *Kantian Consequentialism* (New York: Oxford University Press, 1996).

13. For these criteria, I have relied partially on Frances Kamm's characterization of non-consequentialism in her elegant article: "Non-consequentialism, the Person as an End-in-Itself and the Significance of Status," *Philosophy and Public Affairs* (1991): 354-89.

14. Kamm, "Status," 354. See also: B. Aune, *Kant's Theory of Morals* (Princeton, NJ: Princeton University Press, 1979); M. Baron, *Kantian Ethics Almost Without Apology* (Ithaca, NY: Cornell University Press, 1995); T. Hill, Jr., *Dignity and Practical Reason in Kant's Moral Theory* (Ithaca, NY: Cornell

University Press, 1993); and R. Sullivan, *An Introduction to Kant's Ethics* (Cambridge: Cambridge University Press, 1994).

15. Kant, *The Doctrine of Right,* which is the first part of *Metaphysics,* 24 (P 230-1).

16. Pogge, "Justice," 408-33. See also: A. Rosen, Kant's *Theory of Justice* (Ithaca, NY: Cornell University Press, 1993), 80-115; L. Mulholland, *Kant's System of Rights* (New York: Columbia University Press, 1994), 140-54; P. Benson, "External Freedom According to Kant," *Columbia Law Review* (1987): 559-79; and R. Pippin, "On the Moral Foundations of Kant's *Rechtslehre,*" in R. Kennington, ed. *The Philosophy of Immanuel Kant* (Washington, DC: Catholic University of America Press, 1985) 107-42.

17. Kant, *Right,* 90 (P 312).

18. Rosen, *Theory,* passim. See also Pogge, "Justice," 408-33 and J. Waldron, "Kant's Legal Positivism," *Harvard Law Review* (1996).

19. Kant, *Right,* 25 (P 231).

20. Kant, *Right,* 23-35 and 44-45 (P 229-45 and P 256-57).

21. Kant, *Right,* 45-86 (P 257-308).

22. The "foremost issue" quotation is at I. Kant, *Theory and Practice,* trans. by T. Humphrey in his ed. *Immanuel Kant: Perpetual Peace and Other Essays,* 78 (P 298). The other quotations are from I. Kant, *Perpetual Peace,* in Humphrey, ed., 114 (P 353) in the footnote.

23. Kant, *Right,* 23-26 (P 229-33) and 45-86 (P 255-307). See also Mulholland, *System,* passim; S. Shell, *The Rights of Reason* (Toronto: University of Toronto Press, 1980), passim; M. Gregor, "Kant on 'Natural Rights'," in Beiner and Booth, eds., *Legacy,* supra note 5, 50-75; and M. Gregor, "Kant on Property Rights," *Review of Metaphysics* (1988): 566-90.

24. Quotations at Kant, *Theory,* 72-73 (P 290-91).

25. Kant, *Right,* 90-95 (P 313-16).

26. Kant, *Theory,* 83-84 (P 305). See also: Pogge, "Justice," 408-33; Rosen, *Kant's,* passim; Mulholland, *System,* passim; Shell, *Reason,* passim; H. Arendt, *Lectures on Kant's Political Philosophy* (Chicago: University of Chicago Press, 1982); K. Baynes, *The Normative Grounds of Social Criticism: Kant, Rawls and Habermas* (Albany, NY: SUNY Press, 1992); W.B. Gallie, "Kant's View of Reason in Politics," *Philosophy* 54 (1979): 19-33; B. Ludwig, "The Right of a State in Immanuel Kant's Doctrine of Right," *Journal of the History of Philosophy* (1990): 403-15; J. Murphy, *Kant: The Philosophy of Right* (London: Macmillan, 1970); P. Riley, *Kant's Political Philosophy* (Totowa, NJ: Rowman Littlefield, 1983); H. Williams, *Kant's Political Philosophy* (Oxford: Oxford University Press, 1983); W. Kersting, "Politics, Freedom and Order: Kant's Political Philosophy" in P. Guyer, ed. *The Cambridge Companion to Kant* (Cambridge: Cambridge University Press, 1992), 342-67; and, for a different perspective on the substance of Kant's domestic theory of justice, H. Van der Linden, *Kantian Ethics and Socialism* (Cambridge: Cambridge University Press, 1988).

27. I. Kant, *Universal History with a Cosmopolitan Intent,* in H. Reiss, ed. *Kant: Political Writings* trans. H. Nisbet (Cambridge: Cambridge University Press, 1995), 47 (P 24).

28. Examples of such praise can be found at Gallie, *Philosophers,* 13-14, and Teson, "Kantian," 53-54.

29. There are at least four relevant passages to consider in this regard:

    1) In the theory of domestic justice detailed in the *Doctrine of Right,* Kant asserts that each of the three branches of a just republican constitution are themselves "moral persons"—and, since we have seen that for Kant the three branches are all emanations, so to speak, from the one sovereign and legislative general will which is synonymous with the state, it seems to follow, quite clearly, that the state as a whole is a moral person;

    2) Kant, when broaching his international theory of justice in the *Doctrine of Right,* says that the state of nature, internationally, is a condition (to be detailed shortly) "in which each state, as a moral person...";

    3) In *Perpetual Peace,* Kant argues that a state cannot be grafted artificially onto another state, through means such as inheritance, because that would "terminate its existence as a moral personality and make it into a commodity"; and

    4) In the *Doctrine of Right,* Kant says that, if a state were to violate certain prohibitions in wartime, "it would render itself unfit in the eyes of international right to function as a person in relation to other states and to share equal rights with them."

    The first quotation is at Kant, *Right,* 93 (P 316); the second at Kant, *Right,* 114 (P 343); the third at I. Kant, *Perpetual Peace: A Philosophical Sketch,* in H. Reiss, ed. *Kant: Political Writings,* trans. H.B Nisbet, 94 (P 344); and the fourth at Kant, *Right,* 117 (P 347).

30. One quotation by way of proof is: "Here [i.e., in the international situation] a state, as a moral person, is *considered as* existing in a state of nature, hence in a condition of constant war" (my emphasis). Another pertinent quote says that if a state were to violate certain prohibitions in wartime, "it would render itself unfit *in the eyes of international right* to function as a person in relation to other states and to share equal rights with them" (my emphasis). These quotes occur at Kant, *Right,* 114 (P 343) and 117 (P 347), respectively.

    Yet another quotation occurs when Kant says that the people who make up a nation can *"from the perspective of rights,"* be *"thought of* as the offspring of a common mother [the republic], constituting, *as it were,* a single family (*gens, natio*) whose members (the citizens) are all equal by birth" (all italicized passages are my emphasis except for the last one with the Latin words, which is Kant's). It occurs at Kant, *Right,* 114 (P 343).

31. M. Walzer, *Just and Unjust Wars* (New York: Basic Books, 1991, 1st ed. 1977), 51-74, and H. Suganami, *The Domestic Analogy and World Order Proposals* (Cambridge: Cambridge University Press, 1989). Another discussion of Kant's doctrine of the moral personhood of states is: S. Byrd, "The State as a 'Moral

Person',", H. Robinson, ed. *Proceedings of the Eighth International Kant Congress,* vol. 1 (Milwaukee, WI: Marquette University Press, 1995), 171-90.

32. While it also, as in the domestic case, entails a third principle—namely, that above and beyond these requirements the interstate system ought to foster indirectly the growth of enlightenment and good will—Kant is essentially silent on how this might be achieved, focusing all of his attention and energy on the first two concerns. His vague allusions to free trade between states is perhaps an exception.

33. The most relevant texts are Kant, *Theory;* Kant, *Perpetual;* and especially Kant, *Right.*

34. Kant, *Perpetual,* 105-108 (P 358-61). By "hospitality," Kant refers to a kind of freedom of movement and interaction, especially to the allowance by states for commercial contracts to be forged between their various citizens.

35. The first quotation is at Kant, *Right,* 114 (P 344). The second is at Kant, *Theory,* 91 (P 312).

36. Pogge, "Justice," 428.

37. Gallie lists such scholars at Gallie, *Philosophers,* p. 9, n. 7.

   There is considerable textual evidence in favour of this world government reading of Kant. Kant speaks of the necessity of introducing a "civil constitution" at the international level, even of a "cosmopolitan constitution," saying that "[m]en are compelled to reinforce this law by introducing a system of *united power,* hence a cosmopolitan system of general political security" (my emphasis). Kant, *Universal,* 49 (P 26).

   Kant even, at least twice, employs the term "world-republic." "There is no possible way," he points out, "of counteracting this [i.e., the international state of nature] except a state of international right, based upon *enforceable* public laws to which each state *must* submit."(my emphases). The "world-republic" quotes are at Kant, *Religion,* 30. The other quote is from Kant, *Theory,* 92 (P 312).

   Perhaps the clearest expression of the pro-world-state interpretation is when Kant proclaims that: "There is only one rational way in which states coexisting with other states can emerge from the lawless condition of pure warfare. *Just like* individual men, they must renounce their savage and lawless freedom, adapt themselves to public, coercive laws, and thus *form an international state*" (my emphases). Kant, *Perpetual,* 105 (P 357). Pogge, "Justice," 427-33 and Carson, "What," 173-214, have excellent summaries of this scholarship.

38. Kant, *Perpetual,* 113-14 (P 367).

39. Kant, *Perpetual,* 103 (P 354) for the quote and also 114 (P 357).

40. Kant, *Perpetual,* 105 (P 357).

41. Kant, *Perpetual,* 104 (P 356).

42. Kant, *Perpetual,* 104-105 (P 356).

43. Kant, *Perpetual,* 104 (P 356).

44. Kant, *Right,* 123-24 (P 355). This contention, that by "federalism" Kant does not envision or advocate an actual federal structure between nation-states,

finds support in: Mulholland, "War," 25-41 and his *System,* 348-72; Riley, *Political,* 114-34; Gallie, *Philosophers,* 3-36 and F.H. Hinsley, *Power and the Pursuit of Peace: Theory and Practice in the History of Relations between States* (Cambridge: Cambridge University Press, 1963), pp. 62-79. Thus, I find one of the most frequently offered criticisms of Kant's international theory, namely that he fails to specify the institutional details of his posited federation, to be misplaced. This popular criticism can be found, for example, in Bourke, "Doctrine," 324-33. See also I. Ward, "Kant and the Transnational Order: Towards a European Community Jurisprudence" *Ratio Juris* (1995): 315-29.

45. Kant, *Right,* 122 (P 353).

46. Kant, *Perpetual,* 118 (P 373) in the note.

47. This reading is also supported by Riley, *Political,* 114-34; Williams, *Philosophy,* 244-69; and L. Mulholland, "Kant on War and International Justice," *Kant-Studien* (1987): 25-41 and his *System,* 348-72. On the public use of reason, see O.O'Neill, "The Public Use of Reason," *Political Theory* (1986): 523-51. Other relevant sources on Kant's theory of international justice include: G. Cavallar, "Kant's Society of Nations: Free Federation or World Republic?" *Journal of the History of Philosophy* (1994): 461-82; and T. Donaldson, "Kant's Global Rationalism," in T. Nardin and D. Mapel, eds., *Traditions of International Ethics* (Cambridge: Cambridge University Press, 1992), 136-57. I treat some of these, and related, issues in my "Kant on International Law and Armed Conflict," *Canadian Journal of Law and Jurisprudence* (July 1998): 329-81.

CHAPTER 2 _____

Kant's Just War Theory

Kant's general conception of international justice and law, sketched out in the previous chapter, is essentially an ideal theory. But he admits that this ideal is far from real; there are times when rogue states will defect from the rules of international justice, sometimes with the force of arms. The question then becomes: how are we to deal with such rogue states? One answer, provided the defection is sufficiently grave, is that we may resort to armed force and war in order to vindicate the ideal system of international law. It will be contended in this chapter that Kant concurs with this answer; while we may not use force "positively" to found a world republic, or to force recalcitrant states to join a cosmopolitan federation, we may employ it "negatively" to repeal blatant international injustices.

To contend that Kant permits the resort to armed force by states, under certain conditions, is to contend that Kant has a just war theory. For the baseline proposition of just war theory is that, sometimes, war is morally legitimate and thus ought to be permitted legally. This chapter will assert that Kant has a just war theory and explain its systematic and suggestive substance. Attention will first be paid to the prevailing scholarly view that Kant has no just

Notes to chapter 2 are on pp. 61–64.

war theory. Following that, effort will be made to overturn this traditional understanding: first by showing, negatively, that Kant does not subscribe to the two main rival doctrines on the issue, namely, realism and pacifism; and second by demonstrating, positively, how the core propositions of just war theory are consistent with Kant's basic moral and political principles, as developed in chapter 1. Finally, extensive exegesis and reconstruction will reveal the full substance of Kant's just war theory, which is divided into accounts of *jus ad bellum, jus in bello* and *jus post bellum.*

The Traditional Reading: No Just War

Most of those commentators on Kant's international theory of justice who discuss the problem of war in any detail believe that Kant not only has no just war theory, but that he is, moreover, a vicious critic of the core propositions of classical just war theorists, such as Augustine, Aquinas and Grotius. Howard Williams, for example, says that "Kant has no theory of just war ...[j]ustice and war are in conflict with one another and it is our duty as human beings to try to overcome war." Fernando Teson contends that "Kant dismisses the idea that there could be a just war," and Georg Geismann asserts that, for Kant, "there is no such thing as a just war." Similarly, W.B. Gallie comments that "Kant agreed...that nothing but confusion and harm resulted from regarding any wars as just." There is a bevy of quotes in the Kantian corpus to support this reading.[1]

One prominent anti-just war quote occurs in *Perpetual Peace,* when Kant reflects on the contributions of traditional just war theorists and arrives at the following judgment: "It is therefore to be wondered at that the word *right* has not been completely banished from military politics as superfluous pedantry, and that no state has been bold enough to declare itself publicly in favour of doing so. For Hugo Grotius, Pufendorf, Vattel and the rest (sorry comforters as they are) are still dutifully quoted in *justification* of military aggression, although their philosophically or diplomatically formulated codes do not and cannot have the slightest *legal* force, since states as such are not subject to a common external constraint" (all his italics).[2]

Kant also says that "international right... becomes meaningless if interpreted as a right to go to war."[3] Furthermore, his insistence on the destructiveness of war in general, and his core notion that the international state of nature is unjust, both add credence to the anti-just war interpretation of Kant. Kant does, after all, assert that war is "the scourge of humankind"; "the greatest evil oppressing man"; "the source of all evils and moral corruption"; and "the destroyer of everything good."[4] We might also mention the passage where Kant seems to claim that war is inconsistent with human rights; namely, when he says that "hiring men to kill and be killed seems to mean using them as mere machines and instruments in the hand of someone else (the state), which cannot easily be reconciled with the rights of man in one's own person."[5] Finally, we might cite the clearest such passage in Kant, when he intones that "moral-practical reason within us pronounces the following irresistible veto: *There shall be no war*" (his italics). And this is the case because "war is not the way in which anyone should pursue his rights."[6]

One of the main purposes of this chapter—indeed, this book—is to prove that the above quotes can, by and large, be reconciled with the claim that Kant *has* a just war theory. In fact, an argument will be made that the weight of the textual evidence points clearly in favour of a pro-just war reading of Kant, and that any view to the contrary can only be sustained by a partial and selective reading of the relevant texts. The common tendency to read only *Perpetual Peace* (something which both Teson and Gallie seem guilty of) is, in particular, a prime source of this confusion. It leads people like Teson to say that Kant advocates a form of "extreme pacifism."[7] We will see that this claim is demonstrably false. The related tendency to put disproportionate emphasis on *Perpetual Peace*, even when drawing on such other crucial texts as the *Doctrine of Right* (something which both Williams and Geismann seem guilty of), leads to the same error. So, the aim here is to show that Kant *has* a just war theory and to explain *what* it is.[8]

Neither Realism nor Pacifism

One necessary aspect of any attempt to establish the fact of Kant's being a just war theorist is to show that he does not subscribe to the theory's main rivals. There seem, at bottom, to be three basic perspectives on the ethics and legality of war and peace, with realism and pacifism at the extremes and just war theory in the middle. The phrase "basic perspectives" does not necessarily imply that these three doctrines logically exhaust possible perspectives on war and peace. At the same time, it does not preclude such a view, which has some *prima facie* plausibility to it. In any event, in terms of incisive and well-articulated traditions of thought about war and peace, these three stand out as far and away the most prominent and plausible alternatives.

Realism

Realism is a protean doctrine. There exists a wide variety of perspectives that fall under its rubric. In general, all realists share a strong suspicion about applying moral concepts and judgments to the conduct of international affairs. Moral concepts should not be employed as descriptions of, or as prescriptions for, state behaviour on the international plane. Realists are also united by their emphasis on the salience of power and security issues, on the perceived need for a state to maximize its self-interest and, above all, by their view of the international arena as irreducibly one of fearful anarchy, which is intended to ground their claims about the primacy of power.

Referring specifically to war, realists believe that it is an intractable part of an anarchical world system; that it ought to be resorted to only if it makes sense in terms of national self-interest; and that, once war has begun, a state ought to do whatever it can to win. So if adhering to a set of just war constraints hinders a state in this regard, it ought to disregard them and stick soberly to attending to its fundamental interests in power and security.[9]

Kant's attitude towards realism is complex, but in the end constitutes a rejection. Consider first realism's descriptive side. On the one hand, Kant does believe that the international arena really is a state of nature. He also believes that states stubbornly refuse to accept any interpretation of their rights and interests other than their own—and that the result is a quite insecure and fearful environment in which the outbreak of war is always a danger and sometimes a devastating reality. He believes, in addition, that the instinctual side of our nature inclines us towards selfishness and power-seeking. At the same time, Kant insists that, due to the duality of our nature, there is also an aspiration for something more, namely, the realization of a more just world. He says that the very fact that states often seek to justify their self-serving actions in moral terms reveals that even states in the midst of anarchy display this longing. We long for such things, Kant states, because of our rational nature, in which we actually find our deepest sense of self and identity.[10]

Moreover it is clear that, for Kant, it is both possible and meaningful to evaluate state behaviour on the international plane in terms of moral concepts. Indeed, his entire international theory of justice would not make sense unless that were the case. Kant does not believe that state behaviour is utterly determined by the demands of realpolitik; rather, he sees states as formulating intentional choices and policies, some of which may well be moral in motivation. And Kant adamantly refuses to accept war as an endemic reality of international life. We shall see, shortly, that the bulk of his just war theory is aimed at progressively limiting the incidence and destructiveness of war—a process whose end-state, he hopes, is one of perpetual peace.

So, with regard to realism's descriptive side, Kant believes that states can and ought to act morally, and that we can and ought to judge their behaviour in moral terms. Yet he also believes that, in the status quo of international affairs, states are, on the whole, inclined to be self-seeking. In the absence of progressive reform towards a cosmopolitan federation, states will tend to be egoistic and focused on their relative level of power and security.

At first glance, Kant seems to reject utterly the prescriptions of realism. For nowhere does Kant advocate a foreign policy based on a prudential strategy of maximizing national interests; rather, he staunchly advocates heeding the demands of justice, as contained in the UPJ and the SUPJ. Just as we are not individually to order our personal lives based on the instinctive pursuit of prudence and happiness, so states as moral persons are not to run their foreign policies with an eye towards national interest and calculations of power and benefit. Kant is adamant that the purely prudential approach to foreign policy is "immoral and opportunistic." A purely prudential foreign policy betrays our most fundamental identity as rational beings responsive to the demands of morality and justice.

Not only is such a prudential approach to war both immoral and unjust, Kant also doubts its very feasibility, repeatedly questioning our capacity to predict accurately, in a dispassionate light, all possible relevant consequences of launching a particular war in the national interest. "[R]eason," he proclaims, "is not sufficiently enlightened to discover the whole series of predetermining causes which would allow it to predict accurately the happy or unhappy consequences of human activities...But reason at all times shows us clearly enough what we have to do in order to remain in the paths of duty."[11] Indeed, Kant hints that such sham calculations could well result in wars disastrous to the national interest. They could also result in far more wars than following the dictates of just war theory. Far clearer and more plausible, he contends, to follow the system of state rights and duties, SRs 1-5 and SDs 1-5, outlined in chapter 1 in his theory of international justice and law.[12]

While we do have Kant's clear and forceful remarks on the need to reject as implausible and unjust any kind of prudence-based foreign policy, we will see that he himself, on closer inspection, employs calculative reasoning. One example of this would be when he discusses and defends "the right of anticipatory attack." Anticipation, of course, necessarily involves complex judgments of probability about the opponent's intentions and future behaviour. And it does seem as if Kant believes that, in the face of serious non-compliance and egoism on the part of other states, states may well tend to their own for the sake of protection and security. There is the further complication that, for Kant as for Plato, adherence to the dictates of morality and justice is also to the long-term prudential benefit of all (*as* rational agents). So a sharp prudence-morality split is perhaps, at least in the international sphere, not as thoroughly sustainable as certain of Kant's remarks indicate he would like it to be.[13]

Perhaps the most charitable and consistent reading would be to say that, for Kant, those circumstances which morally justify the resort to war (to be discussed below) also provide complementary, but much weaker, prudential grounds for doing so. This view clearly privileges the moral over the prudential in vintage Kantian fashion without committing Kant to various implausibilities, ironies or problems of self-reference that would seem to follow adherence to a sharp split between them.

Pacifism

The above considerations have only served to rule out realism as Kant's perspective on the ethics of war and peace. What remains to be done in this section is to demonstrate how Kant is not a pacifist. Pacifism, of course, is the view that no war is or could be just. As Jenny Teichman quips, "Pacifism is anti-war-ism."[14] In short, pacifists categorically oppose war as such, though their reasons tend to vary (from an extreme version, which eschews any kind of violence or killing as an intrinsic harm to a more plausible version, which contends that it is the kind and scale of violence or killing that war involves which is insurmountably objectionable). So, unlike some realists, pacifists do believe that it is both possible and meaningful to apply ethical judgment to questions of international relations. In this they agree with just war theorists. But pacifists differ from just war theorists by contending that the substance of such moral judgments is always that we should never resort to war.[15]

So for Kant to be a pacifist would be for him to oppose all wars—for him to deny the justice, or the right, or the moral permissibility, of ever fighting a war. But Kant, in the *Doctrine of Right*, says that it is the "original *right* of free states in the state of nature to make war upon another (for example, in order to bring about a condition closer to that governed by right)" (my emphasis). He also says that "[i]nternational right is thus concerned partly with the *right to make war*, partly with the *right* of war itself, and partly with questions of *right* after a war, i.e., with the *right* of states to compel each other to abandon their war-like condition and to create a constitution which will establish an enduring peace" (my emphases).[16]

Furthermore, when we think back to the passage in *Perpetual Peace* mentioned at the outset of this chapter, where Kant claims that hiring men to kill and be killed is at odds with their human rights, the explicit emphasis is on the *hiring* of those men for dread purposes. The passage is an anti-mercenary passage, not a pro-pacifist one. We know this because, immediately following it, he says that "it is quite a different matter [and thus, presumably, not a violation of human rights] if the citizens undertake voluntary military training...in order to secure themselves and their fatherland against attacks from outside."[17] Indeed, this last clause seems to indicate what for Kant may well be a just cause in fighting a war: the defence of one's state from external aggression. Perhaps most clearly, Kant says that: "In the state of nature, the *right to make war* (i.e., to enter into hostilities) is the *permitted means* by which one state prosecutes its rights against another" (first italics his, second mine). "Thus," Kant continues, "if a state believes that it has been injured by another state, *it is entitled to resort to violence*, for it cannot in the state of nature gain satisfaction through legal proceedings" (my emphasis).[18] It seems quite clear, in light of these remarks, that Kant believes there are some circumstances in which states have the right to go to war. This is to say that there is the possibility of a just war for Kant, which means that Kant cannot be a pacifist.

Traditional Just War Theory

We have seen that Kant must be a just war theorist. What remains to be done is to lay out and explain the specific principles of Kant's just war theory, as a contribution to reflection on the appropriate nature of the laws of war. Before launching that investigation, it would be helpful here to list the traditional elements of the just war doctrine.

Just war theory, at least in terms of what we might call the Just War Tradition (composed of thinkers like Augustine, Aquinas, and especially Grotius),[19] typically makes a fundamental distinction between *jus ad bellum* and *jus in bello*. *Jus ad bellum* concerns the justice of fighting a war in the first place. It sets the normative criteria which must be met by any state considering the resort to armed force. Most typically, the traditional *jus ad bellum* criteria (JWT, for "just war tradition") include the following:

JWT 1. Just cause. A state must have a just cause in launching a war. The causes most frequently mentioned by the just war tradition include: self-defence by a state from external attack; the protection of innocents within its borders; and, in general, vindication for any violation of its two core state rights: political sovereignty and territorial integrity.

JWT 2. Right intention. A state must intend to fight the war only for the sake of those just causes listed in JWT 1. It cannot legitimately employ the cloak of a just cause to advance other intentions it might have, such as ethnic hatred or the pursuit of national glory.

JWT 3. Proper authority and public declaration. A state may go to war only if the decision has been made by the appropriate authorities, according to the proper process, and made public, notably to its own citizens and to the enemy state(s).

JWT 4. Last resort. A state may resort to war only if it has exhausted all plausible, peaceful alternatives to resolving the conflict in question, in particular through diplomatic negotiation.

JWT 5. Probability of success. A state may not resort to war if it can reasonably foresee that doing so will have no measurable impact on the situation. The aim here is to block violence which is going to be futile.

JWT 6. (Macro-) proportionality. A state must, prior to initiating a war, weigh the expected universal good to accrue from its prosecuting the war against the expected universal evils that will result. Only if the benefits seem reasonably proportional to the costs may the war action proceed.

JWT 7. Comparative justice. This final criterion is hotly disputed, even within the just war tradition. Grotius, for instance, vehemently denounced it as incoherent, whereas Vattel insisted upon it as being essential to moderation within war.[20] The idea here is that every state must acknowledge that each side to the war may well have some justice in its cause. Thus, all states are to acknowledge that there are limits to the justice of their own cause, thus forcing them to fight only limited wars.

Only if JWT 1-6 (and perhaps 7, depending on the theorist) are jointly satisfied is a state justified in going to war.

Jus in bello, by contrast, sets out the normative criteria for determining the justice of particular actions undertaken once war has begun. There are two traditional *jus in bello* criteria:

JWT 8. (Micro-) proportionality. Similar to JWT 6, states are to weigh the expected universal goods/benefits against the expected universal evils/costs, not only in terms of the war as a whole but also in terms of each significant military tactic and manoeuvre employed within the war. Only if the goods/benefits of the proposed action seem reasonably proportional to the evils/costs, may a state's armed forces employ it.

JWT 9. Discrimination. It is sometimes wryly noted that just war theory is the one area in political philosophy in which discrimination is acceptable. The key distinction to be made here is between combatants and non-combatants. Non-combatant civilians, unlike combatant soldiers, may not be directly targeted by any military tactics or manoeuvres; non-combatants, thought to be innocent of the war, must have their human rights respected.

It is only when a state fulfils both JWT 8 and 9 that it can be said to be fighting a war justly.

Two further comments are relevant here. The first is that most just war theorists insist that *jus ad bellum* and *jus in bello* are separate (though this is more clouded with those theorists who accept comparative justice). The idea here is that a war can begin for just reasons, yet be prosecuted in an unjust fashion. Similarly, though perhaps much less commonly, a war begun for unjust reasons might be fought with strict adherence to *jus in bello.* The categories are at least logically or conceptually distinct. The second comment is that the *jus ad bellum* criteria are thought to be the preserve and responsibility of political leaders whereas the *jus in bello* criteria are thought to be the province and responsibility of military commanders, officers and soldiers.[21]

The Principles of Kant's Just War Theory

Using traditional just war theory as our model, we can profitably distinguish between *jus ad bellum* and *jus in bello* within Kant's thoughts surrounding just war theory and the laws of war. We can also credit Kant for really being the first great thinker to stress, in a way the Just War Tradition had failed to do, the topic of justice after war, *jus post bellum*.[22]

Jus ad Bellum

In terms of *jus ad bellum*, Kant seems to stipulate the following criteria KJWT (Kant's Just War Theory):

KJWT 1. Just cause. A state may resort to armed force if and only if its rights, SRs 1-5, have been violated. The key principle here is the defence, protection and vindication of the fundamental rights of political communities and their citizens. Kant says that a state can resort to war either in response to "actively inflicted injury" (particularly an invasion or attack) or to "threats" (presumably the credible and imminent threat of such an invasion or attack). So, the right to go to war is, for Kant, not purely or literally defensive; provided there is a serious enough threat, "the right of anticipatory attack" can also be legitimate.[23]

What exactly, for Kant, grounds the right of armed self-defence on the part of a state? His main argument is perhaps best understood as the following chain of propositions:

1. All states have moral rights, SRs 1-5, and duties, SDs 1-5, vis-à-vis other states. The function of these rights is to enable states to help secure the human rights of their individual citizens. These state rights and duties are the bedrock, and most fundamental priority, of concern for international justice for all. Their fulfilment would constitute freedom for all in an era of perpetual peace.

2. These rights, SRs 1-5, entitle states to employ reliable measures necessary to secure the objects of these rights and protect them from violation.

3. There is no reliable or effective international authority that can currently assure states in the possession of the objects of their rights. Thus, states are on their own with regard to such assurance.

4. Currently, the most effective and reliable form of such self-help assurance with regard to rights-protection, at least in the last resort, is the use of armed force.

5. Thus, faced with serious violation of their rights, such as armed aggression, states are entitled to employ armed force and war in order to repeal the aggression of the rights-violator, to

vindicate their rights and to resecure their objects and those of their citizens' human rights.

It is important to understand that states do no wrong in responding to rights-violating aggression with armed force. A war in such a case, for Kant, is not merely one of evil compounding evil. It is, rather, a matter of repealing the wrong of aggression and of asserting and defending, in an effective fashion, one's own status as a rights-bearer. The pith and substance of Kant's justification, then, is two-fold and intertwined: a state may resort to war both to defend itself and to repeal the aggression which made the defence imperative. "Thus," Kant says, "if a state believes that it has been injured by another state, it is entitled to resort to violence, for it cannot in the state of nature gain satisfaction through legal proceedings." So, in the international arena, "the right to make war...is the permitted means by which one state prosecutes its rights against another."[24]

Another way of making this point, at the most fundamental level of Kant's moral philosophy, is to show how wars of self-defence against aggression do not violate the categorical imperative. We saw, in chapter 1, that the categorical imperative mandates that all rational agents act in such a way that: 1) all rational agents could (also) act on the exact same principle of action; and 2) in acting, full respect is paid to the rational agency which is the hallmark of our humanity.

It is crystal clear how we can universalize the following maxim or policy: "When faced with rights-violating aggression, I reserve the right to employ those measures, including armed force, necessary for self-defence." Every rational agent, whether individual or collective, can endorse such a maxim of permissible self-protection: no contradiction is involved in doing so. A system of international law allowing all states to defend themselves from aggression, with force if need be, is entirely consistent and universal: the course of action in question is open to all who fulfil its conditions. Secondly, we do not disrespect rational agency when we respond with armed force to aggression because: 1) we hold the aggressor state responsible for its actions (and thus treat it as a fully deliberative agent); and 2) we are, in doing so, actually vindicating the system of rules and laws designed to secure for all the elements of their rational agency, notably law and order and human rights. We are resisting and punishing a rogue state which has violated the fundamental ground rules of a just and well-functioning international system. We are hindering a hindrance to all our freedom as rational agents. And we have seen previously that hindering a hindrance to freedom is precisely how Kant defines a just use of force.[25]

So much for Kant's understanding of the right of self-defence against an aggressor who violates SRs 1-5. What about the so-called "right of anticipatory attack" that Kant also defends? What are its justifying conditions? Kant's reasoning runs as follows: if we do not attack state S, there is a very high probability that S will violate our rights. Thus, we ought to launch a pre-emptive strike against S. Even though the emphasis with regard to an anticipatory attack may seem different than that with regard to self-defence, in abstract terms we can see how this conception of anticipatory attack can be squared with Kant's main justification of the resort to war. This justification has been framed in terms of the defence of rights, punishment of rights-violation, and the achievement of rights-vindication. The looser formulation of coercion being justified as a "hindrance to a hindrance of freedom" is relevant here: the imminent and credible threat by S to violate the rights of T (i.e., S presenting a clear and present danger to T) is no less a hindrance to T's freedom than is the actual rights-violation by S because the effect of the threat is intended to do the same thing as the actual attack, namely, to coerce T into succumbing to S's unjust designs. T may reasonably and permissibly respond with lethal force in either case.

KJWT 2. Right intention. A state may go to war only with the intention of upholding its just cause, as specified in KJWT 1. This norm seems implicit in Kant's stipulation that, even in the midst of war, there must be "some sort of trust" between the belligerents; and it is clearly in line with his general condemnation of any kind of lying or duplicity with regard to policy and action.[26]

KJWT 3. Proper authority and public declaration. This is a very important *jus ad bellum* criterion for Kant. He stresses that the head of state does not have the right to declare war with impunity; rather, the people must be consulted, in some unspecified sense, on each and every declaration of war. "For a citizen," Kant intones, "must always be regarded as a co-legislative member of the state (i.e., not just as means, but also as an end in himself), and he must therefore give his free consent through his representatives not only to the waging of war in general, but also to every particular declaration of war. Only under this limiting condition may the state put him to service in dangerous enterprises."[27] The war in question must be justifiable to the people as rational co-legislators; which is to say, it must be consistent with Kant's principles of justice. Furthermore, the resort to armed force must be publicly proclaimed to the enemy state so that, once more, duplicity and deceit do not mar the process.

KJWT 4. Last resort. Kant appears to have something like this in mind when he says that "an act of retribution ... without any attempt to gain compensation from the other state by peaceful means is similar in form to starting a war without a prior declaration" (his italics).[28] Some serious attempt at a reasonable non-violent solution, perhaps through diplomatic negotiation, is to be made before resorting to war.

There is nothing in Kant that parallels the traditional *jus ad bellum* criteria of probability of success and (macro-) proportionality. This is, perhaps, not that surprising, since they make explicit appeals to consequentialist and/or prudentialist considerations, such as determining probabilities, relying on calculative reasoning, weighing costs and benefits, seeking to maximize interests and so on. And we have seen that there is a strong non-consequentialist streak in Kant's moral and political thinking which explicitly eschews such concerns. Although mention has been made of how such consequentialist concerns need not be, and perhaps are not, utterly alien to Kant's views on these matters, there are simply no passages in the relevant works that even hint at his endorsement of these two just war criteria, which were common currency during his time. It would thus seriously strain textual credibility to attribute them to him. Even though such need not be the case, and even though their absence may well constitute a flaw of a kind, Kant does not include in his theory these two standard *jus ad bellum* criteria.

Whether there exists a criterion of comparative justice in Kant is more difficult to say. On the one hand, he does make some comments to the effect that the anarchy of the international arena rules out any determinate conception of morality and justice. He denounces what he calls "one-sided maxims backed by force."[29] On the other, appeal to the criterion of just cause would seem to question whether both sides can always have some justice in their cause. If one state S attacks another T (in the absence of any reason to justify an anticipatory attack), what is the comparative justice of S's cause?

It seems that, on balance, there is something like comparative justice in Kant's just war theory. For the lack of central international authority, and thus of a fully determinate positive system of juridical state rights and duties, does leave room for interpretative conflict between states regarding the justice of their respective causes. Of course, Kant is not here advocating some kind of thoroughgoing subjectivism with regard to the application and interpretation of *jus ad bellum* criteria; he does believe that his principles clearly rule out some actions and clearly justify others. However, there is enough residual indeterminacy regarding the international rules for it to be a requirement of reason to acknowledge self-critically some kind of limit to the justice of one's cause.[30] Thus:

KJWT 5. Comparative justice. Although KJWT 1 is sufficiently determinate for us to make accurate and authoritative judgments regarding the justice of war, the lack of total determinacy makes it reasonable to require that all states self-critically acknowledge limits to the justice of their own cause and thus the imperative of fighting only limited wars, circumscribed by the criteria of *jus in bello.*

KJWT 6. Consistency with the ideal of perpetual peace. This suggestive yet imprecise criterion seems to serve two functions. The first is to underline the fact that a state may resort to warfare only for the purpose of vindicating and upholding the universal system of law and order, SRs 1-5 and SDs 1-5, which Kant constructs. The second, and arguably more important, function is to force a state resorting to armed force to consider in advance whether it can do so while adhering to norms of *jus in bello* and even to those of *jus post bellum.* In other words, KJWT 6 seeks to run a normative thread through all three just war categories: a state considering resorting to war must not only fulfil all the *jus ad bellum* criteria but commit itself in advance to avoiding, as far as possible, any breach of the norms of *jus in bello* and *jus post bellum* as the war unfolds. This forward-looking commitment to just conduct and appropriate war termination is needed, Kant suggests, if the idea of perpetual peace following warfare is ever to have a chance of becoming practical reality.

Jus in Bello

The principal aspect to note about Kant's account of *jus in bello* is that it is conspicuously weak and diffuse, at least relative to that of the Just War Tradition and to his own concerns with *jus ad bellum* and *jus post bellum*. In terms of the first standard criterion of jus in bello, Kant makes no mention of any criterion of (micro-) proportionality, presumably for non-consequentialist reasons similar to those stated above in connection with (macro-) proportionality. He does, however, appear to make one mention of discrimination: "[T]o force individual persons [in a conquered state] to part with their belongings...would be robbery, since it was not the conquered people who waged the war, but the state of which they were subjects which waged it through them."[31] Unfortunately, this is not a terribly precise account of the discrimination familiar from the Just War Tradition. The glaring omission in Kant is any kind of explicit mention and endorsement of non-combatant immunity. This is indeed disappointing, given the importance of the principle, but it seems that we can safely infer that Kant must have some such rule in mind because: 1) the quote just mentioned does enumerate an immunity of a kind upon the non-combatant civilian population; and 2) nowhere does Kant mention a right to deliberately kill innocent people, which noncombatant civilians are presumed by traditional just war theory to be. It is only rational actors (whether states or individuals) who either actually attack, or are imminently about to attack, that may be responded to with lethal armed force. So:

KJWT 7. Discrimination between combatants and noncombatants. Non-combatants are not to be made direct targets of armed force.

KJWT 8. No intrinsically heinous means. This seems to be the only truly explicit *jus in bello* category for Kant. For him, this rather vague and sweeping criterion rules out any wars of "extermination," "subjugation" and "annihilation." Civilian populations cannot be massacred or enslaved. It also means that states cannot employ "assassins or poisoners," or even spies.[32] In short, "[t]he attacked state is allowed to use any means of defence except those whose use would render its subjects unfit to be citizens. For if it did not observe this condition, it would render itself unfit in the eyes of international right to function as a person in relation to other states and to share equal rights with them."[33] Such a state would, in effect, be an outlaw and unjust state. So, it is clear that, for Kant the non-consequentialist, the end does not justify the use of any means to attain it. Kant asserts this quite clearly when he says that "[t]he rights of a state against an unjust enemy are unlimited in quantity or degree, although they do have limits in relation to quality. In other words, while the threatened state may not employ every means to assert its own rights, it may employ any intrinsically permissible means to whatever degree its own strength allows" (his italics).[34]

KJWT 8 is explicitly and repeatedly connected up with what we might call, again for added emphasis, KJWT 9: *No means may be employed which are inconsistent with the long-term ideal of perpetual peace.* In Kant's words, "a state must not use such treacherous methods as would destroy that confidence which is required for the future establishment of a lasting peace."[35] As we saw in connection with *jus ad bellum*, this rather sweeping principle of "consistency with perpetual peace" enjoins upon the state in question a commitment not to violate the other relevant just war categories. In particular, in its *jus in bello* form, this criterion demands that states not undertake measures that would undermine the process of war termination and thereby render very difficult the search for a just peace treaty as the war draws to an end.

Jus post Bellum

Kant, unlike most members of the Just War Tradition, is not content to rest with the two standard categories of *jus ad bellum* and *jus in bello*. Indeed he essentially invents a new just war category, *jus post bellum*, to consider in detail the justice of the move from war back to peace. In terms of *jus post bellum*, we need to distinguish between more immediate and more distant rights and duties, as well as between particular wars and the problem of war in general. When it comes to talking about the relevant rights and duties of states in the immediate period after a particular war,

Kant is, if anything, more elusive than he is about *jus in bello.* On the one hand, he firmly believes that victory in war does not, of itself, confer rights upon the victor which the vanquished is duty bound to obey. Might does not equal right. The victor thus has no right, through the raw fact of military success, to punish the vanquished or to seek compensation. In fact, the victor must respect the rights of the people of the vanquished country to be sovereign and self-determining. But against a vanquished enemy who was clearly unjust in terms of the war (for instance, by being the rights-violating aggressor), Kant says the people of such a state "can be made to accept a new constitution of a nature that is unlikely to encourage their warlike inclinations."[36] This latter remark seems to form a limiting condition to what may be done to states in the aftermath of a war: provided that there was a clear aggressor S and that S has been defeated, the very most that can be done to S in vindication of international law and order is the establishment of a more peaceable (presumably republican) constitution in S. There is no mention by Kant of anything like holding war crimes trials for political leaders or soldiers.[37]

In terms of more distant duties of *jus post bellum,* and with a focus on war in general, Kant's very original and suggestive theory of *jus post bellum* is essentially that contained in his famous list of the six preliminary, and three definitive, articles of perpetual peace.[38] These articles seem to constitute the final proposition of Kant's just war theory. Let us refer to this as KJWT 10: *Commitment to the articles of perpetual peace.* These articles are as follows:

The Preliminary Articles

PA 1. "No treaty of peace shall be considered valid as such if it was made with a secret reservation of the material for a future war."

PA 2. "No independently existing state, whether it be large or small, may be acquired by another state by inheritance, exchange, purchase or gift."

PA 3. "Standing armies will gradually be abolished altogether."

PA 4. "No national debt shall be contracted in connection with the external affairs of the state."

PA 5. "No state shall forcibly interfere in the constitution and government of another state."

PA 6. "No state at war with another shall permit such acts of hostility as would make mutual confidence impossible during a future time of peace. Such acts include the employment of *assassins or poisoners, breach of agreements, the instigation of treason* within the enemy state, etc." (his italics).

The Definitive Articles

DA 1. "The civil constitution of every state shall be republican."

DA 2. "The right of nations shall be based on a federation of free states."

DA 3. "Cosmopolitan right shall be limited to conditions of universal hospitality."

We have encountered these articles of long-term *jus post bellum* in some detail in chapter 1, albeit not as organized in this way. What is relevant here is to point out that most of these articles (e.g., PAs 1, 2, 5 and 6, and DAs 2 and 3) essentially mandate a postwar rededication to realizing Kant's ideal system of international justice: to fulfilling SRs 1-5 and SDs 1-5, within the context of a cosmopolitan federation. What is perhaps most significant about these articles is that they mandate not just international, but also domestic, reform (e.g., in DA 1, and PAs 3 and 4). A more just and peaceful world requires that states become republican (i.e., human rights-respecting, as enjoined by MPJ 1) and that they take confidence-building measures (e.g., weapons reductions and decreased military spending), which can substantially reduce the fearful tensions inherent in the current world system. The emphasis on republicanism is key for Kant: he believes that when power is dispersed, when the people are sovereign, and when they have their human rights fulfilled on the domestic front, states will face dramatically reduced incentives to resort to war. A just and lasting peace, for Kant, begins at home with respect for human rights, and is to be aided and abetted, on the international plane, by gradual and voluntary confidence-building measures and joint covenants on the pacific resolution of disputes.

So, even though Kant allows warfare (albeit under certain rigorous constraints), he never gives up on his hopes for a more enduring solution to "the scourge of mankind." Indeed, this theory of "justice after war" is a direct outgrowth of his earlier insistence that "there shall be no war"—that one day, we ought to have progressed to the point where there are no remaining grounds for resorting to the brutalities of war. To get to that point, states are to come together, to renounce both warfare and certain actions that incline states to go to war in the first place. States are to reform themselves internally in a republican, human rights-respecting fashion and, eventually, to structure the international arena in such a way that all SDs and SRs stipulated by the SUPJ can be actually realized and fulfilled, as if there were an effective cosmopolitan federation of peace uniting each and every one of them.

As Kant would say, these long-term prescriptions are intended to secure his foremost political value, freedom: freedom from war, suffering and indignity; and freedom to live our lives in the peaceful and lawful pursuit of whatever we happen to see fit, as we enjoy the substance of our human rights. Kant may well, in this regard, share the sentiments expressed by one of his greatest teachers, Jean Jacques Rousseau, who wrote: "Rich or poor, I shall be free. I shall not be free in this or that land, in this or that region. I shall be free everywhere on earth."[39]

Conclusion

It has been argued here that, contrary to the traditional reading, Kant does in fact have a just war theory. Kant is neither a realist nor a pacifist, and his belief that resort to war can be morally justified is consistent with his own core principles of morality and justice. War is just if and only if armed force is required to vindicate universal principles of international justice, notably the protection of rights. If a state violates the just rules of international law (say, by aggressing against another state), then other states (particularly the attacked one) have the right to repulse the aggressor and to protect their own status as rights-bearers through the force of arms.

Attention was then paid to developing the detailed set of rules constitutive of Kant's just war doctrine. Knowledge of these rules, KJWT 1-10, reveals that Kant differs from traditional just war

theory by: 1) explicitly eschewing consequentialist or prudentialist appeals to proportionality and probability of success; and 2) by
going beyond the tradition's standard criteria of *jus ad bellum* and
jus in bello by constructing an ambitious and forward-looking
account of *jus post bellum*.

It seems that Kant's just war theory, thusly construed, is quite
coherent and both morally and politically defensible. It seeks to
constrain the outbreak of war by limiting its justifying conditions
to those of rights protection and repulsion of aggression; it
attempts to moderate fighting within war by placing firm rules on
appropriate conduct; and it strives to provide imaginative yet
plausible proposals for putting the entire international system on
a more peaceable and secure footing of principled cooperation.
At the very least, Kant's just war theory is a systematic and suggestive account of the ethics of war and peace, as viewed by one of
the true giants of moral and political philosophy.

Notes

1. H. Williams, "Judgements on War: A Response," in H. Robinson, ed.,
   Proceedings of the Eighth International Kant Congress, Vol. 1, Part 3
   (Milwaukee, WI: Marquette University Press, 1995), 1393; F. Teson, "The
   Kantian Theory of International Law," *Columbia Law Review* (1992): 90; G.
   Geismann, "World Peace: Rational Idea and Reality. On the Principles of
   Kant's Political Philosophy" in H. Oberer, ed. *Kant: Analysen, Probleme,
   Kritik* (Germany: Konigshausen und Neumann, 1996), 286; W.B. Gallie,
   Philosophers of Peace and War (Cambridge: Cambridge University Press,
   1978), 19-20.
2. I. Kant, *Perpetual Peace,* in H. Reiss, ed. *Kant's Political Writings,* trans. H.
   Nisbet, 103 (P 355).
3. Kant, *Perpetual,* 105 (P 356).
4. War as "scourge" is in I. Kant, *Religion within the Limits of Reason Alone,*
   trans. T. Greene and H. Hudson (New York: Harper, 1969), p. 29 in the note.
   War as "the greatest evil" is at I. Kant, *Speculative Beginning of Human
   History,* trans. by T. Humphrey in his ed. *Immanuel Kant: Perpetual Peace
   and Other Essays* (Indianapolis, IN: Hackett, 1983), 58 (P 121). War as the
   "source of all evils" is at I. Kant, *Theory and Practice,* in H. Reiss, ed. *Kant:
   Political Writings,* trans. H. Nisbet, 91 (P 312). The other references are all at
   I. Kant, *The Contest of Faculties,* in H. Reiss, ed. *Kant: Political Writings,*
   trans. H. Nisbet, pp. 183, 187 and 189.
5. Kant, *Perpetual,* 95 (P 345).

6. I. Kant, *The Doctrine of Right*, in H. Reiss, ed. *Kant: Political Writings*, trans. H. Nisbet, 174 (P 354).

7. Teson, "Kantian," 90.

8. Not all scholars deny that Kant has a just war theory, or something approximating it. The works of Leslie Mulholland (e.g., "Kant on War and International Justice," *Kant-Studien* [1987]: 25-50, and Thomas Mertens (e.g., "War and International Order in Kant's Legal Thought," *Ratio Juris* [1995]: 296-314) seem much more congenial in this regard. They both anticipate versions of some of the claims that follow.

9. Prominent classical realists often mentioned include Thucydides, Machiavelli and Hobbes. More contemporary realists include Hans Morgenthau, George Kennan, Reinhold Niebuhr and Henry Kissinger, as well as so-called neo-realists, such as Kenneth Waltz and Robert Keohane. Notable realist tracts include Morgenthau's *Politics Among Nations* (New York: Knopf, 1973), Kennan's *Realities of American Foreign Policy* (Princeton: Princeton University Press, 1954) and Waltz's *Man, the State and War* (Princeton: Princeton University Press, 1978). See also R. Keohane, ed., *Neorealism and Its Critics* (New York: Columbia University Press, 1986); and S. Forde, "Classical Realism," 62-84, and J. Donnelly, "Twentieth Century Realism," 85-11, both in T. Nardin and D. Mapel, eds. *Traditions in International Ethics* (Cambridge: Cambridge University Press, 1992).

10. Kant, *Perpetual,* 102-03 (P 355).

11. Kant, *Perpetual,* 116 (P 370).

12. Kant, *Perpetual,* 116-20 (P 370-86).

13. I am indebted to both Thomas Pogge and Jonathan Neufeld for discussions on this point.

14. J. Teichman, *Pacifism and the Just War* (Oxford: Basil Blackwell, 1986).

15. The two most sophisticated defences of pacifism in the recent English literature are: R. Holmes, *On War and Morality* (Princeton: Princeton University Press, 1989); and, indirectly, R. Norman, *Ethics, Killing and War* (Cambridge: Cambridge University Press, 1995). See also J. Narveson, "Pacifism: A Philosophical Analysis," Ethics (1967) and G.E.M. Anscombe, "War and Murder," in R. Wasserstrom, ed., *War and Morality* (Belmont, CA: Wadsworth, 1970).

16. Quotes are at Kant, *Right,* 164-65 (P 343-44) and 167 (P 346), respectively.

17. Kant, *Perpetual,* 95 (P 345).

18. Kant, *Right,* 167 (P 346).

19. Contemporary restatements of traditional just war theory can be found in: Holmes, *War,* 114-82; M. Walzer, *Just and Unjust Wars* (New York: Basic, 1977); W.V. O'Brien, *The Conduct of Just and Limited War* (New York: Praeger, 1981); J.B. Elshtain, ed., *Just War Theory* (Oxford: Basil Blackwell, 1992); R. Wasserstrom, ed., *War and Morality* (Belmont, CA: Wadsworth, 1970); R. Regan, *Just War: Principles and Cases* (Washington, DC: Catholic University Press of America, 1996); R. Phillips, *Can Modern War Be Just?*

(New Haven, CT: Yale University Press, 1984); and P. Ramsey, *The Just War: Force and Political Responsibility* (New York: Charles Scribner's Sons, 1968).

In terms of the actual figures and corpus of the Just War Tradition, notables include Augustine, Aquinas, Grotius, Suarez, Vattel and Vitoria. The best historical studies of this corpus are at J.T. Johnson, *Ideology, Reason and the Limitation of War: Religious and Secular Concepts, 1200-1740* (Princeton, NJ: Princeton University Press, 1981) and J.T. Johnson, *Just War Tradition and the Restraint of War: A Moral and Historical Inquiry* (Princeton: Princeton University Press, 1981). For the primary documents themselves, see St. Augustine, *Basic Writings* (New York: Random House, 1948); Saint T. Aquinas, *Summa Theologica* (London: Washbourne, 1912-22), II, Q. 40, A. 1; Q 64, AA. 6, 7; and the following from J.B. Scott, ed. *Classics of International Law* (Oxford: Clarendon, 1925): H. Grotius, *De Jure Belli ac Pacis Libri Tres;* E. Vattel, *The Law of Nations;* F. Vitoria, *De Indis et De Jure Belli Reflectiones;* and F. Suarez, *De triplici virtute theologica (De caritate, disputatio 13).*

20. P. Christopher, *The Ethics of War and Peace* (Englewood Cliffs, NJ: Prentice Hall, 1994), 86-110.

21. Christopher, *Ethics,* n.19.

22. I owe this emphasis, and the phrase, to Thomas Pogge. It should be noted that some members of the Just War Tradition did indeed deal with some of the issues, such as processes of surrender, contained in *jus post bellum.* However, none did to the same width or depth as Kant; for all practical purposes, we can count Kant as the founder of *jus post bellum* as a separate category of just war analysis.

23. Kant, *Right,* 167 (P 346).

24. Kant, *Right,* 167 (P 346).

25. Perhaps the most helpful source on this complex issue of how Kant can justify the employment of armed force is T. Hill, Jr., "Making Exceptions without Abandoning the Principle: Or How a Kantian Might Think about Terrorism," in R. Frey and C. Morris, eds., *Violence, Terrorism and Justice* (Cambridge: Cambridge University Press, 1991), 196-229. The most relevant primary document is Kant, *Right,* 164-75 (P 343-55). I have dealt with some of these issues in my "Kant on International Law and Armed Conflict," *Canadian Journal of Law and Jurisprudence* (July 1998): 329-81.

26. Kant, *Perpetual,* 96 (P 346-47).

27. Kant, *Right,* 166-67 (P 345-46).

28. Kant, *Right,* 167 (P 346).

29. Kant, Perpetual, 102-105 (P 356-57).

30. See T. Pogge, "Kant's Theory of Justice," *Kant-Studien* (1988): 408 for more on the residual indeterminacy of Kant's moral and political principles. One of my readers felt that these issues of comparative justice and indeterminacy tie into Kant's remarks about permissive law. Permissive law, for Kant, deals with rights which are merely provisional and not peremptory, and thus applies during the long transition phase from the state of nature to civil society. While most of Kant's explicit remarks on permissive law focus on provi-

sional property rights during the transition phase, it is plausible to model not only this requirement of comparative justice but also many of his remarks about just war in light of this conception of permissive law.

31. Kant, *Right,* 168-70 (P 347-48).

32. Kant, *Perpetual,* 96-97 (P 346-47).

33. Kant, *Right,* 168-69 (P 347).

34. Kant, *Right,* 170-71 (P 349).

35. Kant, *Right,* 168 (P 347).

36. Kant, *Right,* 169-71 (P 348-49).

37. One of my readers wondered (as do I) why Kant does not talk about war crimes trials. The trial of soldiers who committed illegal acts during war would seem to pose no problem for his theory of punishment. But they are nowhere mentioned in the texts. What about such trials for political leaders? On the one hand, why wouldn't Kant say that a head of state, for example, could be tried or even deposed domestically for having launched an unjust war? This raises complex issues about Kant's theory of political obligation, in which obedience to the head of state is, at the very least, strongly enjoined upon citizens. This fact, combined with the absence of reference, leads me to be puzzled about whether Kant would have condoned such practices.

38. Kant, *Perpetual,* 93-108 (P 343-60).

39. J.J. Rousseau, *Emile,* trans. A. Bloom (New York: Basic Books, 1978), 472. These and related issues receive additional treatment in my "Kant on International Law and Armed Conflict," *Canadian Journal of Law and Jurisprudence* (July 1998),:29-81, and my "Kant's Just War Theory," *The Journal of the History of Philosophy* (April 1999).

CHAPTER 3

Critical Evaluation of Kant's International Theory

The aim in this chapter is to discover the extent to which we, over two hundred years later, can adopt Kant's groundbreaking theory of international law and justice as our own. What of his theory remains of value? What ought to be rejected as implausible and/or outdated? How can improvements on his account be made? What constitutes the best kind of *contemporary* Kantian theory of international law and just war?

General Criticisms of Some Core Claims

The Dubiousness of the Appeal to Reason Alone

In broad terms, it seems as though Kant is guilty of an overstatement with regard to the demands of morality and justice being the mandates of pure reason, unsullied by any appeal either to empirical evidence or to a set of value-laden views about the good life. Kant's Critical rhetoric about the need for rational purity, about avoiding all reference to human needs and desires, about eschewing any appeal to what we actually find enjoyable and good about life, simply fails to persuade.

Indeed, it seems that even Kant himself cannot remain faithful to his explicit rhetoric regarding his moral and political rationalism. First, it is clear that Kant's core political principle, the UPJ, cannot be fully specified without appealing to certain facts—or, at least, to certain empirical presuppositions—about the kinds of creatures we are and the nature of the social world we inhabit. Such facts include the following: that we inhabit a social world of similar creatures whose ends may conflict with our own; that we are prone to selfishness, subjectivity and violence in the case of such conflict; and that the use of coercion by a state power can effectively deter, and/or rectify, behaviour deemed unjust by the UPJ. Secondly, when it comes to justifying the key move in Kant's political doctrine—that from the state of nature to civil society, both domestically and internationally—he resorts to saying that such a move is necessary because without the lawful and peaceful interpersonal interactions made possible by a just state mechanism, "life on earth would not be worth living."[1] It is doubtful whether pure reason alone, even as Kant conceives it, can tell us when life is, and is not, worth living. More generally, the entirety of Kant's practical philosophy is rooted fundamentally in his understanding of the supposed facts of human nature, namely, as being split between free rationality and animal instinctuality. And his insistence that, of these two elements, we "most truly are" free and rational beings can, not implausibly, be described as a substantive conception of what is good about human life. In light of all these difficulties and problems of self-reference, it seems cogent to concur with Thomas Pogge when he writes that "most of Kant's particular [political] principles and prescriptions cannot be derived a priori."[2]

This is not to say that we ought to reject the content and worth of Kant's theory of morality and justice on this basis. We can easily distinguish between what he claims his methodology and proof are, what he actually employs as his methodology and proof, and how plausible and compelling are the norms of morality and justice he arrives at. Only the first seems questionable.

This is also not to say that appeal should not, or cannot, be made to norms of rationality and political reasonableness. Further,

it is not to say that we ought not to see ourselves, most fundamentally, as agents responsive to such norms. A contemporary
Kantian can still make such claims but, apparently, ought not to
confuse them with the more radical and insupportable view about
relying solely upon reason and making no appeal whatsoever to
complementary conceptions of human nature, of the state of the
world and interpersonal relations and, above all, of the good life.
A more modest and manifold structure of procedure and justification may well succeed where a very bold and precariously narrow
one apparently can not.

The Narrowness of the Theory of Rights

Much of the general structure of Kant's theory of rights seems
persuasive. It is both cogent and commonplace nowadays to
follow Kant in defining a human right as a just claim or entitlement, enforceable by coercion, to objects deemed vital or fundamental to our agency, interests and/or nature as human beings.
But this leads to the following query: are the human rights Kant
posits sufficient to protect, preserve and enhance our vital needs
as rational agents?

There are reasons to believe that, due to what Wolfgang
Kersting has labelled his "a prioristic parsimony,"[3] Kant fails to
specify a sufficient list of relevant human rights. It will be recalled
that, for him, the only innate or natural right is the right to be free:
free from force and fraud; and *free to* be governed by one's own
rational principles. We saw, in chapter 1, that the list of human
rights that Kant purportedly deduces from this central postulate are
the standard civil and political rights enshrined in the Western tradition: rights to private property, to due process in the legal system,
to formal equality before the law, to freedom of conscience and
belief, to freedom of religion, and to vaguely defined aspects of
political participation.

The grounds for doubting that rights to such objects suffice to
protect, preserve and enhance rational agency, even as Kant defines
it, are familiar. They are rooted in the most potent criticism that Karl
Marx had of Kant. Marx contended that any classical liberal political doctrine, such as Kant's, which concerns itself solely with civil
and political rights, will ignore those socio-economic realities,
which can be just as serious a threat to human enlightenment and

emancipation as brute violence and political coercion. The argument is that human agency—our free and rational choice-making capacities—can also be seriously jeopardized and undermined by things like dire poverty and starvation, lack of potable water, serious illness and disease, lack of adequate clothing and shelter, and perhaps a grievous lack of basic education. We are, in short, hard pressed to see how we could possibly be those autonomous agents Kant thinks so highly of unless we were to enjoy some kind of enforceable protection from such standard socio-economic threats. Contemporary Kantianism must thus devise a way in which such socio-economic objects can be brought under the fold of legitimate human rights claims.[4]

Criticisms of the International Theory of Justice

Only States?

For Kant, international justice is exclusively a matter of considering the rights and relations of states. While this narrow focus was perhaps understandable during his time, such a view cannot today be allowed to stand unrevised. Many contemporary scholars have, for example, highlighted the role that non-state associations—such as corporations and non-governmental organizations (NGOs), etc.—play in international relations. So Kant's rather abstracted and artificial concern with the nation-state needs to be weakened. This matter seems adequately taken care of by moving from the (implicit) claim that states are the only actors relevant to international justice to the more defensible notion that, while not alone, they are still the most important actors. States, for all the current pressures on them,[5] remain the primary determinants with regard to the direction and calibre of international relations. Their overwhelming advantage vis-à-vis other entities—in terms of the use of armed force, their awesome revenue-generating capacities (e.g., through taxation) and their control of their borders and membership within them—ensures that states will continue to enjoy such a position of power in the foreseeable future. Thus, it is still quite plausible to focus one's account of international justice on states as primary units of analysis.

The State as a Moral Person: Part One

The most central, and arguably contentious, of Kant's fundamental principles of international justice is that the state exists as a moral person. We have seen that Kant seems to offer two arguments in defence of this all-pervasive postulate: 1) that we cannot make sense of international relations unless we conceive of states as being free and rational actors that are responsive to defensible principles and policies; and 2) that the having of a state is a necessary condition for the citizens of that state having individual human rights. This section shall deal with the first of these claims, the next with the second.

Do we really need to conceive of states as being free and rational agents in order to make sense of international relations and to form cogent judgments about them? I am inclined to believe that this is one of Kant's most plausible uses of his ubiquitous, and notorious, "as if" Critical strategy. It seems cogent to contend that, to make sense of the behaviour of these mammoth, complicated entities (to say nothing of judging such behaviour, either prudentially or morally) we need to employ convenient conceptual devices and assumptions, such as that states can be seen: 1) as having some kind of individuated identity and unity vis-à-vis other states; 2) as having an identifiable nature, a set of needs and desires; 3) as having intentions and forming maxims or policies of action; 4) as being responsive to norms of rationality and justice while being tempted to follow those of prudence; and so on.

It is important to note that making the above kinds of simplifying assumptions—in short, employing some version of the domestic analogy—seems fully compatible with making much finer and more complicated analyses, so that the state is not seen as some kind of crude and artificial monolith. Consider the following example of such a finer analysis: suppose it is contended that the foreign policy of nation-state NS is a function of the commands of its chief executive CE, who is himself reliant on advice from chosen members of an elite within the foreign policy establishment, who in turn are animated by the desire for promotion within the civil service by the CE. It seems that such finer analyses of state behaviour themselves presuppose something like the domestic analogy. This can be seen in the present case by pointing out that the proffered analysis of foreign policy formation in NS is predicated on the notion that there is a more-or-less identifiable policy, that NS has a discernible set of intentions and policies, that NS could have chosen other such policies but did not do so for these reasons, and so on. So, the domestic analogy need not be an obstacle to deeper and more refined analyses of state and interstate behaviour.

It is also compelling to assert that the domestic analogy can be in perfect consonance with a more finely grained *moral* understanding of the behaviour of a nation-state. Consider NS again. NS invades nation-state Q, overthrows the existing regime and establishes its own puppet regime. A critic of NS's foreign policy might contend that moral responsibility for NS's actions resides not with the people of NS on the whole but, rather, with the political and military elites in NS who were at the centre of the decision to perform this act. Once more, it seems as if such more finely grained distinctions—this time prescriptive in nature—themselves do not make sense unless the domestic analogy is presupposed, at least to some degree. If we blame the elites of NS, this is because we think (among other things) that NS itself did something worthy of blame, that NS could have done something else, that we can identify a set of actions and intentions on NS's part that fail the test of moral decency, and so on.

Thus, it appears not unreasonable to follow Kant in employing some version of the domestic analogy when considering the manifold problems of international justice. To do so is not to be guilty of violating the strictures of methodological individualism: indeed, in international relations, it would seem exceedingly difficult even to grasp the vast multitude of actors and factors unless one employs such simplifying assumptions, at least as a groundwork to more refined analyses.[6]

The State as a Moral Person: Part Two

The second aspect of Kant's view that the state is a moral person is not cognitive or interpretative but, rather, moral in nature: the state is to be accorded moral respect as the necessary condition for securing the human rights of its individual citizens, who are moral persons proper. Taken as stated, the view seems plausible enough: the state, if well-ordered, can indeed provide a secure context in which individuals are rescued from the serious dangers of the anarchical state of nature, have much greater assurances of not being routinely exposed to force and fraud, have reliable dispute-resolution mechanisms which are public, predictable and peaceful, and so on. The presence of some context of law and order does seem to be a necessary aspect of a just, rights-respecting social condition. And so the state possesses some moral value.

The problem is that this is hardly the end of the story for Kant. The main difficulty is as Howard Williams has noted: it is unclear regarding what Kant believes are the precise identity conditions of a state subject to international law.[7] In particular, is the bringing of law and order to a people sufficient to establish a state's worthiness as a moral person in the eyes of its domestic, and the international, community? Or, in addition to this descriptive, purely factual ability to govern, must the state in question also satisfy normative requirements, such as respect for human rights? We have encountered this dilemma throughout the exegesis on Kant's theory of justice: it is the tension between priority and justification within the component principles of the UPJ (and thus also of the SUPJ). Following Allan Rosen, I have labelled it Kant's internal tension between his conservative concern with law and order and his more liberal concern with human rights.[8]

The above dilemma gives rise to the following concern: if a state is a legitimate subject of international law solely through its fulfilment of the law-and-order criterion, then it seems doubtful whether it should be seen as a moral person entitled to all the respect and regard due to such an entity. After all, the state in question might be rights-violative in nature. It might be an authoritarian, law-and-order regime that does not recognize rudimentary political liberties and personal freedoms. If such a state were thought by Kant to enjoy the full panoply of state rights, SRs 1-5, then there would be next to no link between the rights of states and the human rights of persons. But this violates a core stipulation of his international theory of justice—namely, that there be such a direct link—and, moreover, seems to create a serious problem for his conception of practical reason. This problem would be that, in the absence of a positive relation between the rights of states and those of persons, there is the possibility of conflict between them. This conflict is quite acute in the real world, where law-and-order states routinely employ their prerogatives to increase repression and rights-violation at home. But, given the stipulated unity and coherence of practical reason, no such conflict in its directives is possible.

The obvious solution would be to assert that *both* law and order *and* human rights fulfilment are required for a state to be deemed worthy as a moral person and thus entitled to the full panoply of state rights, SRs 1-5. The problem here for Kant is that such a solution seems to run afoul of his repeated claims of the priority of establishing law and order. Kant has no clear and compelling answer with regard to this conundrum raised by his conservative-liberal tension. He seems, unrealistically, to pin his hopes on the truth of his descriptive philosophy of history: one day, he assures us, the progress of nature and time will ensure that we enjoy both law and order and human rights. This is, however, a patently deus ex machina solution, as Patrick Riley has pointed out.[9] We are still left wondering what we, on this side of history, ought to do in concrete cases, in a manner becoming our status as free and rational agents.

The Very Idea of an International State of Nature

We might pause, before evaluating Kant's just war theory, to consider whether the chief problem of Kant's international theory of justice—namely, the move from the state of nature to civil society—is itself ill-conceived. In particular, is it the case that the status quo of the international arena really constitutes a state of nature? And, even if it does, is it as robust a state of nature as Kant, following in the footsteps of Hobbes, would have us believe?

Charles Beitz has offered some potent objections to the commonplace theoretical assumption that international relations are, at bottom, still a state of nature.[10] He has four chief points to make:

1. In the state-of-nature postulate, it is assumed that all relevant actors are selfish and fearful of each other and that this sensibility is so potent that it comes to set a firm realist framework for what it would be rational (or not) to do. In particular, it makes some kind of conflict between these fearful egoists, in a world of

scarce resources, appear inevitable, if not intractable. However, as Beitz points out, in current international relations, there actually exist ties and associations (such as corporations, NGOs, churches, family ties, etc.) that straddle the divide between states. States are not the only actors in relations between peoples; there exist sub- and supra-state associations and ties that can serve some kind of conflict-mediating role. Family ties between countries historically linked through immigration and/or colonization, for example, are frequently appealed to in order to diffuse potential conflict between the states in question. The Jewish community in the United States, for example, has been quite successful in influencing American foreign policy to be, on the whole, quite favourably disposed towards Israel.

2. In the state-of-nature postulate, it is assumed that there is a rough equality of power and ability. This is what makes it rational, in the social contract tradition, for all to agree to the terms of the contract that establishes civil society. However, as Beitz points out, this assumption does not seem to hold in the actual state of international relations. It is not at all clear, for instance, what the United States has to fear about the power of any of the nations of sub-Saharan Africa. This fact of a clear inequality of power between nation-states perhaps goes some way to explaining how it is today that there is little appreciable sense of international civil society. In social contract terms, not all of the relevant parties have reason or incentive to join into a juridical condition. Some are so strong and powerful that they have precious little to fear from others.

3. In the state-of-nature postulate, not only are the relevant actors selfish and fearful, they are also thought to be isolated and independent. They have only their own resources and wits to draw upon in the war of everyman versus everyman. However, as Beitz notes, in the real world states are neither isolated nor independent. Even island nations like Japan, which might seem self-sufficient, are in fact heavily reliant on outside sources for imports of certain needed materials, like foodstuffs and energy sources. The ties between states—of trade and commerce, of educational exchanges, of military alliances, and so on—create some considerable degree of interdependence amongst nations. But the fact of interdependence limits the degree to which rational actors can be self-serving egoists. Unlike the pure state of nature posited by

social contract theorists like Hobbes and Kant, cooperation can be very rational and real even in the absence of central authority.

4. Finally, in the state-of-nature postulate, it is assumed that there is no reliable way to enforce common rules and procedures. This fundamental lack of assurance makes self-help, perhaps including resort to armed conflict, the order of the day. Beitz contends, by contrast, that there are reliable ways in which nation-states try to enforce a set of customary rules and procedures, such as those embodied in the positive international law. These ways include diplomatic censure, punitive tariffs, economic boycotts and sanctions and, ultimately, armed force itself, whether unilaterally or multilaterally. Even though we do lack the much greater assurance offered by a full-blown international juridical authority, we have a collection of reasonably effective means for upholding and vindicating a number of core rules and procedures in relations between nations.

Many commentators have applauded Beitz's quite systematic questioning of some of the most prominent assumptions about the international state of nature. After reflecting on these points, Kant himself must back down from his earliest remarks about the severity of the international situation; he does not, in the end, endorse as extreme a state of nature as Hobbes does. Consider, for example, the previously mentioned fact that, unlike the domestic state of nature case, in the international state of nature actors are not permitted to employ armed force to coerce others to join civil society. And that was true because states that have established constitutions ought not to be subjected to force, lest they become destabilized and collapse back into the full-blown state of nature. This means that Kant's international state of nature is different from—and less extreme than—that which might obtain domestically. Pogge has neatly labelled Kant's true version of the international arena as a "semi-juridical condition," caught halfway between a full-blown state of nature and a full-blown civil society.[11]

More proof that Kant cannot subscribe to the extreme portrait of international relations as a pure state of nature is that, in his argument against world government, Kant questions whether a central coercive authority would be needed—truly, whether it could even be effective—in upholding and vindicating a number of morally defensible principles and laws. And his just war theory is predicated on the resort to armed force being one (admittedly desperate and unfortunate) measure that can go some way towards vindicating his set of ideal international principles, at least until states internally reform themselves in such a way as to become republican in nature.

But while it seems right to criticize Kant's most extreme formulations in this regard, it does not follow that the conceptual device of the state of nature is totally without value. On the contrary, it seems that, even taking into account the criticisms of Beitz, some form of descriptive realism is still a quite persuasive account of the actual state of affairs in current international relations. It is, at least, a defensible understanding of the subject matter. Although states are interdependent, they really do tend to pursue what they perceive to be in their own fundamental interests. Indeed, it could be argued that they accept interdependence *precisely because* it is in their interests to do so, for instance by minimizing costs or by gaining access to larger markets. As contemporary contractarians like David Gauthier have pointed out, it can be fully rational and fully egoistic in the long term to constrain one's egoism in the short term.

The reality remains that states currently act, and see themselves as acting, on what they take to be their own well-considered interests. If these interests seem to dictate defection from the common rules of the society of states, then so be it. This is to say that there is still some considerable (though not total) lack of assurance in international relations. And this lack of assurance regarding whether other states, especially powerful ones, will adhere to the rules is a non-trivial source of insecurity in international affairs. It is precisely this lack of sufficiently reliable assurance which seems to leave open a justified space for resort to armed force, as we have seen with regard to Kant himself. So Kant's adherence to a form of descriptive realism, while it needs to be muted by some of Beitz's concerns, nevertheless retains considerable value as an explanatory hypothesis of the actual state of international relations.[12]

Kant's Cosmopolitan Federation

The final problem with Kant's theory of international justice concerns his conception of cosmopolitan federalism. While the presence of such a federation may be able to reduce the international assurance problem—perhaps even to its smallest level possible—it is clear that Kant's vision of its actual instantiation is insufficient. For, every piece of historical evidence we have points to the extreme implausibility of any meaningful international federation existing without some kind of coercive power or institutional structure backing it up, which is something Kant clearly rejects.[13]

Criticisms of Kant's Just War Theory

Kant's just war theory is quite plausible. For its time, it was an excellent theory and one whose contribution ought to be reflected accurately in the historical record, which has so far failed to happen. For example, his theory points out, and attempts to fill, gaps in the standard theory offered by the Just War Tradition, particularly in terms of the requirements of *jus post bellum*. At the same time, there is no denying the existence of deficiencies that require rectification.

Errors of Omission

The first criticism of omission on Kant's part is his failure to take pacifism seriously. His overwhelming attention is paid to realism. On the one hand, Kant's focus on realism is entirely understandable, given that realism was, and is still, the dominant discourse of international relations. On the other hand, when one thinks of what is required to establish a just war theory, it is clear that realism is not the only doctrine that must be argued against, and powerfully. For pacifism says that no war can ever be just. It is hard to think of a more thorough rejection of just war theory than that. A contemporary Kantian just war theory thus needs to take the arguments of pacifism more seriously.

The second error of omission in Kant's account is the weakness of the theory of *jus in bello*, especially as compared with *jus ad bellum* and *jus post bellum*. Even though we have seen that certain standard principles of *jus in bello* can be teased out of a few passages, his lack of explicit endorsement of as basic a *jus in bello* principle as non-combatant immunity renders his commitment to *jus in bello* quite infirm. Kant is not comfortable talking about justice in war. This is related to what Jeremy Waldron has called Kant's "systematic unease" about permitting warfare in the first place. Kant does not want to concede everything to traditional just war theory; and so his attention is overwhelmingly focused on the broader question of progressively limiting the extent to which states might ever justifiably embark down the grim road of war. But it should be added that, even if this is his motivation for paying meagre attention to *jus in bello,* he still seems vulnerable to a serious criticism of incompleteness. To the extent to which he does permit warfare, it seems clear that the actions of states and their officers within war can, and ought, also to be subjected to rigorous and considered moral and political scrutiny. And this is something he patently fails to do.[14]

The third and final omission in Kant's just war theory is his comparative silence regarding the appropriate norms of short-term *jus post bellum,* following a particular war. And yet it is crucial, in terms of developing a comprehensive just war theory, to discover such norms, since the terms of the peace are frequently contentious and are often cited as a *casus belli* for future conflict. Belligerents also tend to prolong fighting on the ground in order to improve their position at the bargaining table, as recently witnessed in Bosnia.[15] It would thus seem a great improvement if such short-term norms—more focused and concrete than Kant's sweeping long-term principles for eliminating war altogether—for "justice after war," during its termination phase, could be developed. In particular, such would constitute an important source for reform of the international law of armed conflict. And this is so because the current law regarding the cessation of hostilities is extremely sparse, and largely focused on purely procedural issues of surrender. Almost no substantive restrictions of justice and legality are currently placed upon the victor of a particular war. There are no firm ground rules regarding what peace treaties should be based on.[16]

Errors of Commission

The largest error of commission in Kant's just war theory centres around his attack on prescriptive realism, which on the face of it constitutes a stridently expressed condemnation and rejection. A cluster of quotes expressing Kant's disdain for following "maxims of prudence" was cited in chapters 1 and 2. It was also suggested that Kant cannot, strictly speaking, be taken at face value in this regard. This is so since his account of anticipatory attack, for example, relies on the same kind of calculative reasoning. It also matters greatly for Kant, in terms of determining the justice of agent A's conduct, what the other agents around A are doing. Finally, Kant is clearly animated, in his just war theory, not simply by an a priori concern over the violation of ideal rules by outlaw agents; he is also moved by a posteriori—prudentialist, consequentialist—concerns regarding war's destructiveness and the immense human misery and suffering it can cause.

A related flaw is that Kant cannot be read as endorsing any norm of proportionality. There is simply no textual basis for this. And yet such a consequentialist norm—along with that of probability of success—plays an important role in constraining warfare and the destructiveness it causes, which is something Kant clearly would have supported. An important task for a contemporary Kantian just war theory is to figure out how to contextualize these storied just war norms within a moral framework that is recognizably Kantian in nature.

Particular Disagreements and Amendments

In terms of the actual content of Kant's just war theory, it seems that a contemporary Kantian account can improve on Kant's by developing a fuller conception of what constitutes aggression and self-defence, along with considering whether, and if so how, the right of anticipatory attack figures in the ethics of war and peace. Kant, we have seen, essentially relies on an unstated appeal to a common-sense understanding of these matters. But subsequent moral inquiry has demonstrated the existence of considerable depth and perplexity about these issues. It is especially challenging to account, in a satisfying way, for how the human rights of persons function within these various scenarios and issues.

More incisive and extensive commentary also seems possible and desirable in terms of some of the other just war criteria, such as right intention and comparative justice. My own view, to be developed in the second part of the work, is that the latter ought to be dropped in favour of a revised version of the former.

Finally, the examination of some historical cases, or even thought experiments, may well shed further, more revealing light on the moral realities at play, as opposed to Kant's sole reliance on principles pitched at a high level of abstraction and generality.

Constitutive Elements of a Contemporary Kantian Internationalism

After considering all these criticisms, omissions, qualifications and amendments of Kant, we might well wonder what of his international theory survives and is of value to us today. Can one be a "Kantian" with regard to these issues in the contemporary era? If so, how? What exactly is implied by that? Since the term "Kantian" is so readily, and sloppily, employed in the current milieu—both for purposes of appropriation and of criticism—it would be a clear contribution to scholarship if some greater specificity could be brought to bear. What follows is a list of interrelated elements which I believe to constitute a very cogent form of contemporary "Kantian internationalism" (or KI). As the best of Kant's international legacy, they will be referred to substantively throughout the second part of the work:

KI 1. Moral universalism, or cosmopolitanism. This includes, in particular, the core principle that every person is entitled to have his human rights respected. Human rights inform us as to how, as a matter of justice, human beings ought to be treated by others and by their social institutions.

KI 2. Rational agency. The justification for satisfying human rights in terms of respect for, and protection of, rational agency. This may involve the further belief that the most central and inescapable feature of our identity and self-understanding as human beings resides in rationality.

KI 3. Institutional focus. Above all, the insistence that legal, political and social structures are to be created, and/or reformed, in such a way that they satisfy human rights, and thereby respect, protect and enhance rational agency.

KI 4. An emphasis on deontology over consequentialism (without any further implication that consequentialism is to be utterly rejected.) The core notion here is that there be some firm, principled restrictions on the means by which a more just world order may be achieved. Such restrictions include, notably, respect for human rights.

KI 5. Rules, principles and laws. The idea here is that a contemporary Kantian approach should, in the footsteps of Kant himself, view the system of defensible international principles called for by KI 1-4 as constituting a more-or-less consistent system of normative direction—a system that can be mapped out in a set of general, yet instructive and action-guiding, rules and laws.

KI 6. Descriptive realism and the domestic analogy. Contemporary Kantian internationalists not only employ the domestic analogy when thinking about international relations, they also subscribe to some form of descriptive realism as an essentially accurate portrayal of the facts on the ground in terms of international relations: in the status quo international system, states are fundamentally, though not irreversibly, inclined to seek out and maximize their own national interest.

KI 7. The maintenance of a prominent role for nation-states. The main idea here is that descriptive realism constrains the set of prescriptions that we can reasonably expect to be fulfilled in the international arena. In particular, we are not to expect or hope for a full-blown world government that takes the place of nation-states. Kantian internationalists do not look forward to a global state, modelled after a central domestic government.

KI 8. Cosmopolitan federalism. What Kantian internationalists do look forward to is a cosmopolitan federation between nation-states, based on the rule of law, human rights and the develop-ment and growth of culture and commerce.

KI 9. Just war theory. In terms of war, Kantian international-ists subscribe to the view that war is justified only if reasonably deemed necessary to uphold and vindicate those universal prin-ciples of international justice (notably, respect for human rights) which, if adhered to by all, would result in a just and peaceful cosmopolitan federation.

KI 10. Jus post bellum. Kantian internationalists, unlike traditional just war theorists, give prominence to the just war category of *jus post bellum*, as invented by Kant. The idea here, we have seen, is that people and states are not only to consider the justice of embarking on war, and of fighting in war, but also what constitutes a just settlement after war and what longer-term institutional reforms need to be implemented to constrain the incidence and destructiveness of war as such.

It seems that these propositions, KI 1-10, constitute a very powerful and distinctive Kantian approach to contemporary questions of international justice. I propose, for purposes of clarity and rigour, that we not call an international theory "Kantian" unless it fulfils each of KI 1-10. These propositions are Kantian because they are, undeniably, propositions to which Kant himself subscribed. And KI 1-10 are distinctive in that, together, they set contemporary Kantian internationalism off from other prominent approaches to international affairs and law. Consider the following, "big picture" distinctions.

KI 1 marks KI off from non-human rights-based approaches to international affairs and law, like realism, statism, Marxism, pragmatism or unreconstructed utilitarianism. It also marks KI off from any unregenerate communitarian or nationalist conception of international ethics, according to which the demands of morality and justice alter radically across national borders. KI 2 distinguishes between KI and other approaches to international affairs and law which are human rights-based, such as the natural law tradition, which is closely allied with what we have called the Just War Tradition, by grounding human rights in a robust conception of autonomous rational agency. KI 1, 2, 3, 8 and 10 set KI off from other conceptions, such as conventionalism or legal positivism, by setting up a critical, non-conventional standard for the evaluation and reform of the international status quo. KI 4 and 5 clearly distinguish KI from various forms of utilitarianism, as well as from any neo-Aristotelian, virtue-based conception, because both of these latter ethical traditions explicitly question the feasibility and desirability of resorting to firm general rules and laws for moral guidance. KI 6 and 7 serve to carve KI off from some of the more unreflective, and unpersuasive, utopian understandings of international justice and law, such as claims that a full-blown world government is the end that we are all duty bound to pursue. Finally, KI 9 clearly distinguishes KI from pacifism, which denies the legitimacy of ever resorting to war in the international arena; and KI 10 establishes another boundary between KI and the natural law Just War Tradition, according to which the only just war criteria are *jus ad bellum* and *jus in bello*.

Contemporary Relevance

There is much of relevance and resonance in the Kantian tradition of thought about international justice and law in general, and that of just war and armed conflict in particular, as it has been reconstructed here. The first thing to note is its powerful insistence on the centrality of both reason and morality to an adequate conception of international law. This marks the Kantian tradition as a formidable and principled alternative to all those traditions of thought which stress the salience, and/or appropriateness, of more primal and unthinking drives, such as those of power, partiality and private interest, at the heart of the international system.[17] It also distinguishes Kantianism from all non-normative approaches to these questions.[18] Indeed, perhaps the greatest contemporary significance of the Kantian tradition is that it remains the most systematic and powerful normative account of international law and justice currently on offer. No other moral doctrine is as deep, as wide, as consistent, or as applied to questions of international justice and law, as is Kant's.

Furthermore, the Kantian tradition offers a comprehensive, principled and inspired vision of the future: of where we ought to be heading in terms of the evolution of international law in general, and that of war in particular. This vision is of a law-based cosmopolitan federation based on respect for human rights, separation and diffusion of power, and for the progressive advance of culture and commerce. This contrasts considerably with the relative confusion and listlessness surrounding many foreign policy questions, following the dissipation of previous dreams of a so-called "new world order."

Perhaps it might be noted how the essentials of the Kantian vision do appear to be present, at least to some degree, in the current international context. These would include such international institutions as the United Nations, the progressive development of freer trading relations amongst people, the growth of wider and deeper ties of international law and cooperation and, above all, the explosive growth of the human rights movement, especially as it has been codified and implemented with increasing effectiveness the world over. In essence, then, the Kantian vision calls for a deeper rededication to certain realities and commitments already present in our international life. In Kant's own terms, he offers us an inspiring challenge to remain true to our own deepest values and commitments as rational agents in the contemporary world.

So much for the continued relevance of Kantianism in general to the contemporary milieu of international justice, law and organization. What about its relevance as focused specifically upon the problem of war? Perhaps the best way to answer this is through demonstration rather than declaration. One plausible answer to the question, in short, is to be found in the book's second part, where the goal is precisely to construct and defend a contemporary Kantian just war theory.

Conclusion

This chapter has sought to show that, even though we must be impressed by, and can no longer downplay, Kant's historical achievements in international normative theory, we cannot simply swallow him whole in the contemporary era. We must be constructively critical of Kant's theory, as we move forward into the book's second part. The task there will be to fashion a compelling contemporary Kantian just war theory which is consistent with the core tenets of contemporary Kantian internationalism, KI 1-10.

Notes

1. I. Kant, *The Doctrine of Right*, in *The Metaphysical Elements of Justice*, trans. and ed. J. Ladd (New York: Bobbs Merrill, 1965), 100 (P 332).
2. Thomas Pogge, "Kant's Theory of Justice," *Kant-Studien 79* (1988): 40, n. 3.
3. W. Kersting, "Politics, Freedom and Order: Kant's Political Philosophy," in P. Guyer, ed., *The Cambridge Companion to Kant* (Cambridge: Cambridge University Press, 1992), 349.
4. On this issue, see W.J. Booth, "The Limits of Autonomy: Karl Marx's Kant Critique," in R. Beiner and W.J. Booth, eds. *Kant and Political Philosophy* (New Haven, CT: Yale University Press, 1993), 245-75. Also relevant is H. Shue, *Basic Rights: Subsistence, Affluence and U.S. Foreign Policy* (Princeton, NJ: Princeton University Press, 2nd ed., 1996), passim, and J. Nickel, *Making Sense of Human Rights* (Berkeley, CA: University of California Press, 1987), 1-60.

   It should be noted that there are a handful of passages in Kant that talk about state-run provisions for the destitute, and about public education. So, it is not as though Kant is ignorant of these considerations. But, generally, these measures are not framed in terms of responding to rights claims, owing to Kant's classical liberalism.
5. These pressures are often now summarized under the heading "glocalization." The term refers to pressure from two directions: one, the "upward" pressure from global institutions and practices, notably competition within the global economy; and the other, the "downward" pressure from regional, state or provincial levels of governance and public service. Nation-states are sometimes seen as being pulled in both directions, and thus under serious pressure in the post-Cold War world. I argue below, however, that all the recent academic discourse about the "death of the state"—while interesting and dramatic—is seriously incorrect.
6. For more on the domestic analogy, see M. Walzer, *Just and Unjust Wars* (New York: Basic Books, 1977), xxv-xxxi and 51-72, and H. Suganami, *The Domestic Analogy and World Order Proposals* (Cambridge: Cambridge University Press, 1989).
7. H. Williams, *Kant's Political Philosophy* (Oxford: Oxford University Press, 1983), 250-51.
8. Allan Rosen, *Kant's Theory of Justice* (Ithaca, NY: Cornell University Press, 1993).
9. Patrick Riley, *Kant's Political Philosophy* (Totowa, NJ: Rowman Littlefield, 1983), 102. For Kant's descriptive philosophy of history, see his *Idea for a Universal History with a Cosmopolitan Purpose*, in H. Reiss, ed. *Kant: Political Writings*, trans. H. Nisbet (Cambridge: Cambridge University Press, 1970), 41-53; and his *Perpetual Peace*.
10. C. Beitz, *Political Theory and International Relations* (Princeton, NJ: Princeton University Press, 1979), 11-66. Comment on these contentions can be found in T. Carson, "Perpetual Peace: What Kant Should Have Said," *Social Theory and Practice* (1988): 186-91.

11. More specifically, the international arena is "semi-juridical" because there do exist legal constitutions within the states. There exists, so to speak, a patchwork quilt of legal regimes here and there. However, it cannot be called a full-blown civil society since there is still absent any overarching cosmopolitan constitution. See Pogge, "Justice," 403-16.

12. D. Gauthier, *Morals by Agreement* (Oxford: Clarendon Press, 1986), passim; T. Pogge, *Realizing Rawls* (Ithaca, NY: Cornell University Press, 1989), 211-80; H. Bull, *The Anarchical Society: A Study of Order in World Politics* (New York: Columbia University Press, 1977); F.H. Hinsley, *Power and the Pursuit of Peace: Theory and Practice in the History of Relations Between States* (Cambridge: Cambridge University Press, 1963); T. Nardin, *Law, Morality and the Relations of States* (Princeton: Princeton University Press, 1983); and H. Morgenthau, *Politics Among Nations* (New York: Knopf, 5th. ed., 1973).

13. Many commentators, such as Riley (*Political*), contend that Kant is wrong if he expects any kind of workable international cooperation—at least on those serious issues over which armed conflict may break out—without some kind of enforcement procedures and institutionalized dispute-resolution mechanisms.

14. As pointed out in the Introduction, this work will follow Kant with regard to this incompleteness. But this is done solely for reasons of focusing on the main and most original tasks and not out of any ignorance or lack of interest regarding *jus in bello*. Such is a job better saved for another time.

15. See, for example, R. Regan, *Just War: Principles and Cases* (Washington, DC: Catholic University Press of America, 1996), 200-12.

16. See M. Reisman and C. Antoniou, *The Laws of War* (New York: Vintage, 1994). This issue will be dealt with, in detail, in the chapter on *jus post bellum*.

17. These rival doctrines range from extreme forms of prescriptive realism to various forms of recent post-modern approaches to legal thought in general and international law in particular.

18. See T. Franck, *The Power of Legitimacy Amongst Nations* (Princeton: Princeton University Press, 1990) for an example of an utterly non-normative approach to international law. Note in particular his appendix, devoted to arguing why justice should not be the concern of international law. A related account can be found in T. Nardin, *Law, Morality and the Relations of States* (Princeton: Princeton University Press, 1983)

PART TWO

A Contemporary Kantian Just War Theory

Contemporary Kantian Internationalism: Human Rights and Ideal Rules of International Law

The goal of the second part of this book is to employ the best of Kant in the construction of a defensible and groundbreaking contemporary Kantian perspective on the ethics of war and peace. This perspective will be infused with those principles, KI 1-10, developed at the end of chapter 3 as the hallmark values of contemporary Kantian internationalism.

There will be three stages in the construction of contemporary Kantian just war theory: 1) an examination of the core principles of international justice presupposed by the just war theory; 2) an exhaustive criticism of realism and pacifism, the two main rivals of just war theory; and 3) an elucidation of the principles of *jus ad bellum* and *jus post bellum* which contemporary Kantianism has to offer.[1]

This chapter's contribution will focus on the first of these stages. In order to fashion a compelling contemporary just war

Notes to chapter 4 are on pp. 121–126

theory, it is essential to develop a conception of international justice in general. Only once that has been achieved has the normative context been set for determining the justice of, in and after war. However, since the main goal of this work is the just war theory, the general conception of international justice cannot be exhaustively detailed. Only the pith and substance of the contemporary Kantian conception will be offered.

This pith and substance was revealed at the end of chapter 3, in the KI 1-10 list of core propositions of contemporary Kantian internationalism. The essence of what those propositions inform us about a contemporary Kantian conception of international justice is at least twofold: 1) that the human rights of individuals are the most important goals of international justice; and 2) that the main actors in the international system—namely, states—ought to be structured so as to make the fulfilment of everyone's human rights not only possible but actual. This chapter will thus be devoted to detailing more of the contemporary Kantian perspective on the nature of human rights in general and on the nature of state rights in particular. The key questions that require plausible answers include: 1) what are human rights, and why are they implicated at the heart of international justice? and 2) which state rights need to be formulated and respected so that persons can enjoy (at least more fully) the objects of their human rights?

Human Rights from a Kantian Point of View

Since human rights form the moral lodestar of contemporary Kantian internationalism, as per proposition KI 1, we must examine in some detail the nature of human rights, as viewed through Kantian lenses. A complete theory of rights, generated from the ground up, is obviously a task well beyond our present ambit. All that is sought here, and offered, is a substantive, comprehensive conception which suffices for the purpose of having a solid normative base for a defensible contemporary understanding of international justice in general and just war in particular. The specific aim is to arrive at a wider and deeper conception of human rights than rival contemporary just war theories which feature human rights, such as Michael Walzer's. The goal is simply to advance the state of the art regarding reflection on rights in times of war.[2]

What Is a Right?

The first question that must be answered in considering the nature of human rights is: what is a right to begin with? A good general answer to this query is that a right is a justified claim, or entitlement, to a certain kind of treatment from other people and from basic social institutions.[3] Furthermore, it is generally thought that a right is not just any justified claim to a certain kind of treatment; rather, it is a very powerful and weighty claim. The very word "right" clearly connotes something forceful and compelling, something which is not to be denied very lightly. In fact, many rights theorists have contended, following Ronald Dworkin, that "rights are trumps," which is to say that, other things being equal, rights have a greater claim on our attention and energies than do rival social claims or norms, such as the growth of GDP, the happiness of the majority, and so on.[4]

So we can think of rights as being *high-priority* entitlements, or justified claims, to certain kinds of treatment. In schematic terms, for agent A to have a right R is for A to have sufficient reasons SR why other persons and social institutions should treat A in certain ways W, and/or should refrain from treating A in certain other ways NW, whichever combination of omission and commission is required to provide for the kind of treatment in question. These reasons SR are so compelling as to make A's right claim R one of very high priority in terms of social attention, respect and satisfaction. To quote Jan Narveson's lovely phrase, a person's rights are as real as his reasons are strong. A person's rights ought to be respected to the extent to which his reasons for others, and social institutions, to respect these rights are strong. By "strong," Narveson clearly intends some reference to a cogent, compelling, non-tendentious and publicly accessible account of the ground of the right in question. A strong reason, in this sense, is one whose nature commands the attention and respect of all reasonable persons. Thus, a reason grounding a right is one that has serious purchase on our attention and action with regard to how we, and our social institutions, ought to treat people. In the final analysis, for the contemporary Kantian, rights are reasons.[5]

By asserting that "rights are reasons," what is meant is that a compelling analysis of them will reveal that, at bottom, the entirety of their purchase on our attention is a set of grounds for the treatment of persons. In particular, a compelling analysis of the concept of rights will not end with the discovery of some property of persons which simply commands our respect, like some faculty of rights we simply intuit. The older, "natural rights" tradition often conveyed this impression. The proper analysis, it seems, will end with nothing more nor less than a set of reasons regarding how, and why, persons are entitled to a specified level of regard from their fellows and their shared institutions.

Two crucial distinctions need to be made before further progress can be achieved. The first is that between a legal right and a moral right. Legal rights are simply those rights—as defined generally above—which are enshrined in positive legal codes and for whose violation there exist concrete legal remedies. This need not be the case with moral rights, which can be said to exist *either* as rights within actually existing moralities *or* as rights posited and grounded within what we might call a critical or justified morality. It is thus very important to note that there may be some overlap between these two kinds of rights: moral rights, in either sense, may find expression in particular legal codes which provide concrete remedies for their violation. But the key differences between the two categories are: 1) moral rights need not have effective legal codification for their existence and claim on our attention, nor effective legal remedies for their violation; and 2) legal rights need not be rights which are morally justifiable.[6]

The second distinction is that between general and special rights. General rights are those rights which make claims on all others and all social institutions. We shall see shortly, for example, that all human rights are general rights. Special rights, by contrast, are thought to be rights which make claims only against particular persons and/or institutions (and usually only at particular times and under certain circumstances). A particular kind of legal right granted to a landlord L in jurisdiction J would be an example of a special right: such cannot be claimed against all other agents, or against humanity at large, but only against, say, the tenants T of the landlord L in J.[7]

But what are the objects of these high-priority justified claims, whether they be legal or moral, general or special? It has already been asserted that, most generally, rights are justified claims or entitlements to certain kinds of treatment. But we measure the calibre of treatment through the possession and/or provision of certain elements. Most rights theorists contend that well-grounded rights are, essentially, claims to freedoms and/or benefits. We judge how well or poorly we are being treated by others and by institutions by determining the degree to which they allow us to enjoy such freedoms and benefits. The precise degree of enjoyment we require, as Thomas Pogge has claimed, is that of "reasonably secure access." This locution is needed in order to account for the fact that, despite our very best efforts, we can never fully guarantee that right-holders will always have complete, perfect and unfailing access to all the objects of all (dimensions of) their rights-claims. We can never entirely guarantee perfect access because of the finitude of our knowledge and information, the finiteness of resources, and unforeseen circumstances and changing conditions. The harsh reality is that satisfying rights (i.e., providing rights-holders with the objects of their rights) comes at a price, requiring the use of scarce resources, absorbing both explicit and implicit costs, the devotion of time and energy, and reliance on information that is not, and cannot be, flawless. And yet, owing to the importance of what rights protect, every effort must be expended to ensure at least reasonably secure access to them. Generally speaking, then, our entitlements are focused on enjoying reasonably secure access to freedoms and benefits.[8]

Thus, a right—whether legal or moral, whether general or special—is a high-priority, justified claim, on other persons and social institutions, to allow and enable the right-holder to enjoy reasonably secure access to some kind of freedom or benefit. The reasons justifying the claim are sufficient to make it one which ought not to be denied. This is to say that the justifying reasons are such that they impose duties on the relevant others and institutions to allow and enable the satisfaction of the right-holder's rights.[9]

What Is a Human Right?

Given this broad conception of rights in general, how are we to view human rights in particular? Perhaps the first question to answer here is: are human rights moral or legal rights? The answer, as with many rights commonly asserted in our time, is both. However, it seems safe to say that the ultimate ground of human rights resides in moral reasoning: such rights have existed, and do exist, first and foremost in terms of propositions in moral and political theory, whether critical or popular. At the same time, it is true that, given the plausibility and appeal of the human rights ideal, some human rights have recently found themselves worked into codes of positive law, both domestic and international. There has been a kind of assuring convergence between moral reasoning and legal reform in this regard.[10]

The second question to answer is: are human rights general or special rights? The answer here, at least in moral terms, is crystal-clear: human rights are general rights, claimable against all other human beings and all social institutions. Such rights do not rely upon special acts or particular relationships for their normative purchase on us. They are universal entitlements.

Human rights differ from other kinds of rights in at least two other ways. The first is that, not only are human rights claimable by all human beings, they are claimable for the exact same reason by each. This reason, loosely stated, is that we may all claim the objects of our human rights on the grounds of our very humanity.[11] The second distinguishing aspect of human rights concerns the fundamental importance of what they are designed to protect. Although more will be said about this in the section on justification, suffice it for now to say that human rights are justified claims to those objects—i.e., to those freedoms and benefits—we vitally need as human beings and which we can reasonably demand from other persons and social institutions. In fact, so important is the substance of what human rights are designed to protect that it seems reasonable to concur with Kant when he says that such may be, where needed, enforced with coercion.

So human rights are high-priority claims, enforceable by coercion, which stipulate how all human beings ought to be treated by each other and by their social institutions. They are claims, morally justified by appeal to our humanity, to those freedoms and benefits that we vitally need and which we can reasonably demand. Human rights, in short, command the performance of those duties—on the part of others and institutions—which will provide the human right-holder with reasonably secure access to the objects of his vital needs. As such, human rights establish what we might call, following John Rawls, the fundamental conditions for political morality and reasonableness in our era. In other words, a social and political system will be minimally just and reasonable to the extent to which it recognizes, respects and satisfies human rights.[12]

The Nature of the Correlative Duties

Given that human rights are claims on others and institutions—claims which entail correlative duties on their part—we need to inquire further into the nature of these duties. Perhaps the best way to proceed in this regard would be in a slightly historical vein, surveying some of the most prevalent views up until the present day before arriving at a considered judgment.

Until the late 1970s, the duties correlative to claims of human right were largely seen as being either negative or positive.[13] It needs to be stressed that this negative/positive distinction was, in terms of the *content* of the duty specified, wholly descriptive in nature: a negative duty was strictly a duty of factual inaction, of omission, of forbearance, or of refraining from doing something, whereas a positive duty was strictly a duty of factual action, of performance, of commission, of assistance or of providing something. Frequently, it was contended that the rights correlative to such duties should, in fact, be named after them: hence, the rights correlative to negative duties were "negative rights," and those correlative to positive ones were "positive rights."

It was often contended, on the basis of such assumptions, that the duties correlative to the so-called civil and political rights (e.g., to life, liberty, property and standard participatory and due process rights) were wholly negative. It was thought, for example, that all that others have to do for one to enjoy one's right to free speech is simply to refrain from interfering with one's speech. Civil and political rights, thusly viewed, appear to have only costs of forbearance in this regard and, as a result, seem very affordable and reasonable. Asking others to control themselves and refrain from interference is clearly not asking too much of them. By contrast, it was often thought that the duties correlative to the so-called socio-economic rights were wholly positive. To enjoy a right to material subsistence, for example, would require that other people and social institutions go out of their way to aid, assist, perform and otherwise supply one with the object of one's subsistence right, namely some level of nutritious food and potable water. By this convenient conceptual linkage, earlier rights theorists were quick to pronounce on the utter illegitimacy of socio-economic rights. Such rights, they said, really are not worthy of the name, due to the immense costs and onerous burdens that their correlative positive duties mandate. Such rights, they said, simply ask for too much, and so they do not constitute "justified claims," as the definition of rights stipulates they must be. So, their conclusion was that socio-economic rights are bogus rights; only civil and political rights, correlative to reasonable duties of non-interference, are truly worthy of the distinguished title of "human rights."[14]

Henry Shue, amongst others, formulated a devastating counterattack to this conservatively inclined conception of human rights and their correlative duties. Keeping the same descriptive understanding of the distinction between "negative" and "positive," he pointed out that some very traditional civil and political rights require the performance of duties that are not simply negative ones of forbearance. Consider, for example, the basic set of due process rights, such as the right to a fair trial by one's peers within a reasonable time period, or the right to be informed of what one has been charged with, or the right to qualified counsel, or the right to question one's accusers, or the right to the presumption of innocence. To enjoy the substance of these rights, is it true that the relevant others need only to refrain from treating oneself in certain ways? The answer, clearly, is no. Obviously, the right to be informed of whatever one has been charged with requires positive action on the part of whomever is to inform one of the nature of the charge. Furthermore, the right to a trial by peers within a reasonable time frame requires that innumerable positive duties be performed: it requires the positive presence and participation of jury members and officers of the court, and so on—in fact, it requires the positive construction and maintenance of an entire judicial system charged with expediting one's case. And it is clear that these positive actions do, in fact, come at a substantial cost.[15]

It follows from the above considerations, as Shue points out, that the enjoyment of some of the most traditional human rights requires the performance of duties that are not merely negative but also positive—and ones that can cost a considerable amount indeed. So, one of Shue's most powerful contentions was that, if one defines the duties correlative to human rights in terms of a binary distinction between empirically negative inaction and empirically positive action, such a binary cannot be sustained. And so the sharp split between so-called civil and political rights, on the one hand, and socio-economic rights, on the other, is fallacious. The conservative critics of socio-economic human rights turned out, on their own terms, to be seriously mistaken. (Indeed, this can be witnessed quite straightforwardly in the fact that the conservatives have long been partial to the right of private property, a right with socio-economic intentions and consequences, if ever there was one.) There is no sharp cleavage within the heart of human rights; they seem, rather, to form a unified and coherent whole.[16]

Shue's alternative understanding of the duties correlative to human rights runs thusly. His conception is not twofold but, rather, threefold. First, Shue still relies of the traditional descriptive/empirical conception of the difference between a negative and a positive duty: a negative duty is still, for him, one of factual forbearance, while a positive duty is still one of factual performance or assistance. However, Shue contends that, correlative to any single human right is not one single duty, which must be either negative or positive; rather, there are actually multiple duties, which mix both negative and positive elements. Specifically, he says that correlative to any single assertion of human right are three correlative duties: 1) negatively, not to deprive the right-holder of the object of his right; 2) positively, to protect the right-holder in his possession of the object of his right; and 3) positively, to aid the right-holder, should someone still manage to violate his right.[17]

Why these three kinds of duty, expressed in this manner? The answer, in Shue's mind, is straightforward and compelling: the performance of these three kinds of duty is, in fact, required to actually supply everyone with (reasonably secure access to) the objects of their human rights. Human rights, we have seen, exist to ensure a certain baseline level of treatment for all persons, usually by providing for them certain freedoms or benefits and by protecting them from standard threats to the enjoyment of such freedoms and benefits. Shue contends, powerfully, that such protection from standard threats is ensured *only* when the relevant actors and institutions fulfil these duties: 1) all persons refrain from violating the right; 2) effective institutions exist to protect the object of the right; and 3) everyone (or, at least, all those causally well-placed) comes to one's aid in case such protection fails. This tripartite structure, in short, is called for because it denotes a comprehensive normative structure which holds the greatest promise in terms of actually ensuring that everyone can enjoy reasonably secure access to the objects of their human rights. Shue's perspective on this matter is thus a refreshing reversal of the earlier doctrine: instead of obsessing about the duties and asking which are reasonable and which excessive, Shue asks instead which duties have to be performed if the right is to be respected, thereby giving priority of emphasis where it seems to belong, namely, on the human rights which are thought to be constitutive of political reasonableness and minimal justice in our era.[18]

It seems that Shue's account is strong, and many have followed him in this regard. But perhaps there may still be an objection: his account seems to run afoul of our considered intuitions, and a long-standing tradition of thought, namely, that negative duties are more powerful than positive ones. This long-standing tradition of thought, furthermore, has been closely allied with deontological perspectives on the nature of morality and justice.[19] My own view is that such distinctions may, in the end, cause more confusion than clarity, and that the most important thing remains to consider what is actually required for everyone to enjoy their human rights. However, since the distinction is still so widespread and since it does possess links to deontology (which Kantianism is committed to, as per KI 4 listed in chapter 3), further comment is required.

We might follow Pogge's lead, in this regard, by offering a thoroughly *normativized* conception of the distinction between negative and positive. A negative duty would thus be redefined as the duty not to harm some person, whereas a positive duty would be redefined as the duty to do someone good.[20] This distinction would seem to allow us to concur with established intuitions with regard to the priority of negative over positive duties without running afoul of the problems of self-reference exhibited in the earlier accounts, which relied on a purely *descriptive* distinction. For a normatively negative duty can still mandate the performance of actions, which are both empirically negative and positive. It may well be, as part of my negative duty not to harm person P, that I not only need to refrain empirically from injuring P myself, but that I need positively to do something to prevent injury from routinely befalling him, such as voting for the appropriate policies come election time, or coming to his aid in an emergency when doing so is at little cost to me, and so on.

The conception of the duties correlative to human rights defended here therefore runs as follows. Generally speaking, we ought to respect human rights because to fail to do so is to do grievous harm to the bearer of the rights. So, our reasons for performing the duties correlative to claims of human right may be seen as negative, *in the fully normativized sense.* However, under this general rubric, there is still the question of which actual mix of action and inaction is called for in order to provide for reasonably secure access to the objects of human rights. And this actual mix seems best thought of in terms of Shue's tripartite distinction, relying on the descriptive understandings of positive and negative. The view of the duties correlative to human rights is hence:
1. Negatively, not to deprive the right-holder of the object of his right (applies to all persons and social institutions).
2. Positively, to protect the right-holder in his possession of the object of the right. This is applied most directly to social institutions, which are much more capable, cost-effective and causally implicated in this regard. Yet, as Pogge would say, this does not unburden individual persons, whose part in this duty would seem to involve some kind of political activism and engagement, to

ensure that the institutions in question are appropriately structured.

3. Positively, to aid the right-holder, should the institutional protection fail and someone violate their duty of forbearance (applies to causally well-placed individuals and is subject to a constraint of reasonableness of burden).

To summarize the findings thus far: human rights are high-priority justified claims. They are general claims on all persons and shared institutions and are morally justified on the grounds of humanity demanding some baseline level of treatment. The duties correlative to human rights claims are simply those whose performance is required to actually provide for reasonably secure access to the object of the right. The object of the human right will be either a freedom or benefit vitally needed by the right-holder. It was suggested that, although the main reason for respecting human rights is normatively negative, the actual actions involve a mixture of elements which are descriptively negative and positive.

The Justification of Human Rights

The justification and the specification of human rights are two very closely intertwined issues: for our appraisal of the justification of human rights claims will, in large measure, depend on exactly what human rights are being claimed; and, conversely, our list of human rights will (and should) stick very closely to the grounds offered for their justification. So, one cannot talk about the one without the other. In this sub-section, I will concentrate on elaborating contemporary Kantian grounds for thinking we have human rights, which will allude to what we might have human rights to, a topic that will be expounded upon more fully in the next sub-section.

So what reasons do we have for postulating human rights? The reasons we have for postulating human rights are intrinsically linked with what human rights most centrally are: claims to certain kinds of treatment. The key question then is: how ought human beings to be treated by one another and by their social, legal, economic and political institutions? What is the baseline requirement of just treatment, from one's fellows and from one's social structure, which is due to every person and which can and ought to be coercively enforced where needed?

One of the most compelling contemporary Kantian justifications of human rights begins by offering a conception of what is meant when it is said that we all have human rights by virtue of our humanity. A Kantian, typically, will follow Kant himself and conceive of the property of humanity in terms of the conjunction of animal instinctuality and free rationality, with rational agency—our capacity for choosing deliberately between alternative courses of action—enjoying pride of place as our deepest sense of self. Our most precious possession, Kantians will assert, is our ability to live and direct our own lives as rational agents.

Our humanity, thusly conceived, no doubt imposes on us a set of needs. To need x is, in its most fundamental sense, to be dependent on x; importantly, it is to be harmed if one is deprived of, or lacking, x. For an agent A to vitally need x is for x to be a requirement for A's functioning as the kind of creature A is. A vitally needs x if A requires x for A's living a minimally good or worthwhile life for the kind of creature A is. To follow the schema of David Wiggins, A vitally needs x if: 1) the deprivation, or lack, of x would harm A's functioning as the kind of creature A is; 2) there are no readily available and/or acceptable substitutes for x; and 3) x is thus constitutive of A's living a life of minimal value.[21]

The interesting and important thing to note, in this regard, is the astonishingly similar structure between claims of (vital) need and claims of (human) right: they are both urgent, high-priority claims to the provision of some kind of object, for which we have very powerful reasons for complying with that claim. It is thus compelling to contend that there must be a deep linkage between these two notions.

But the linkage is not straightforward. There is not, so to speak, a one-to-one reduction, or equivalence, between vital needs and human rights. It is crucial, in particular, to note that the having of a vital need for x is not, of itself, sufficient for having a human rights claim to x. Judith Thomson has illustrated this point vividly with her famous case of the dying violinist. Even though said violinist will die unless he is hooked up to both of your kidneys, it seems clearly wrong to say that he has the human right for you to be so hooked up. It seems wrong because it mandates an incredibly onerous burden on you, thus constituting a serious infringement on your rational agency—your ability to live your own life—which is the deepest hallmark of your humanity. Even though he vitally needs you to be hooked up, he has no right either to claim it or enforce it.[22]

The obvious conclusion to draw is that a needs-based justification of human rights must include the notion that the correlative duties impose only reasonable burdens. The essence of this justification, then, is that A has a human right HR to x if and only if: 1) A vitally needs x as a human being; and 2) the correlative duties required for A to enjoy x are not excessive, *which is to say* that they will not undermine the rational agency of other persons. Which objects—which vital needs—fulfil both criteria?

Given that we do indeed seem to be complex composites of animality and rationality, with rationality arguably expressing our deepest self-understanding, it seems plausible for a contemporary Kantian account to stipulate that the list of relevant vital needs would include the following abstractly defined items: 1) personal security; 2) material subsistence; 3) equality; 4) freedom; and 5) recognition (or sociability, or membership). These are at least some of the objects of our vital needs as human beings which we can, at the same time, reasonably claim from others, with coercive enforcement if need be. We can conceive of, and implement, a system of rights wherein these objects can be provided reasonably for all: we can devise strategies and order our conduct such that everyone can have reasonably secure access to personal security, material subsistence, liberty, equality and recognition without undermining the rational agency of anyone.[23]

Personal security means security from serious violence which can endanger one's life and the core aspects of one's physical and mental well-being. Material subsistence means having one's fundamental physical needs met—notably a minimal level of nutritious food, potable water, fresh air, clothing, shelter and basic preventative health care—and/or having an income sufficient to provide such necessities for oneself. Equality means our need as moral beings to be regarded as equal in intrinsic value with other rational beings, and not to suffer from arbitrary and groundless discriminations. Freedom means the need to pursue one's own goals, and to make one's own rational choices, to be free from interference within a certain defined private space and to develop a degree of personal identity, integrity and autonomy. Finally, recognition means our deep need as social beings for acknowledgement of our own humanity, of our own rational potential and worth, and of our own belonging to, and full membership within, the human community. These are things, a contemporary Kantian will contend, without which complex creatures like us cannot imagine living lives of even minimal value. To use a term familiar from previous chapters, these are the things we require to protect and enhance our rational agency as human beings.[24]

We know this by reflection on what our lives would be like in the absence of (reasonably secure access to) these posited objects of human rights claims. I dare say, following theorists like Shue and Alan Gewirth, that we are hard pressed to see ourselves as rational, purposive agents at all in social contexts wherein we systematically lack potable water and nutritious food, where we have inadequate clothing and no shelter, where we have little or no education, where we live daily in an atmosphere of violence and fear of serious personal injury, where others do not recognize us as their equals in essential worth, and where they do not respect our own choices but, rather, seek to impose on us a certain way of life. The living of such a life seems scarcely imaginable for creatures like us; indeed, it is not clear how long we could survive at all under such miserable conditions. What is clear is that, in the absence of (reasonably secure access to) such objects—in the absence of protection of these objects from serious, standard threats to them—we cannot see ourselves as self-respecting and purposive rational agents possessed of intrinsic worth. To borrow and revise Kant's phrase, without the objects of our reasonable vital needs as rational agents, life on earth does not seem worth living.[25]

So, the core of this justification for human rights is that human beings ought to be treated in such a way that they can have (reasonably secure access to) what they vitally need as rational agents, *provided* such needs can be met without undermining the rational agency of others. They ought to be so treated because: 1) to fail to treat them in this way is to do them serious harm as the kinds of creatures they are; and 2) it is (*ceteris paribus*) one of our clearest, most potent and most broadly shared duties of morality and justice not to do serious harm to human beings.

It is my contention that mandating, with coercive force if necessary, the performance of the duties necessary to provide everyone with (reasonably secure access to) security, subsistence, equality, freedom and recognition would infringe on the agency of no one. This is to say that it is not too much to ask of us that we refrain from seriously harming our fellow human beings: that we refrain from depriving right-holders of the objects of their rights; that we do our part in structuring social institutions so that they reliably protect the objects of all our rights; and that we come to the aid of victims of rights-violation, provided that we are causally well-placed and can do so at a reasonable cost to ourselves. Performing such duties in no way seems to undermine our status as rational agents who have their reasonable vital needs fulfilled. Indeed, we might go further and agree with Kant when he opines that such performance would actually be an expression and affirmation of our deepest sense of self.

And coercion ought to be employed, or at least permitted, with regard to enforcing these duties, owing to its effectiveness in securing compliance and the enormous importance that people and institutions actually comply. We are, after all, talking about those elements we all require if we are to lead lives of even minimal value as human beings. We are talking about the minimal requirements of political morality in our era. As Kant would say, any coercion needed to secure such elements is no threat to, but rather necessary for, fundamental justice in our conduct and our social arrangements.

Approached from a slightly different angle, we might follow Narveson in contending that the having of a human right implies having the further right to employ the means necessary to realize that right: if this were not the case, we would fail to have the "right" as a right at all. Since, in our world, coercion and force are at times required to stave off rights-violation, and to secure rights-realization, then it follows that to have a human right is to have moral title to employ coercion, where needed, in defence and protection of its object.[26]

The basic structure of this justification of human rights, then, is as follows:

1. We all have vital needs as rational agents, the fulfilment of which poses no threat to the agency of others. These are the

things without which we cannot live lives of minimal value as the kinds of creatures we are. Indeed, it is not clear whether we can survive for very long at all in the absence of reasonably secure access to the objects of our vital needs. Examples of such vital needs, which can be satisfied reasonably by and for all, include: security; subsistence; equality; freedom; and recognition.

2. We cannot make more potent claims on the conduct of others, or social and political structures, than that they meet, or at least enable the meeting of, our vital needs as rational agents.

3. We cannot make more potent claims than this because:

a) Primarily, to fail deliberately to satisfy reasonable claims of vital need, or to fail deliberately to protect the objects of such need from standard threats, or to pose such a threat oneself, is to do serious harm and grievous injury to human beings, things which it is one of our most powerful and broadly shared moral duties to avoid doing.

b) Secondarily, social and political structures would be lacking in rationale if they failed to meet such fundamental claims. After all, what could justify social and political institutions that failed to provide the means to living lives of even minimal value? What reasons could be offered to justify the creation or maintenance of institutions that systematically failed to provide for—or perhaps even positively thwarted—our reasonable vital needs as rational agents? Rational agents, it seems, could not consent to live under such institutions.

4. Such claims of reasonable vital need ought to be seen as being co-extensive with claims of human rights. We all have human rights to those objects we vitally need as the kinds of creatures we are and whose provision to us poses no threat to the agency of others.

5. Thus, we can make no more potent claim on persons and institutions than that they perform the correlative duties necessary to realize our human rights claims, as sketched out last section: they refrain from rights violation; they structure social institutions so that rights are protected; and they come to the aid of victims of rights violation.[27]

The Specification of Human Rights: Vindication of the Universal Declaration

Having offered a reasonably detailed contemporary Kantian conception of the nature, meaning, weight, scope and justification of human rights claims, greater attention must now be paid to specifying which human rights we have, based on the foregoing principles and concepts. What I should like to do, in this regard, is to offer a brief vindication of the list of human rights contained in the United Nation's 1948 Universal Declaration of Human Rights (UDHR), which has come to exert hegemonic influence on mainstream contemporary thinking about what human rights we have. I would like to show how the majority of the human rights listed in the Declaration can be given a cogent explanation and justification within the contemporary Kantian perspective that has been developed thus far. It will be recalled that there seemed to be five basic, abstractly defined objects of the most fundamental of our human rights claims: security; subsistence; equality; freedom; and recognition. The central contention in this section is that we can interpret the UDHR in such a way as to show it being protective of each of these five key objects.

Consider first personal security. A number of articles in the UDHR, particularly Articles 3-6, 8-11 and 14-15, appear expressive of this vital human need. Article 3 stipulates that everyone has the right to *"life,* liberty and *security of the person"* (my emphasis). Articles 4 and 5 posit, respectively, a human right not to be enslaved or held in slavery and not to be subjected to torture or cruel and unusual punishment. Articles 6 and 8-11 are all human rights to certain kinds of legal guarantees and protections. Article 6 stipulates that everyone has the human right to recognition as a person before the law wherever they may be; Article 8 mandates that all have the human right to an effective remedy for having their rights violated; Article 9 maintains that no one shall be subjected to arbitrary arrest, detention or exile; Articles 10 and 11 guarantee fair trial and due process rights, notably the presumption of innocence, no *ex post facto* prosecution and the constitution of a competent and impartial judiciary. Articles 14 and 15 concern one's right to seek asylum in a foreign country, if one faces groundless persecution in one's own country, as well as a right not to be deprived arbitrarily of one's nationality, which in the modern world is a very important element regarding one's recognition as a person: stateless or nationless people, such as refugees, face very insecure conditions in a world dominated by nation-states.

This brings us to a consideration of which human rights listed in the UDHR are protective, and expressive, of the baseline of material subsistence which is required for all of us, in the contemporary world, to live lives of even minimal value as rational agents. Articles 17 and 22-26 seem to be the ones most relevant in this regard. Article 17 is the human right to own property and the right not to be arbitrarily deprived of one's property. Article 22 is the right to social security; Article 23 is the right to work and to social assistance in the event of prolonged unemployment; Article 24 is the right to rest from work and to enjoy leisure; Article 25 is the right to a minimal level of satisfaction of one's vital physical needs, notably food, clothing, housing, medical care and "necessary social services"; and Article 26 is the right to (basic primary and secondary) education.

Even though it was pointed out previously that socio-economic rights are just as legitimate as more traditional civil and political rights, it must be admitted that certain formulations of *these* socio-economic rights, within the UDHR itself, seem controversial. Most notorious in this regard is the section in Article 24 that includes "holidays with pay" as part of the human right to some respite from work. It is hard to see how lack of a paid holiday seriously threatens functioning as a rational agent—even if one agrees that a life without at least some free time is brutal even to contemplate, much less live. Furthermore, many of these socio-economic rights in the UDHR are at their most plausible when they are interpreted rather cautiously: for instance, when the right to work is not seen as implausibly mandating the creation of jobs for all but, rather, as stipulating the lack of arbitrary and confining restrictions on employment and the existence of social security payments in the event of chronic, non-voluntary unemployment. In my view, the core human rights here are Article 25, material subsistence; Article 26, primary and secondary education; and then some further right implied by the others to economic and employment opportunities and to the provision of a subsistence income in the event of chronic, non-voluntary unemployment.

Equality is captured in Article 7, which guarantees equality and non-discrimination before the law, as well as in Article 6, which guarantees everyone's right to be recognized as a person. Indeed, to the extent to which every single right listed in the UDHR is affirmed as a human right claimable by all, the entire Declaration is a resounding endorsement of human equality with regard to basic, dignified treatment by others and by social and political systems.

To what extent do the human rights listed in the UDHR protect freedom and liberty? A number of articles are relevant here. Article 3, previously mentioned, enshrines the right to "life, *liberty* and security of the person" (my emphasis). Article 12 stipulates that one has the right to be free from "arbitrary interference" with one's private life. Article 13 protects freedom of movement within borders and the right to emigrate across them. Article 16 says that we all have the right to found a family with the partner of our own choosing, while Articles 18 and 19 protect freedom of thought or conscience and freedom of expression and belief. Article 20 enshrines the right to freedom of association with others. Article 21 mandates the right of positive liberty to take part in government, particularly to vote in democratic elections and to run for office.

In terms of recognition and membership, we have seen that the very important Article 6 mandates that all have the right to be recognized as persons before the law and that Article 15 stipulates that one has the right to one's nationality and is not to be deprived arbitrarily of it. The right to recognition and membership also seems implied in Article 20's right to freedom of association with others, Article 21's participatory rights, and Article 27's right to participate in "the cultural life of the community."

The preceding has been an attempt to interpret the UDHR in terms consistent with the contemporary Kantian view of human rights, which has been defended throughout this chapter and rooted in the KI 1-10 principles of Kantian internationalism described in Part 1 of the book. The only articles in the UDHR which have been left out are those from 28-30. Article 28 only serves to corroborate one aspect of the present interpretation, in that it stipulates that everyone has the right to "a social and international order in which the rights, and freedoms set forth in this Declaration can be fully realized."

Articles 29 and 30 set out a number of restrictions and qualifications on the human rights listed in the rest of the UDHR. The restrictions and qualifications here are far too numerous and sweeping, in my judgment. A contemporary Kantian ought not to be too quick to endorse these two articles. The credible point these articles do make, however, (and one which has been previously dealt with) is that respect for human rights comes at a cost, and so reasonably secure access to their objects, and protection from only standard threats to them, is all that we can plausibly claim. However, given the extreme importance of such objects to our living lives of even minimal value, it seems to follow quite clearly that the threshold level required for "reasonably secure access" must actually be quite high.[28]

International Justice in General

Human rights are the highest priority goal of a contemporary Kantian perspective on international justice. They may be defined as justified and enforceable claims, on others and social institutions, that we all have regarding how we ought to be treated. Human rights are claims to those freedoms and benefits—specified in the UDHR—that we all need to lead lives of minimal value in the contemporary era. They establish the baseline quality of life and the minimal level of treatment and regard owed to rational beings. They constitute the essentials of a just contemporary society.

While individual persons, and their rights, are the most important normative focus of contemporary Kantian internationalism, they are not the main actors on the international stage: states are. It is, descriptively, the actions of states that largely determine the calibre of international relations and their impact on human rights fulfilment. We have seen, in connection with Kant, that the causal role that states play in the satisfaction of the human rights of their citizens imbues them with some moral worth. Rational persons found and adhere to state structures for the sake of securing the objects of their rights from standard threats to them. The key question of international justice, for Kantians, is thus: what are the appropriate rights and duties of states? What do states need to be entitled to, and what do they need to be duty-bound to do, in order to do their part on the international stage to advance human rights satisfaction?

It is absolutely essential to note how this focus on state rights and duties is consistent with individual human rights. There are two things to appeal to here. The first is the just-mentioned descriptive claim about the important causal link between the existence and structure of state mechanisms and the satisfaction of individual human rights in our era. The second is a prescriptive claim that we ought to ascribe to states only those rights whose objects they require to satisfy the human rights claims of their citizens. States, truly, have a legitimate existence only to the extent to which they can and do protect, preserve and enhance the rational agency of their members, and do so in a way that does not detract from the ability of other states to do likewise for their members. No state has any right to violate the individual rights of its own member citizens, nor indeed those of other states. To the extent to which this is true, we see that there is nothing to the acceptance of state mechanisms that is intrinsically at odds with a fully globalized and pro-human rights conception of justice: the task becomes to make sure that all states can realize the human rights of all their member citizens and that all states refrain from violating anyone's human rights. The order of the day is then to specify such universal and ideal principles of state rights and duties as are compatible with this directive, and then to consider what more adequate structures might be required to help bring that conception towards practical reality.

What is a state and why, exactly, does it have rights? A state is a political association of peoples, formed to be the authoritative source of governance for them. A state is the most authoritative political decision-making structure, backed up with a monopoly on the authorized use of coercion to enforce its decisions, within a demarcated territory. Usually, it is composed of legislative, executive and judicial branches, with a bureaucratic structure to support and implement its decisions and activities. One of the prime functions of state mechanisms, we have seen, is to bring law and order to a collection of peoples, providing them with an authoritative and peaceful means of resolving their disputes between them. This is to say, in Kantian terms, that a core function of a state mechanism is to rescue its people from the force, fraud and anarchy of the state of nature and to institute a civil society based on public and enforceable positive law. It is to try and ensure that lawful, moral behaviour is not folly, that it has a safe context in which it can develop and eventually flourish. But law and order is not the sole raison d'être of a state.

The other prime domestic function of a state mechanism, in Kantian terms, is to secure for its peoples their human rights, at least to the best of its ability. Indeed, to the extent to which security is itself a human right, these two core functions of a state— law and order, and human rights fulfilment—share a powerful linkage. States are to satisfy human rights, to the best of their ability, because that is what their peoples vitally need as human beings and because that is what they can reasonably claim from their political structures, by way of dignified and humane treatment. We have seen that it would literally be pointless for a rational agent to agree to be governed by a state structure that systematically failed to do its part in the meeting of his vital needs as a human being.

Related to these two central domestic functions are the further international functions of a state, namely, protecting its people vis-à-vis the unjust encroachments of other peoples or organizations, and of representing its people, and acting on their behalf, in a minimally just manner, vis-à-vis other states. When we talk about the rights and duties of states on the international plane, we are talking precisely about their rights and duties vis-à-vis other states and their populations, on behalf of their own domestic citizenry. We are talking about the rights and duties they need to protect and satisfy the human rights of their member citizens.

So states have rights only because human beings have rights. States are entitled to rights in the international arena because their citizens are entitled to the objects of their rights. People found and adhere to state structures to the extent to which those structures are able to satisfy their reasonable vital needs as human beings. And state structures will succeed in doing their part in the human rights fulfilment of their member citizens if, and only if, they fulfil four criteria: two domestic and two international. It seems cogent to argue that these four criteria must be met in order for a state to be well-ordered, or minimally just, at all. Specifically, then, a state entitled to rights is a minimally just (MJ) state which meets a threshold level of reasonableness with regard to the following functions: MJ 1) providing its people with domestic law and order; MJ 2) providing its people with reasonably secure domestic access to the objects of their human rights; MJ 3) protecting its people from outside attack and other forms of dele-terious interference by non-members; and MJ 4) representing its people vis-à-vis outsiders in a minimally just manner. Only states that satisfy MJ 1-4 are entitled to state rights.[29]

What is the nature and substance of the state rights to which minimally just states are entitled? The first thing to note is that, as rights, state rights are justified claims to those objects they vitally need to fulfil their nature or function. The function of a state is, at the least, to fulfil MJ 1-4 consistently over time. State rights are high-priority reasons for action which stipulate how political communities are to be treated by others, on behalf of their indi-vidual members. Notably, state rights serve as side-constraints which preclude the doing of serious harm to communities and the people of which they are composed.

Based on reasoning previously developed in this work, espe-cially Kant's list of state rights and duties, I would like to offer what follows below as an illustrative list of the general kinds of state rights and duties suggested by this contemporary Kantian conception of international justice.[30]

State rights (SRs) of minimally just states:

SR 1. Political sovereignty. This is the right of a people, orga-nized by its state mechanism: 1) to be free from the use of force and fraud by other states; and 2) to be free to be self-governing, in a minimally just fashion, without deleterious interference by other states.

The political sovereignty of states is rooted in the rights of its citizens to liberty, in particular, to be autonomous and self-direct-ing. In short, sovereignty is rooted in the right of people to make for themselves the most important decisions in their (political) lives. Given the sheer importance of the state in people's lives, people ought not to be forced to adhere to the rule of a state mechanism they do not accept as rational agents and so, conversely, they ought to be able to found their own state and to shape it in accordance with their wishes, *subject to MJ 1-4.*

SR 2. Territorial integrity. This is the right of a people, organized by its state mechanism, to ownership of the land and resources contained within the territory they inhabit, *subject* to the constraint provided by SR 3 and SD 5.

The right of territorial integrity is entirely parasitic, in terms of its justification, on the political sovereignty enumerated in SR 1. States are entitled to territorial integrity simply because peoples have to exercise their right of political sovereignty *somewhere.* States and peoples have to exist on some piece of land and they must have secure possession of that land vis-à-vis others. They must be able *to count on* that possession, if they are to fulfil MJ 1-4 for their citizens in a reliable manner. States have to exercise their rights and pursue their further political goals within a certain secured geographical space, and with the material wherewithal needed, otherwise political sovereignty will be practically meaningless. So states have the right, on behalf of their people, to be considered by other states to be the owners, or proprietors, of the territory—and any natural resources therein, subject to SR 3 and SD 5—over which their authority is acknowledged.

This is not to say that the principle of territorial integrity renders the current regime of national borders somehow sacrosanct or immutable. The prevailing principle, as Walzer suggests, ought to be that the land is to follow the people: a people ought not to be forced to be ruled by a state mechanism which it does not recognize as legitimate and which fails to be minimally just. Where such situations occur, the claims over who has authority over what territory will be overlapping, and a complicated process of negotiation and accommodation is no doubt in order, perhaps resulting in the establishment of a new state. The particular result will obviously depend on the situation in question. The point here is that there is nothing intrinsic to the right of territorial integrity, as here conceived, which would render the status quo untouchable. The bottom line, with regard to the practical import of this state right, is this: any invasion or serious boundary-crossing by one state into another is at least a prima facie violation of the right of territorial integrity because it attacks the ability of the invaded state to fulfil MJ 1-4 for its people. As such, the invader constitutes a serious threat to the invaded state's people. Only an overwhelming demonstration of the fact that the invaded state failed to meet MJ 1-4 can overturn this presumption.[31]

SR 3. Resources. This is the right of those states which, owing to the present state of boundaries, lack the resources necessary for providing their peoples with the objects of their human rights claims. It is a right for them to be provided with an amount of resources from surplus countries which: 1) will enable the poor states to make serious and sustained efforts at human rights fulfilment; and yet 2) does not deprive surplus countries of the means necessary to fulfil the human rights claims of their citizens.

The right of territorial integrity, we have seen, is not sweeping and rigid. In particular, the notion that state mechanisms are to be seen by other states as being the owners of all the natural resources therein obviously needs to be qualified in a world in which there is such dire poverty and such a poor record of human rights (especially subsistence rights) fulfilment. Just as property owners within a state can be taxed for the rights-fulfilment of themselves and other members of their community, so too it seems reasonable to claim that surplus nations within the global community can be taxed, in some fashion, for the rights-fulfilment of themselves and those whose vital needs and human rights are currently going unfulfilled.

There have been many realistic attempts at, and proposals for, such a transfer of rights-protecting resources. These range from multilateral and bilateral aid programs, to trade and financing preferences, to technical assistance and educational exchanges. But it is clear that much more needs to be done if the structure of the global economy is to progress further towards the provision of objects that can fulfil all human rights claims. For example, recourse might well be made to some minimal level of taxation of global currency trading, of investing in global securities, of international air travel, or much heavier taxes on cross-border arms sales and the like. Another option would be Pogge's detailed proposal of a Global Resources Tax or Dividend. Many experts, including some Nobel Prize laureates for economics, have proclaimed not only the plausibility and the desirability of such global institutional reforms, but also the sheer magnitude of the resources to be captured in relatively painless fashion. (A small tax on currency speculation is an especially clear example of this latter claim.) Of course, substantial institutional reforms within recipient countries would have to be made—and somehow monitored—by the global community to ensure effective delivery of the objects of human rights to the citizenry. This, too, points to the need for greater levels of global cooperation and interstate institutions which can assist us in the pursuit of greater international justice for all.[32]

SR 4. Equality. This is the right of all peoples, as organized and represented by their states, to be considered as equals in the interstate system.

The reasoning behind this state right is that actual levels of state power and influence ought not to be the sole, and/or determining, arbiter of relations between states. They ought not to be so because such is inconsistent with our human right, as rational beings, to be governed by right and not by raw might. No individual's claim to liberty and autonomy, for instance, is any the less for that person's not being the strongest, or the smartest, or the luckiest. From a strictly Kantian point of view, all individuals' claims to liberty, security, equality and so on, are equal. Analogously, no people's claim to political sovereignty is morally weaker than any other. All states, as representatives of their people on the international stage, are thus to be recognized as equals, *qua* holders of state rights and bearers of correlative state duties.

SR 5. Recognition. This is the right of all states to be recognized as such, *provided* that they meet a threshold of reasonableness with regard to the requirements of minimal justice, MJ 1-4.

The criterion of meeting a certain threshold of reasonableness as a state, is, of course, imprecise and colloquial. Yet it is clear that such is precisely the criterion with which we actually do, and have to, work. It is clearest and most compelling as a criterion when we consider, negatively, what would not be a reasonable job of fulfilling the posited functions of a minimally just state, namely: 1) the presence of anarchy, widespread law-breaking and hooliganism and prevalent violence amongst private citizens over conflicting rights-claims; 2) gross human rights violations, such as the severe persecution of a sizable portion of the domestic population, lack of regard and respect for civil and political liberties, the failure to provide legal guarantees and due process, serious and systemic socio-economic deprivation, and other familiar conditions which have been painstakingly analyzed and categorized by the international community of human rights organizations;[33] 3) the utter inability of the state in question to protect its members from outside attack; and 4) the failure of the state to act internationally in accordance with minimal rules of appropriate conduct, for instance by launching an aggressive attack against another state. States in which any of these four scenarios hold true do not have the right to be recognized as states entitled to the full panoply of state rights. They fail to be well-ordered and fully fledged members of the global community.

SR 6. Contract. This is the right of a state, based on liberty, to undertake contractual agreements on behalf of its people with other states and their peoples, regarding any matter they wish, provided that such agreements do not violate the requirements of international justice as here specified.

SR 7. Self-defence and the resort to force. States have the right to defend themselves from external attack, to defend other states from such attack, and to vindicate these universal principles of international justice in general, if necessary by armed force.

Much more, obviously, will be said about this topic later, since it is one of the main foci of the second part of this book. The general idea is that we fail to respect these state rights—indeed, *we fail to have these rights* in any meaningful sense[34]—unless we can employ those measures (including armed force) that are necessary to secure their objects from standard threats to them, such as violent aggression. In other words, it would be entirely fatuous to specify these state rights and duties were they not, in some sense, enforceable, and thus realizable.

SR 8. Protection of nationals. States also have special prerogatives concerning the safety of their own citizens or nationals who are working, travelling or temporarily residing in another country. Such prerogatives might include the right to make special representations and demand explanations for poor treatment of their nationals, perhaps to sue on behalf of their nationals in that country's court system, and so on. The uppermost limit to such prerog-atives would be, in an extreme case of severe persecution against its nationals, to launch an armed rescue operation on their behalf.

SR 9. Aid during disasters. States have at least a prima facie claim to some reasonable level of assistance from others in the event of a serious humanitarian emergency, such as an earth-quake, famine, flood, epidemic and so on.

What is the nature of the state duties correlative to these state rights, SRs 1-9? In general, state duties share the same general structure as those duties previously discerned in connection with individual human rights. There seems to be a set of negative duties of forbearance, positive duties of institutional protection and reasonable aid, all of which are descriptively defined aspects of the one overarching duty, a normatively negative one, not to do serious harm to minimally just communities and their citizen members. More specifically, it seems as though the following duties must be performed by all states if any state and its people are to enjoy reasonably secure access to the objects of their rights:

States duties (SDs) correlative to SRs 1-9:

SD 1. Recognition of all other states. This is the duty, correl-ative to SRs 4 and 5, to recognize all states as such and as equally entitled to the full panoply of state rights, *provided* that they are doing a reasonable job of fulfilling the four criteria of minimal justice, MJ 1-4.

SD 2. Non-interference with other states. This is the duty, correlative to one aspect of SR 1, not to interfere with the self-governance of another minimally just state, in terms of a purely domestic matter.

SD 3. No force, unless justified by SR 7. This is the duty, correlative to another aspect of SR 1, not to resort to force and fraud in one's dealings with another state, unless such a resort to force is justified by SR 7. There is thus a heavy presumption against the resort to force in international life. This implies a commitment to the peaceful resolution of interstate disputes, wherever possible and plausible.

SD 4. No invasion or capture of territory. This is the duty, correlative to SR 2 and closely related to SD 3, not to violate another state's right to territorial integrity (unless, again, such is reasonably deemed a necessary aspect of the resort to force permitted by SR 7).

SD 5. Resource transfer. This duty, correlative to SR 3, is that of surplus nations to devise some fair and universal mechanism for the transfer of some resources to those poor countries who need them to be able to fulfil their functions as reasonable states that satisfy the human rights of their citizen members.

SD 6. Keep all just, freely made contracts with other states. This duty is correlative to SR 6.

SD 7. Adherence to the norms of just war. Should war be justified, as according to SR 7, then states are duty bound to commit themselves to following the norms of just war in prosecuting the armed vindication of their rights: *jus ad bellum, jus in bello,* and *jus post bellum.*

SD 8. Hospitality for foreigners. This is the duty correlative to SR 8 and it stipulates that foreigners on one's soil are to be treated with (Kantian) hospitality and thus not to have their human rights violated during their stay.

SD 9. Reasonable aid to disaster-stricken states. This is the duty correlative to SR 9, and it mandates that, in the event of a humanitarian disaster in State A, there is a general presumption in favour of providing some reasonable level of required assistance to A.

Such seems to be, at least, a plausible and substantive contemporary Kantian list of state rights and duties. These rights and duties seem to be ones that states ought to have and respect; their doing so would constitute clear progress towards a more just global order, in terms of human rights fulfilment. If all states were minimally just, and performed SDs 1-9, and enjoyed the objects of SRs 1-9, there would seem to be little reason why all their citizen members would not be much closer to having reasonably secure access to personal security, material subsistence, liberty, equality and recognition. The international arena would really be doing its part in forwarding human rights-based justice for all. The sheer plausibility of these state rights and duties has been an important reason why the majority of them have already found their way into the positive codes of international law.[35] That being said, it must be stressed how this conception of state rights and duties importantly differs from the status quo of positive international law, in at least four respects:

1) The only states thought to be entitled to the full panoply of state rights are those that meet, on the domestic front, the threshold criterion of reasonableness with regard to *both* the securing of law and order *and* the fulfilment of human rights. This differs from traditional international law, where only the law-and-order criterion requires satisfaction prior to a formal duty of recognition (though this is thought by some experts to be changing).[36] The important consequence of this is that states which fail to fulfil the criteria of reasonableness are, by definition, outlaw states. As such, they do not enjoy the rights of states, as listed, though from this it does not follow that other, lawful states have no duties with regard *to the people* of such outlaw states, should they decide to interfere with them.

2) Relatedly, the present Kantian conception differs from traditional, positive international law particularly with regard to the rigidity of political sovereignty and territorial integrity. In opposition to the quite rigid claims of the past, which entitled any law-and-order-based state to full sovereignty and integrity, the present conception contends that sovereignty is grounded legitimately only when MJ 1-4 have been reasonably fulfilled. Similarly, the territorial integrity enshrined in contemporary Kantianism is not unreflective: rather, it is grounded in the normative principle of the land following the autonomous wishes of the people who inhabit it, and it is constrained by the resource-transfer principles of SR 3 and SD 5. Here too some international law experts have thought the content of the international law to be changing more in accord with contemporary Kantianism.[37]

3) There is no mention in contemporary international law of anything like SR 3 and SD 5, which deal with economic justice in the international order, and the meeting of subsistence human rights claims. A contemporary Kantian, following the lead of Pogge, will contend that it is very important to the functioning of a just international system to consider not only how states relate formally and whether or not they use force against each other, but also to what extent economic factors are at play in causing some of the gritty realities present in international

relations. To the extent to which economic factors play a considerable causal role in the calibre and direction of international relations, they too need to come under reflective principles of justice with regard to interstate transactions and capabilities.[38]

4) One of the reasons why positive international law, despite its containing many of these Kantian state rights and duties formally, has not been more effective at guiding us towards a more just and peaceful global order concerns the lack of effective enforcement machinery between states for the realization of these rights and duties. The suggestion has previously been made, following Kant's lead, for some kind of effective cosmopolitan federation between states as a cogent mechanism by which such rights and duties might be more fully realized. What might a contemporary Kantian have in mind with regard to such a global civil society—i.e., to such an effective and just scheme of greater interstate cooperation? The answer seems better dealt with later on in this work, since a cosmopolitan federation, as envisaged by proposition KI 8, constitutes a central aspect of long-term *jus post bellum*.

The main point here, therefore, is that this list of Kantian state rights and duties is a normative list which is reformist in spirit, as all Kantian conceptions must be. It does not, in the words of Pogge, present "the essentials of the status quo as unalterable facts."[39] Although it shares, nominally, many of the same rights and duties as positive international law, it does not share them all, nor in the same way, nor in the context of the same conception of justice and political aspiration.

Conclusion

The goal of this chapter was to lay one of the foundations for the construction of a contemporary Kantian just war theory, drawing on KI 1-10, the principles of contemporary Kantian internationalism. And this foundation concerned the general conception of international justice presupposed by the theory of just war. The general conception fashioned was composed of two parts: 1) of the human rights of persons; and 2) of the rights and duties of states in the international system. The foremost goal of justice offered by contemporary Kantian internationalism is the protection of individual human rights, as enshrined in the UN's Universal Declaration. But such rights require protection and the founding of states is the principal manner in which persons have attempted to secure such protection. Since this is true, and since states dominate international life, plausible considerations of international justice in our time must revolve around the state and its rights and duties. It was contended in this regard that: 1) only minimally just states are entitled to state rights, SRs 1-9, in the international system; and 2) minimally just states will perform those correlative duties, SDs 1-9, required for the realization of SRs 1-9.

This condensed conception of international justice is related to just war theory in the following way: as Kant had stipulated, one just cause for a state to resort to war is to defend its rights and to repulse those outlaw states that violate principles of global justice. We now have a fuller understanding of those rights and principles, which our just war theory presupposes. But before we can discover the nature of contemporary Kantian just war theory, we need to show how its two main rival doctrines are radically flawed. The criticism of realism and pacifism thus forms the goal of the following chapter.

Notes

1. It will be recalled from the Introduction that this work will not deal with *jus in bello,* since contemporary Kantianism has little to contribute to the state of the art. The current laws of war regulating conduct within war, and the efforts of the Just War Tradition in this regard, offer much more thorough and satisfying analyses of *jus in bello* than Kantianism. For an example, see the Geneva Conventions on the Treatment of Prisoners of War, in W. Reisman and C. Antoniou, eds., *The Laws of War: A Comprehensive Collection of Primary Documents* (New York: Vintage, 1994).
2. Walzer, as noted in this work's Introduction, relies on rights systematically (as a contrastive foil vis-à-vis a utility-based conception) yet eschews a comprehensive account and/or justification of them. M. Walzer, *Just and Unjust Wars* (New York: Basic Books, 1977), xxx and passim.
3. What is meant here by the phrase, "basic social institutions"? The reliance here is on Thomas Pogge's neo-Rawlsian conception, developed in his *Realizing Rawls* (Ithaca, NY: Cornell University Press, 1989), 1-65.

A basic institutional structure of a social system is the set of the most important ground rules governing the external conduct and interrelations of those persons affected by it. The "most important" ground rules are those whose effects, whether established (direct) or engendered (indirect), are "profound, pervasive, inescapable and present from birth." (Pogge, *Rawls,* 23-25)

A reasonably exhaustive list of such core social institutions would be: the nation-state and the interstate system; the constitution of the particular state in question and its governing bodies, as well as the distribution of powers between them (i.e., its most pervasive and important decision-making procedures and bodies—executive, legislative, judicial and bureaucratic—and the constraints on them); its legal system (particularly the fundamental legal rights, duties, powers and immunities accorded to those living under it); its mode of economic organization (particularly the system of property entitlements, the tax system, the kind of means of exchange, such as money, whether or not competitive markets are present and how they are structured and constrained, the kinds of sectors its economy features and the kinds of work activity available); its socially sanctioned system for using coercion and armed force, both domestically and internationally; its system for producing and distributing such crucial goods as food, potable water, clothing, means for shelter, education and health care; and the kinds of family structure it permits and to which it gives rise.

Not only are human rights claims on discrete, concrete individuals, they are also claims on how these basic institutions, which exert such enormous causal influence over our lives, ought to be shaped and operated.

4. R. Dworkin, *Taking Rights Seriously* (Cambridge, MA: Harvard University Press, 1977). On the whole idea of rights as claims, see the seminal work of W.N. Hohfeld, *Fundamental Legal Conceptions as Applied to Judicial Reasoning* (New Haven, CT: Yale University Press, 1919).

5. J. Narveson, *Moral Matters* (Philadelphia, PA: Temple University Press, 1985), passim, and J. Feinberg, "The Nature and Value of Rights," *The Journal of Value Inquiry* (1970/71): 243-57.

6. I am indebted to both Christian Barry and Thomas Pogge for stressing the importance of this distinction. The issue also receives cogent treatment in J. Nickel, *Making Sense of Human Rights* (Berkeley, CA: University of California Press, 1987), 13-36.

7. Hohfeld, *Legal,* passim; P. Jones, *Rights* (New York: St. Martin's, 1994), 12-26; and J.J. Thomson, *The Realm of Rights* (Cambridge, MA: Harvard University Press, 1992), passim.

8. J.J. Thomson, *Rights, Risk and Restitution* (Cambridge: Cambridge University Press, 1986); Thomson, *Realm*; Jones, *Rights,* 26-44; J. Raz, "The Nature of Rights," *Mind* (1994); T. Pogge, "How Should Human Rights Be Conceived?" *Jahrbuch fur Recht und Ethik* (1995): 103-20; Pogge, *Rawls,* passim; and H. Shue, *Basic Rights: Subsistence, Affluence and U.S. Foreign Policy* (Princeton, NJ: Princeton University Press, 2nd ed., 1996).

9. The correlativity of claims and duties was stressed by Hohfeld, *Judicial,* and has been echoed ever since.

10. And so it may be worth contending that, even if the subsequent justification of human rights in moral terms fails to persuade completely, there is still the positivist contention to fall back on: nearly every nation in the world today has legally ratified the United Nation's Charter, which mandates a commitment to respect and fulfil human rights. Thus, all states ought to respect and fulfil human rights because they have all, in a meaningful sense, already acknowledged their existence and committed themselves to adhering to them.

11. More will be said about the specific meaning of this claim in the subsequent section on justification.

12. This is fully in accord with propositions KI 1 and 2, laid down last chapter as foundational principles of contemporary Kantian internationalism. See Nickel, *Making,* 36-85; Jones, *Rights,* 72-92; H.L.A. Hart, "Are There Any Natural Rights?" *Philosophical Review* (1957): 54-66; the collection of essays in J.R. Pennock, ed. *Nomos, XXIII: Human Rights* (New York: New York University Press, 1981); A. Gewirth, *Human Rights: Essays on Justification and Applications* (Chicago: University of Chicago Press, 1982); Carlos Nino Santiago, *The Ethics of Human Rights* (Oxford: Clarendon Press, 1991); and J. Rawls, "The Law of Peoples" in S. Shute and S. Hurley, eds. *On Human Rights* (New York: Basic Books, 1993), 40-81.

13. In the exclusive sense of "either/or."

14. M. Cranston is one of the most infamous critics of socio-economic rights in this regard. See M. Cranston, *What Are Human Rights?* (New York: Basic Books, 1973). In general, the preceding position is adhered to by libertarian rights theorists, such as Robert Nozick and Jan Narveson. While it might be tempting to see Kant as fitting into this category, it would not be wholly accurate to do so. For, while Kant rejected most socio-economic rights (with the telling exception of private property), he did not reject stipulating the existence of positive moral duties. See the *Groundwork* for more on this.

15. Shue, *Basic,* passim; Nickel, *Making,* 147-70; R. Peffer, "A Defence of Rights to Well-Being," *Philosophy and Public Affairs* (1978/79): 65-87; D. Lyons, "Human Rights and the General Welfare," *Philosophy and Public Affairs* (1976/77): 113-29; and J. Donnelly, *International Human Rights* (Boulder, CO: Westview, 1993): 13-39.

16. Donnelly, *International,* n. 15.

17. Shue, *Basic,* 3-65.

18. Shue, *Basic,* passim.

19. See Pogge, *Rawls,* passim.

20. Pogge, *Rawls,* passim, and T. Pogge, "The Bounds of Nationalism," in J. Couture et al., eds. *Rethinking Nationalism* (Calgary, AB: University of Calgary Press, 1998), 463-504.

21. The linkage between human rights and basic needs has been mentioned and elaborated at a number of points in the literature: Shue, *Basic,* passim; Jones,

Rights, 94-119 and 146-71; Pogge, *Realizing,* 134-46; J. Feinberg, *Rights, Justice and the Bounds of Liberty* (Princeton: Princeton University Press, 1980), passim; Dworkin, *Rights,* passim; J. Raz, "Nature," 194-214; J. Raz, "Rights and Individual Well-Being," *Ratio Juris* (July 1992); D. Wiggins, "Claims of Need" in his *Needs, Values and Truth* (Oxford: Basil Blackwell, 1986), 1-57; Santiago, *Ethics* (Oxford: Basil Blackwell, 1992), passim; O. O'Neill, "Hunger, Needs and Rights," in S. Luper-Foy, ed. *Problems of International Justice* (Boulder, CO: Westview, 1987), 67-83; M. Nussbaum, "Human Functioning and Social Justice," *Political Theory* (1992) 202-46; A. Sen, "Rights and Agency," *Philosophy and Public Affairs* (1982), and J.J. Thomson, "Some Ruminations on Rights," in *Risk,* 49-65 (esp. 63-65).

22. Thomson, *Risk,* 12-55.

23. This raw stipulation of these five abstract objects of human rights claims might seem unsatisfactory in at least one sense: why these five, as opposed to others? Is there not some unified conception to which one might appeal here?

    The unified conception, while sparse, will follow below: it has to do with the avoidance of doing harm to others and with the having of the requirements of a life of minimal value as a rational agent. While these requirements may seem, as it were, philosophically "plunked down," this is neither the intent nor, I think, the effect. These requirements can be gleaned not only from an understanding of the human rights literature but also from a reasonable, non-doctrinal reflection upon human functioning and aspiration. While I would prefer a more extended grounding of this claim, I fear that in order to advance to the main topic of current just war theory, I must leave the matter with these contentions, as elucidated below.

24. Thomson, *Risk,* n. 21.

25. Shue, *Basic,* passim; Gewirth, *Essays,* passim; and Thomson, *Risk,* passim.

26. J. Narveson, "Force, Violence and Law," in J. Brady and N. Garver, eds. *Violence, Law and Justice* (Philadelphia, PA: Temple University Press, 1991), 134-49.

27. It should be pointed out that this is by no means the only possible contemporary Kantian option regarding the justification of human rights. One might, for instance, employ a dignity-based justification, and simply assert that the nature of a human being qua rational agent simply demands that we treat them with a certain kind and quality of treatment—enshrined, for instance, in human rights. Kant himself is clearly open to such a contention, given his assertion that rational agents have a "dignity beyond all price." My own sense, however, is that dignity-based appeals, of themselves, lack the substantiality that needs-based approaches bring to the table. Rhetorically, the former are incredibly powerful but, given the relative slipperiness and conflictual readings of "human dignity" (compared to a listing of a slim set of core needs), they seem to lack the grit and bite of the latter. My own preference is to contextualize a dignity-based account into the needs-based one, making the secondary point that to fail to protect the reasonable vital needs

of others, or to positively thwart the meeting of such needs, is not only to do serious harm to those others, it is to fail to treat them with the dignity owed to human persons.

Another contemporary Kantian option might be called the Rawlsian one. This justification would be that we ought to satisfy human rights because that is what rational agents would choose to do under ideal conditions. I shall not belabour what is a very familiar theoretical structure, dealing with the original position, the veil of ignorance, and rational representatives choosing social and political principles for ordering society based on the maximin criterion. The only point here is that it is quite plausible to suggest that rational agents would, under ideal conditions, want their reasonable vital needs fulfilled. This seems about as clear an instance of rational choice as there is. Not knowing who they are representing behind the veil, or what kind of social position they will occupy after the veil is lifted, rational agents would seem quite clearly to want a guaranteed minimal level of treatment (in case they themselves or those they represented should find themselves in precisely that position in the post-veil world). And what better guaranteed minimum could they all agree upon if not for ordering external conduct, and basic institutional structures, such that everyone enjoys (reasonably secure access to) the objects of their human rights? Rawls' collective term for such objects is "social primary goods," and among them he lists freedom and opportunity, income and wealth and "the social bases of self-respect." His list is not unlike the one offered here. See Rawls, *Justice,* passim.

28. Copies of the UDHR and other relevant international law documents on human rights can be located in the appendix of Nickel, *Making,* as well as in the very handy *Twenty-Five Human Rights Documents* (New York: Center for the Study of Human Rights at Columbia University, 1994).

29. This is the contemporary Kantian way out of the dilemma Kant faced earlier—as we saw in Part 1 of the book—with regard to the tension between law-and-order and human rights.

30. For the Kant material, see previous chapters, notably chapter 1. As can be seen, the list of rights and duties is composed as a set of general rules and laws, as per proposition KI 5, outlined in chapter 3. Other sources drawn on for the construction of this list include: M. Walzer, *Just and Unjust Wars* (New York: Basic Books, 2nd ed., 1991); J. Rawls, "The Law of Peoples," in S. Shute and S. Hurley, eds., *On Human Rights* (New York: Basic Books, 1993), 40-82; T. Nardin, *Law, Morality and the Relations of States* (Princeton, NJ: Princeton University Press, 1983); T. Buergenthal and H.G. Maier, *Public International Law* (St. Paul, MI: West, 1990); M. Forsyth, "The Tradition of International Law," 23-41, and D. Jones, "The Declaratory Tradition in Modern International Law," 42-61, both in T. Nardin and D. Mapel, eds. *Traditions of International Ethics* (Cambridge: Cambridge University Press, 1992); I. Brownlie, *Principles of Public International Law* (Oxford: Clarendon, 2nd ed., 1979); and J.L. Brierly, *The Law of Nations* (New York: Waldock, 6th ed., 1963).

31. Walzer, *Wars*, 51-73; M. Walzer, *Spheres of Justice* (New York: Basic Books, 1983), 18-35; M. Walzer, *Thick and Thin: Moral Argument at Home and Abroad* (Notre Dame: University of Notre Dame Press, 1994); and J. Lichtenberg, "National Boundaries and Moral Boundaries," in P. Brown and H. Shue, eds., *Boundaries: National Autonomy and Its Limits* (Totowa, NJ: Rowman Littlefield, 1981), 79-100.

32. T. Pogge, "An Egalitarian Law of Peoples," *Philosophy and Public Affairs* (1994): 195-224; T. Pogge, "A Global Resources Dividend," in D.A. Crocker and T. Linden, eds., *Ethics of Consumption* (Lanham, MD: Rowman Littlefield, 1998), 501-36; Pogge, "Bounds," 463-504; Shue, *Basic,* passim; and T. Eichengren, James Tobin (the Nobel laureate in economics) and C. Wyplosz, "Two Cases for Sand in the Wheels of International Finance," *The Economic Journal* 105 (1995): 162-73. Also relevant is the 1994 *Human Development Report,* published in New York by the United Nations.

33. See, for instance, *Twenty-Five Human Rights Documents* (New York: Columbia University's Center for the Study of Human Rights, 1995); H. E. Spirer and L. Spirer, *Data Analysis for Monitoring Human Rights* (Washington, DC: The American Association for the Advancement of Science, 1993); and the annual reports of such human rights organizations as Amnesty International and Human Rights Watch. The annual country-by-country human rights review of the U.S. State Department can also be useful.

34. J. Narveson, "Force, Violence and Law" in J. Brady and N. Garver, eds., *Justice, Law and Violence*, 149-69 and Shue, Basic, passim.

35. The most important primary source of international law in this regard would be the UN Charter. Secondary sources would include: Brierly, *Nations*; Brownlie, *Principles*; Buergenthal and Maier, *Public*; Forsyth, "Tradition," 23-41; Jones, "Declaratory," 42-61; L. Henkin, *How Nations Behave: Law and Foreign Policy* (New York: Columbia University Press, 1979); H. Lauterpacht, *International Law* (Cambridge: Cambridge University Press, 1977-78); and G. Van Glahen, *Law Among Nations* (New York: Macmillan, 1986).

36. See Rawls, "Law," 41-82; Buergenthal and Maier, *Public*; editorial comment by M. Reisman, "International Law After the Cold War," *The American Journal of International Law* 84 (1990): 859-76; T.J. Farer, "Human Rights in Law's Empire," *The American Journal of International Law* 85 (1991): 117-27; and the symposium in the Summer 1995 issue on the future of sovereignty in *Harvard International Review*.

37. Reisman, "Law," 859–76.

38. An important point in this connection is that economic deprivation and resentment, on the one hand, and lust for profits, on the other, have played an important causal role historically in the initiation of warfare. A comprehensive just war theory must thus pay attention to these economic issues. For more, see Pogge, *Rawls,* passim.

39. Pogge, "Peoples," 224.

CHAPTER 5

The Refutation of Realism and Pacifism

In chapter 4, we surveyed some of the core elements of a contemporary Kantian approach to questions of international law and order, on the one hand, and the ethics of war and peace, on the other. We also described and defended, in some detail, a Kantian conception of human rights, which forms the basis of contemporary Kantian internationalism. The tasks that remain, when it comes to offering a reasonably comprehensive contemporary Kantian understanding of just war theory, are: 1) to refute, in this chapter, both realism and pacifism, the two most potent challengers to just war theory; and then 2) to construct, in subsequent chapters, plausible doctrines of *jus ad bellum* and *jus post bellum.*[1]

The word "refute" has been chosen with some thought. Realism and pacifism are obviously not hopelessly benighted doctrines, nor are they literally self-contradictory. It does not seem possible to "prove" that they are the wrong perspectives to take on these matters. Perhaps the best that can be hoped for, between such rival conceptions, is a strong argumentative clash between

Notes to chapter 5 are on pp. 169–74.

them, similar to a reasoned public debate or a court case. So, the aim in this chapter is simply to provide strong arguments, from a contemporary Kantian point of view, aimed at refuting the central tenets of both realism and pacifism.

Realism

We have already encountered realism in some detail in chapter 2, which dealt with Kant's just war theory. But the aim there was solely exegetical: to determine the substance of Kant's views with regard to realism. Here, by contrast, the aim is twofold: 1) to explain, in a rigorous and novel fashion, the different kinds of contemporary realism most relevant to our issue; and then 2) to argue against what might be called those "strong" elements of realism which present the most forceful challenge to the tenets of just war theory.

It will be recalled that all realists are united by a strong suspicion about applying moral concepts and judgments to the conduct of international affairs. They are also united by their emphasis on the realities of power and security, on the need for national egoism and the protection of one's best interests, and, above all, by their view of the international arena as irreducibly one of a fearful anarchy, which seeks to ground their claims about the primacy of power. Archetypal realists often mentioned are characters like Thucydides, Hobbes and Machiavelli; and prominent twentieth-century realists have been figures like Hans Morgenthau, George Kennan, Reinhold Niebuhr and Henry Kissinger, as well as so-called neo-realists such as Kenneth Waltz and Robert Keohane.[2] The following chart, offered as a substantial advance on how just war theory usually characterizes realism, might be employed to illustrate the main kinds of realism relevant to the debate on just war theory:[3]

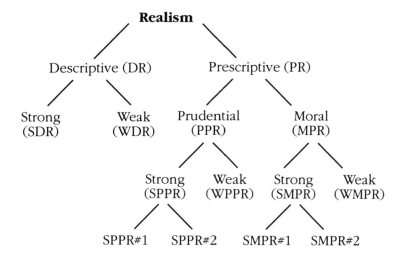

Descriptive Realism and Criticism of SDR

Descriptive realism (or DR) is the doctrine according to which states, the primary actors in the international arena, are in fact motivated by considerations of power, security and national interest, and not by those of morality or justice. The basic starting point for descriptive realism is an understanding of the nature of the international arena as one of anarchy. Because there is no international authority, all states are fundamentally insecure: they are always vulnerable to the attacks and encroachments of others. At the very least, they have no reliable assurances from the others that they will not attack or interfere deleteriously in their affairs. This assurance problem makes states fearful and insecure. Furthermore, the lack of central authority means that, in the final analysis, states can rely on no one other than themselves to secure their rights-claims. So self-help is the order of the day. It follows that, given the international state of nature, each state will be and is concerned, first and foremost, with its own power and security vis-à-vis other states. Each state will, and does, act so as to maximize what it takes to be its own enlightened self-interest, and this will tend to involve relying on armed force, trying to assert and forward its own power and security, and in general doing the best it can vis-à-vis other states in terms of cultural, commercial, political and military competition.[4]

Within this general conception of DR, distinction needs to be made further between strong and weak descriptive realism. Strong descriptive realism (SDR) is the doctrine—adhered to by Morgenthau, for instance—that we cannot speak meaningfully of state behaviour in terms of moral concepts and judgments. The only meaningful kind of discourse surrounding international relations is that centred on power, interests and security. Moral concepts are literally inapplicable to the realm of international affairs. To appeal to moral judgment in international relations would be to commit a category mistake.[5]

It is very difficult to see precisely in which sense "inapplicable" is being used in this regard. But the core notion seems to be that states are in no way motivated by moral concerns, and thus appeal to such concerns is idle. The idea here is that the extreme circumstances of the international arena render moral motivation essentially impossible for any state actor concerned with survival and security. Indeed, some SD realists frequently contend that the international arena is not even a place wherein choice plays a meaningful role. These realists frequently speak of the "necessity" of state action in the global context: states have no meaningful choice but to act on the basis of power and interest if they are to survive at all, much less thrive. The one thing that looms large in all such accounts is the bleak and dangerous picture of the international arena. On this SDR view, war is seen as an entirely predictable, even intractable, reality of the interstate system: it is a simple fact that the clash of national egoisms will sometimes spill over into armed conflict. It is another simple fact that states will do whatever they can in the midst of war to win; to hope otherwise is to engage in wishful thinking about the brutal facts on the ground in the international arena. So attempting to limit or constrain warfare, for instance with a set of just war rules and laws, is, as Carl von Clausewitz contended, at odds with its very nature and the very animating force behind state action.[6]

What is wrong with this SDR perspective? How to argue effectively against its claims from a just war point of view? Perhaps a cogent modus operandi would be to contrast SDR with the virtues of weak descriptive realism (WDR), which need not be opposed to just war theory. WDR is the doctrine that, while we can meaningfully evaluate state behaviour in moral terms (i.e., we do not commit a category mistake when we do so), it is never-theless true that, on the whole, states currently behave in accor-dance with their own conception of their national interest. They do so owing to the fundamental assurance problem that remains at the heart of international relations.[7]

The first criticism that the WDR theorist can level at SDR is simply the manifest ambiguity of its omnipresent appeal to "inap-plicability." Some have argued that such a claim is false, contend-ing that states sometimes do act on the basis of moral commitments, even when such actions seem manifestly at odds with their national interests. Although such examples are always complex and open to controversy, some have contended that Britain's efforts in the nineteenth century to outlaw the slave trade constitute one such example. Others cite American participation in World War I as another case of moral motivation at odds with even expansively conceived national interest.[8]

A second criticism is that these SDR charges of "inapplicabil-ity" fly in the face of long-standing practice: we have had a very long history of utterly coherent normative thought about interna-tional relations in general and warfare in particular. Just war theory is only one example in this regard. It would seem to take substantially more than sweeping (and condescending) assertions of category mistakes to overturn the salience and import of such practices.[9]

A related criticism of SDR is that all its discourse surround-ing the "necessity" of state self-regard is quite misleading and ill-founded. As Michael Walzer says, rarely is a state credibly threatened with extinction; and so the day-to-day reality of inter-national affairs is much more a matter of probability and risk than it is of strict necessity and of adhering to the fierce requirements of survival. States, it seems, are much more free to choose between alternative courses of action than SDR theorists contend. This means that they are free, in some sense, to choose to act on the basis of moral commitments and conceptions of justice, as well as upon considerations of their own national interest.[10]

The most severe criticism of SDR, apart from the above accu-sations of profound vagueness, opposition to established practice and exaggerated inaccuracy, is that it seriously misunderstands the nature of moral discourse, particularly with regard to war. As

Walzer has contended, war is an intentional human activity: states, after much consideration, choose whether or not to take the dramatic step of embarking down the road of war. They deliberately decide whether it is in their best interests to do so. (So all SDR pretence of states being "forced" or "determined" to go to war, one might be tempted to say, is a dubious piece of mystification.) And it is an important fact about moral discourse that any intentional human activity can be subjected to moral scrutiny. Of any prospective choice in the realm of human action, we can always meaningfully ask: "What ought the agent to do?" Furthermore, war is not just *any* intentional human activity subject to moral scrutiny: it is one of the most extreme and destructive activities there is. The very activity inherent in warfare—namely mass killing and destruction for political purposes—is so serious and far-reaching in its impact on our lives that it clearly demands moral judgment. Thus, all these considerations seem to put paid to the SDR theorist's vague, yet vehement, convictions regarding the "inapplicability" of moral concepts to international relations. We can, we ought, and we actually do make meaningful moral judgments with regard to international relations in general and war in particular.[11]

Perhaps, before moving on to consider prescriptive realism, we ought to reflect on how it is that WDR is compatible with just war theory. The key here is that WDR does not preclude the employment of moral values in either the motivation or evaluation of international conduct in the way purported by SDR. So state adherence to moral norms, such as those of just war, is not impossible, even though the current geo-political configuration militates against having much confidence in such norms eliciting staunch adherence. Another important fact is that, like just war theory, WDR does not necessarily view war as an intractable aspect of international relations, for which little by way of constraint can be achieved.

Prescriptive Realism and Criticism of SPPR and SMPR

Prescriptive realism (PR) is the view that states should only care about maximizing what they take to be their own enlightened national interest. It seems that here too we can discern an important distinction, namely, that between a prudential and a moral prescriptive realism.

Prudential prescriptive realism (PPR) stipulates that nation-states ought, prudentially, to be motivated in their international relations only in terms of national interest. The bottom line with PPR is that basing a foreign policy solely on an informed and sober understanding of national interest is simply the smartest and most advantageous thing to do. It seems possible and plausible to distinguish once more between strong and weak forms.

Strong PPR (SPPR) would be the view that, regardless of what other states are doing, a state ought (prudentially) to attend only to maximizing its national interests. There seem to be two prominent contemporary grounds for advocating SPPR. The first grounding of SPPR, SPPR #1, would be predicated on SDR: given that morality has no meaningful purchase on states in the inter-national sphere, what else *ought* they to do, save to maximize their enlightened self-interest? SPPR #1 stipulates that a state ought only to care about its own well-being, regardless of what other states are doing, because the only relevant norms of rationally defensible action to appeal to for guidance, in this case, are those of self-regarding prudence.[12]

The second kind of grounding offered for SPPR, SPPR #2, is not based on any form of DR. It is the more universalized claim that all states should be motivated solely in terms of prudence in their international relations because everyone would thereby be better off. If only every state minded its own business, and from a purely hard-nosed prudential perspective, the world would be a much better place. SPPR #2 views moral motivation not as impossible but, rather, as the source of serious (potential) conflict and instability in the international system. So it counsels that we would do best to leave morality off the international agenda.[13]

Weak PPR (WPPR), by contrast, eschews SDR in favour of WDR as its base, and stipulates that *only* in the face of serious non-compliance and egoism on the part of other states should a state forgo moral values and stick to the sober dictates of prudence. In light of the empirical salience of WDR, states that were motivated by moral ideals in their foreign policy would place themselves at enormous risk of being taken advantage of, or getting "suckered," by other states less scrupulous. It is simply the best bet, the most prudent wager, to base one's foreign policy on a sober, considered calculus of national interests.

In terms of war, both forms of PPR appear to recommend that such is to be undertaken only if it is in that nation's best interests to do so. Generally speaking, since war is such a momentous, costly and risky undertaking, both kinds of PPR will want to recommend war only in very serious cases where the nation's fundamental interests are demonstrably at stake. Furthermore, once a war has begun, the only principle that is to guide a nation's actions is again one of prudence: one should do whatever will maximize one's interests in terms of the war. Whether or not that involves adhering to just war rules constraining wartime action depends entirely on whether the nation in question sees such behaviour contributing to its end of victory (and, at least in the case of WPPR, whether the other belligerent is adhering to the laws of war or not). There is here no question of adhering to a set of restrictions as a matter of principle, or right; the guiding light emanates solely from the notion of protecting and enhancing national security and power.[14]

Contemporary just war theory, when reflecting on the cogency of prudential prescriptive realism, will reject at least SPPR, on either of its proffered grounds. One of the most powerful objections to the SDR-based SPPR, which we have labelled SPPR #1, is precisely that it is based on SDR, which was portrayed above as a dubious and inaccurate construct. National egoism for its own sake—and/or because one "has no other choice" but to act in accord with its dictates—does not appear to be a defensible doctrine.

Additionally, there is no reason why SPPR, on either of its grounds, should be thought to be more sober, or stabilizing, or advantageous, than alternative understandings of the imperatives of foreign policy, especially given its lack of heed to what other states are doing and how they are being animated. Every state, according to SPPR, is to be a headlong, self-regarding prudentialist. Indeed, one can easily imagine SPPR recommending more aggressive foreign policies—perhaps even more wars—than, say, a justice-based account of foreign policy. This is especially the case for a powerful state, which has less to lose and more to gain by exercising its influence, perhaps even by resorting to armed force. And this is not just an idle thought experiment; even the most cursory glance at the historical record shows the deleterious consequences of states basing their mutual dealings solely on the basis of national egoism and the strategic struggle for power. Indeed, to the extent to which SPPR recommends national egoism (indeed, even without regard to what others are doing)—and to the extent to which such headlong national egoism is thought to be at the heart of the assurance problem which is the very essence of the international arena—*SPPR would actually seem itself to undermine the security of the interstate system.* This is a version of the familiar prisoner's dilemma: co-operation in the solution of a common problem predictably leads to greater benefits than the pursuit of egoism. Yet, in the absence of assurance or mutual trust between the actors, the rational choice they will both make will be the egoistic option, thereby placing them both in a worse-off position. Far from saving us from morally charged adventurism, SPPR in either form may well condemn us to another kind of adventurism, a strategic one, whose costs would seem not predictably less than those of the putative first kind. So, SPPR might even verge on the self-defeating.[15]

And this last point is quite separate from whether morality can plausibly be seen as the source of conflict which the free-based form of SPPR, which we have labelled SPPR #2, contends it is. Contemporary just war theory, by contrast, perceives the existence of a universal core of values shared by all the world's diverse ethical traditions. In its political manifestation, that core revolves around protecting and respecting human rights. This point shall be elaborated upon in conjunction with MPR; for now, the only claim is that not all moral motivation in international affairs would give rise to the kinds of tensions, threats and inse-curities as are endemic to the purely prudential approach. Indeed, as Thomas Pogge has contended, shared moral commitments serve as more promising bases of a secure international system in that they are by no means as prone to change and renunciation as are those resulting from the latest cost-benefit calculation. *Ceteris paribus,* people keep their moral commitments, even when doing so leads to a sub-optimal result in terms of personal prudence: this is part of what it means truly to have a moral commitment. So moral animation in foreign policy, provided that it is universally accessible and minimally conceived—limited, say, to respecting human rights—need provide no grounds for worry about stoking the fires of interstate distrust and deviousness.[16]

Another flaw with SPPR, on either of its basings, is that it is incapable of ruling out from consideration state actions that are blatantly immoral. To that extent, SPPR seems at odds with some of our deepest commitments, which do indeed levy definitive prohibitions. As Jack Donnelly says, there is nothing in SPPR that would be at odds with, say, colonialism or imperialism—or even slavery and genocide—provided the right conditions and calculations were met. The familiar point here is that the recommendations of SPPR (indeed, any PR) are always contingent; there are no firm rules or side-constraints that states are to adhere to on principle. And this feeds back into the instability which SPPR, contrary to its self-image, fuels and furthers. If a state's foreign policy is always malleable (because it is based on the latest conditions and calculations), then this can only add to the insecurity which all states feel in wondering about the motives and future manoeuvres of other states and what they ought to do next to forward their own power and security.[17]

A final serious flaw of SPPR is that it really seems to mark a capitulation to being governed by might and not right. Less dramatically and more precisely, SPPR, in either form, favours and legitimizes the actions of the most powerful states in the interstate system. SPPR benefits and buttresses the actions and interests of the most powerful. If states ought to do what it is in their best interests to do (again, regardless of what other states are doing), and if the most powerful states have the greatest capability to do what they want to do, then the result appears to be a legitimation of the fact that powerful states are able to exert such incredible power over the interstate system in general and smaller states in particular. And yet this may well be at odds with other of our commitments, for instance to democracy and the self-determination of political communities. Also, if the only criterion for praise and blame in the realm of foreign policy is a prudential one, this conveniently deprives smaller, less powerful states of what is often their most powerful claim for international reform: moral criticism.

The question of whether a contemporary just war theorist ought to reject WPPR is more complex. On the one hand, as a PPR, WPPR seems open to a number of objections just levelled at SPPR, especially with regard to the insecurity implied by animation on the basis of mere prudence and the bias in favour of strong states. However, being grounded in WDR and not SDR, WPPR obviously sports a more attractive empirical base than does SPPR #1. And any complete just war theory must avail itself of at least some element of calculative, prudential and/or consequentialist concerns, for instance in the form of the criterion of proportionality. Furthermore, it does make clear sense to contend that, in the face of serious non-compliance and egoism on the part of other states, rational states ought, prudentially, to tend to their own when they act on the world stage, lest unreflective moralizing expose them to serious risk. It would indeed seem naive to contend that, regardless of what other states are doing, a state ought only to be concerned with how well it fulfils the imperatives of morality and justice. Indeed, when it comes to those core issues of just war theory—the protection and survival of peoples and the objects of their rights—it is clear that the norms of *both* prudence and morality/justice are deeply implicated and perhaps even interconnected.

This much seems clear with regard to reflections about WPPR: if the propositions of WPPR can find a place in contemporary just war theory, it is clear that they can do so only alongside—in fact, in a position subordinate to—those of morality and justice. The notion here is that those circumstances which morally ground the resort to war also provide some complementary prudential grounds for doing so. Such a view clearly privileges the moral over the prudential in vintage just war fashion, without committing ourselves to the implausibilities that would perhaps result from rejecting WPPR out of hand.

The forgoing in this section has only examined one line of the branch of prescriptive realism, with the conclusion that SPPR, in both forms, ought to be rejected while WPPR can perhaps be seen as compatible with certain aspects of contemporary just war theory. The other kind of prescriptive realism, we have seen in our chart, is not prudential but moral. Moral prescriptive realism (MPR) is the notion that, morally, nation-states ought to be motivated in their international relations only in terms of national interest. Morality itself, it is said, demands prudence on the international stage. There seems to be one final distinction between strong and weak forms in this regard. Strong MPR (SMPR) would claim that, regardless of what other states are doing, a state ought, morally, only to be motivated on the international stage in terms of its national interest. Weak MPR (WMPR), by contrast, would be the view that it matters importantly what other states are doing: only if they are seriously and systematically tending to their own ought the state in question, as a matter of fulfilling its moral duty of protection, to tend to its own, in the form of being animated on the international stage in terms of self-regarding prudence.[18] It is not merely the smart thing, but also the right thing, to focus on protecting one's interests when those around you are doing the same.

There seem to be two prominent grounds for SMPR, just as there were for SPPR. The first ground, SMPR #1, is impersonal or universal. The notion here is that all states ought (morally) to be animated internationally only in terms of self-regarding prudence because moral animation makes states intolerant, inflexible and disrespective of the autonomy of other peoples, particularly those committed to a different set of moral values.[19]

The second grounding for SMPR, SMPR #2, is more particularist or nationalist in nature. This particularist SMPR is commonly predicated on the notion that there are no non-voluntary cosmopolitan moral duties. Moral demands alter radically along national borders; indeed, they alter so radically that only norms of prudence ought to be adhered to internationally. The most powerful reasons why this is thought to be the case are: 1) a legitimate national government is a trustee, or advocate, or agent of its people and as such its overwhelming and overriding duty is to look out for the well-being of its people, and only its own people; and 2) individual identity is very closely tied to national membership. Shared values, languages, historical experiences and customs tie together a moral community based on mutual recognition and regard—a kind of mutuality which is simply not present at the international level. Whether universal or particular in terms of its grounding, SMPR, in terms specifically referring to war, counsels that it is not only prudent but moral to base decisions to go to war on a calculation of national interests. And in the conduct of war, the best that a national government can do, morally, is to do the best it can by its own citizens, namely, by winning the war as quickly as it can, with as little cost to itself and its people as possible.[20]

SMPR, regardless of kind of grounding, is a powerful and influential doctrine. Kennan, one of the chief architects of post-World War II foreign policy in the U.S., repeatedly contended that "the primary obligation" of a national government "is to the interests of the national society it represents...its military security, the integrity of its political life, and the well-being of its people."[21] And Kissinger, another influential figure, has repeatedly claimed that it is morally offensive for states to be morally charged, contending that the world is thereby made worse off.[22] Yet a contemporary just war theorist will reject such a view. On what grounds?

The first thing to note is that, as a strong prescriptive realism, SMPR shares a number of flaws with SPPR, such as: the commendation of a doctrine which if widely adhered to would result, and has resulted, in serious international instability; and the implicit bias built in favour of the most powerful nation-states. In fact, it is arguable that SMPR is more offensive than SPPR with regard to this last remark because it grounds pure national self-regard *morally*, as opposed to prudentially. It therefore offers moral cover and justification for the dominance of the most powerful and privileged states. The implicit reasoning would be: it is moral that states base their foreign policies on national self-interest; and the most powerful states have the most capability to pursue their self-interest; thus, it appears morally legitimate that the most powerful states have the most capability to shape the interstate system to their own benefit. The morally dubious character of this inference is readily apparent. Indeed, it seems to reveal that SMPR verges on the paradoxical: offering a headlong moral recommendation of an (at best) amoral foreign policy. In the case of the impersonal form of SMPR, SMPR #1, the paradox is doubled: morally recommending, at the universal level, a particularist regard for prudence alone.[23]

One way of honing in on the other serious flaws in SMPR is to consider the grounds offered in support of its prescriptions.

Consider first the impersonal, universalist grounding for SMPR, SMPR #1. The notion here is that moral motivation in international affairs is a source of intolerance and perhaps paternalism. Since there is radical moral diversity in our world, states ought not to base their dealings with the rest of the world in terms of their own (presumably provincial) morality. A contemporary just war theorist will object to this grounding of SMPR for the reason that it proffers an excessively balkanized conception of morality, hardly allowing for the existence of any shared moral values between admittedly diverse ethical traditions. Consider human rights. Nearly every state on earth has ratified the United Nations' Charter, which mandates commitment to human rights. Human rights have thus been committed to, in a non-trivial sense, by representatives of every major ethical tradition on the globe. Furthermore, the grounds typically offered for respecting human rights are utterly non-provincial, invoking plausible conceptions of the vital needs of the human person and the very widespread norm not to do serious harm to such persons. There are thus grounds for contending that a morality limited to respect for such human rights—such as that advocated here—will avoid this criticism of SMPR #1. So it appears false to contend that a human rights-based foreign policy would produce intolerance or paternalism.[24]

So much for the impersonal grounds of SMPR #1. What of the particularist or nationalist ones of SMPR #2? The first particularist claim is that a legitimate national government is one that is a trustee or agent of its people and, as such, has an overriding moral duty to look after the interests and well-being of those it represents. There is obviously an important political truth in this claim, especially if one subscribes to values like democracy and the self-determination of communities freely organized into states. The real question here is not whether such a claim is morally compelling; rather, it is: what does its compellingness legitimately ground? In particular, does its compellingness justify the posited non-existence of cosmopolitan duties? To what extent does its truth allow national governments to put the interests and well-being of their citizens over those of foreigners?

By way of response to these queries, consider that a trustee or agent of X is not morally entitled to do something that X may not himself do. A defence lawyer, for example, is neither morally nor legally entitled to do anything and everything on behalf of his client. He is not permitted, for instance, to bribe the judge or to murder a damaging witness. The lawyer has to maintain a set of rules; but within the parameters established by those rules, he is entitled to argue vigorously and especially on behalf of his client. We might say that, within a minimal set of fair and just standards applicable to all, the agent or trustee is entitled to be partial to the interests of his client. Are there any such minimal standards operative at the international level?

Following reasoning developed previously, it seems defensible to contend that the Universal Declaration of Human Rights (UDHR) can meaningfully be seen as establishing the minimal set of rules and principles of justice which states are duty bound to uphold on the international level. This is to say that human rights, and the rights of minimally just states, form the minimal threshold level required by a defensible and contemporary theory of international justice. Such rights are, as Rawls has said, the baseline requirements of political reasonableness and just conduct in our era. This claim puts paid to the SMPR #2 ignorance, or degradation, of non-voluntary cosmopolitan duties, substituting for its denial the claim that all legitimate national governments are duty bound not to violate human rights, regardless of the nationality of the rights-holder. They are not to violate any human rights because to do so is to do serious harm to human beings, something which (*ceteris paribus*) no one is morally entitled to do. National governments may not do something which their own citizens may not themselves do; there are thus real, powerful and principled limits on the degree of partiality which SMPR #2 can plausibly justify.[25]

It is important to note that this just war claim is compatible with *one aspect* of the SMPR #2 claim that national governments owe some degree of partiality to their own citizens. Just like the case of the defence lawyer, it seems cogent to contend that, above and beyond the minimal, universal threshold of human rights fulfilment required by international justice, national governments may feel free to do the best they can for those they represent. Above and beyond respect for human rights, and the rights of minimally just states, national governments need not treat all claims of foreigners on par with those of their own citizens, for instance with regard to membership, access to government subsidies, social programs and welfare benefits, participatory rights and so on.[26]

But what of the second nationalist claim often advanced on behalf of the extreme moral partiality defended by SMPR #2, namely, that moral duties are the irreducible products of a sense of moral community and belongingness that only obtains at the national level? It needs to be admitted, in response, that the global community obviously does not constitute a community in any way near as strong as that of a nation-state. It also seems as though a considerable part of an individual's self-understanding is shaped by his cultural and historical membership and thus that our communities enjoy a privileged position in our political thinking, especially when it comes to the international plane. But, that being said, there are serious limits and ambiguities to this grounding of SMPR #2.

The first thing to note with regard to such limits and ambiguities is that individuals can also feel quite alienated and disillusioned with their own communities—and to place greater personal value on leaving them behind rather than on preserving their traditions and customs.

Furthermore, it is very difficult to speak clearly and consistently about a shared, coherent national culture or identity worthy of the exalted status often claimed by nationalists or communitarians, given that no national culture is homogenous. The reality on the ground is that every so-called "nation-state" is actually a multinational state, with majority-minority dynamics and tensions, differences of language, race, custom, interest, historical perception, political ideology and so forth. In fact, we know from the historical record that most "shared cultures" have come to be that way through very questionable practices, such as wars of genocide, persecution of minorities and dissidents, propaganda campaigns and so on. So, even if there were a truly "shared culture," and even if it did play an enormous role in individual self-understanding, it would seem to be (at least somewhat) morally tainted by the way it came into being historically. At the very least, such knowledge cautions us from claiming too much on behalf of the nation-state. It certainly seems to prevent us from agreeing with the SMPR #2 claim that such is the exalted moral status of the nation-state that, internationally, it ought only to act to forward its own power and interests vis-à-vis neighbouring communities—and, moreover, to do so without regard to how they are being motivated and acting on the international stage.[27]

Pogge has come up with a very telling point in this regard. Consider the human association that seems clearly to be most constitutive of identity and self-perception, namely, the family. Even though we acknowledge many special measures and steps on behalf of families in our social structures, we do not think that family ties justify *any* act on behalf of the family. We do not think that moral duties radically alter, perhaps to the point of dissolution, as soon as one walks out the front door of the house. We do not encourage families to think in terms of a prudential struggle of "us versus them," of doing the best they can amongst themselves without regard to how their acts impact upon their neighbours. And if we are not inclined to extend such permissive privileges to the family, why should so many believe we ought to do so when it comes to the nation-state?[28]

Another dubious aspect of SMPR #2 is that, as Charles Beitz has contended, it seems to constitute another kind of groundless discrimination. Membership, on an SMPR #2 account, is all-important: a state is only duty bound to look after the interests and well-being of its own members, let the interests of others fall where they may. But what is political membership based on? In the majority of states, and for the majority of the world's people, membership is based on the place of one's birth. And yet no one had a choice where or when they were born, just as no one had a choice what sex or race they were born into. And we do not argue on principled grounds in favour of racism or sexism. So how can we argue on principled grounds that political membership is to be determinative of how one gets treated in the contemporary world, especially during times as dangerous as those of war? Membership, by and large, is an arbitrary, unchosen characteristic for which no one can be held responsible; so how can so much turn on it, morally, in terms of what governments may and may not do to people?[29]

We see these issues in bold relief in terms of what SMPR #2 recommends in times of war: namely, an efficient victory, with minimal costs to one's own citizens. In the words of Michael Gelven: "The value we place on the concerns of peace ... are challenged by those of war, which make up our communal meaning and allow us to posit the worth of what is ours against the challenge of what is alien." An even stronger claim is that "war [is] grounded in the existential concern for the priority of the We over the They."[30] This communalism implies the existence of only voluntary restraints upon the conduct of war with regard to foreigners. As with SPPR, there are here no firm principles, such as rules of just war, restraining a nation's conduct during war. There is nothing that might be called the employment of intrinsically heinous means: everything is entirely contingent upon the situation and upon the wishes of the nation in question. But surely this is morally dubious and grinds against our other commitments. The employment of mass rape campaigns, for example, or weapons of mass destruction, are usually actions we want to level non-contingent prohibitions against. And these are not idle thought experiments: SMPR, with its emphasis on ending the war as quickly and as favourably as possible, and without regard to what the other belligerent is actually doing, would seem open to recommend and endorse the employment of dirty means against the enemy state. For what quicker and more thorough way to crush an enemy and minimize the total costs to one's own people than by rapidly deploying overwhelming, disproportionate and indiscriminate force? Quick, dirty, ugly and despicable wars are the predictable result of state adherence to SMPR.

These considerations support the cogency of the core argument made previously. Nation-states are to adhere, as a minimal condition of international justice, to the code of human rights as developed in the UDHR. Even during times of war, human rights form the bedrock of cosmopolitan moral duties. (Indeed, just war norms are designed to secure human rights as best they can be secured amid the grim circumstances of war.) But above and beyond the threshold level of minimal justice established by human rights, states may justifiably pay more attention, and give greater weight, to the interests of their own citizens. It does not, in other words, seem defensible to support national partiality all the way down, as SMPR #2 does. There remains a residual yet stubborn threshold level of moral universality and cosmopolitanism. Compatriots may well owe each other more than they do foreigners, but they are never utterly free of all obligations with regard to even the most distant of strangers. Community, fellow-feeling, and even the maintenance of (a part of) one's sense of self, do not justify doing serious harm and grievous injury to other human beings.

It seems that the previous remarks about WPPR can be repeated when it comes to considering WMPR. It does not need to be radically at odds with contemporary just war theory, provided that it is contextualized, and ultimately subordinated, within a broader theory of morality and justice. In the face of systematic and serious non-compliance and egoism on the part of other states, there may well be some justification for prudently tending to one's own, out of the moral duty of protection (but without any further implication that the carrying out of such a duty implies the non-existence of any cross-border moral demands).

So, it has been suggested that there may well be some space within contemporary just war theory for both WPPR and WMPR. This is most clearly seen in the just war criterion of proportionality. Strictly speaking, then, the refutation of realism offered in this section is a rejection of the strong and robust forms of realism, whether prudential or moral in animation. It is these strong forms that pose a clear and potent challenge to the norms of just war theory, and thus must be called into doubt by any compelling and comprehensive account of it. The weaker forms of the doctrine, by contrast, seem at least not inconsistent with a broader and deeper concern for justice, both within and across borders, whether in war or peace.

Pacifism

This section will proceed much like the last one: attempt will be made to characterize pacifism in its most compelling contemporary fashion and then arguments will be levelled against those aspects of it that pose a serious challenge to just war theory.

The most formidable and relevant conception of pacifism revolves around Jenny Teichman's definition of pacifism as "anti-war-ism." Quite literally and straightforwardly, a pacifist rejects war in favour of peace. It is not violence in all its forms that the most challenging kind of pacifist objects to; rather, it is the specific *kind and degree* of violence that war involves to which the pacifist objects. A pacifist objects to killing (not just violence) in general and, in particular, objects to the mass killing, for political reasons, which is part and parcel of the wartime experience. So, a pacifist rejects war, and believes that there are no moral grounds which can justify resorting to war. War, for the pacifist, is always wrong.[31]

Having come to a working definition of pacifism as anti-war-ism, we can now consider some of the reasons that have been offered in its favour. Many such reasons have been offered, but not all of them are apposite to our concern in this article. Religious justifications of pacifism, for instance, are not to the present point because they rest on beliefs that are too contentious and exclusionary.[32] The most relevant and accessible pro-pacifist grounds, it seems, include the following: 1) a more consequen-tialist form of pacifism (or CP), which maintains that the benefits accruing from war can never outweigh the costs of fighting it; and 2) a more deontological form of pacifism (or DP), which contends that the very activity of war is intrinsically unjust, since it violates foremost duties of morality and justice, such as not killing other human beings.[33] Most common and compelling amongst contem-porary secular pacifists, such as Robert Holmes, is a mixed doctrine which combines both CP and DP. It terms of the just war tradition, we can see that these pacifist objections essentially amount to the conviction that the traditional principles of just war, both of *jus ad bellum* and *jus in bello*, can never actually be satis-fied. So destructive and heinous is war, it is thought, that no suffi-cient grounds exist for ever launching a military campaign, much less "fighting it cleanly" once war has begun.[34]

Pacifism, like (strong) realism, undoubtedly has something substantial to it. Specifically, pacifism seems laudable for its belief that international relations can and ought to be evaluated morally, for its critical attitude towards the use of political violence, and for its humanitarianism and inspired long-term vision of peaceful problem-solving between states. But just as (strong) realism, in spite of its strengths, was found seriously deficient as a compelling understanding of the ethics of war and peace, pacifism seems likewise vulnerable to forceful objections.

Before offering these objections, perhaps mention should be made of a very popular criticism of pacifism which will not here be employed. This criticism is that pacifism amounts to an indefensible "clean hands policy." The pacifist, it has often been thought, refuses to take the brutal measures necessary for the defense of himself, or his nation, for the sake of maintaining his own inner moral purity. This argument is easily overstated and has sometimes been so exaggerated as to amount to a cheap shot. It is important to note, in response, that, to the extent to which *any* moral stance will commend a certain set of actions or intentions deemed morally worthy, and condemn others as being reprehensible, the "clean hands" criticism can be so malleable as to apply to nearly any substantive moral and political doctrine. Every moral and political theory stipulates that one ought to do what it deems good or just and to avoid what it deems bad or unjust. The very point of morality itself, we might say, is to help keep one's hands clean. So this popular just war criticism of pacifism is not especially appealing. Besides, the very idea of a selfish pacifist simply does not ring true: many pacifists have, historically, paid a very high price for their pacifism during wartime (through severe ostracism and even jail time), and their pacifism seems less rooted in regard for inner moral purity than it is in regard for constructing a less violent and more humane world order. So, this argument against pacifism seems to fail; but others, now to be discussed, appear to succeed in questioning the tenability of its core principles, at least relative to those of just war theory.

Criticizing CP

The CP element of contemporary pacifism, we have seen, is the notion that the costs of war always outweigh the benefits from undertaking war. In essence, this pacifist objection asserts that the proportionality criteria of traditional just war theory can never be fulfilled. The first critical question to raise here, by way of response, is: what kind of costs and benefits are being appealed to here? Short-term or long-term costs and benefits, or both? Prudential or moral costs and benefits, or both? And costs from whose point of view? No contemporary pacifist tract offers a detailed breakdown of war's costs and benefits; the preference instead is to gesture towards very general—almost clichéd—understandings of war's destructiveness. Could this tendency exist due to a lack of confidence in the results of a more finely grained analysis?[35]

One important counterpoint to note in this regard is that we have to consider not only the explicit costs of war action (i.e., both military and civilian casualties, and the destruction of property) but also the implicit costs of war inaction: not resorting to war to defend political sovereignty and territorial integrity may well be tantamount to rewarding aggression in international relations. The lack of armed resistance and forceful punishment allows the aggressor state to keep the fruits of its campaign, thereby augmenting the incentives in favour of future aggression. And to what extent can we have a well-functioning and stable, much less a just, international system in which aggression between nations is thusly rewarded? We might call this the "macro-cost of war inaction": the rewarding of interstate aggression, which leads to the long-term weakening of the interstate system of peaceful dispute resolution.

We might also discern the "micro-costs" of not resorting to war to defend one's own populace from an aggressive invader. Such a pacifist strategy seems to run enormous risks with the safety and well-being of one's populace, not to mention their right to be self-governing and not subject to a conquering regime. In light of this, we might ask: does pacifism make sense at the level of collective agents, like states, *especially* if those collective agents are charged with the responsibility of protecting and serving their citizen members? Is there too great a reliance, by the pacifist, on the intuitive appeal of the interpersonal case (of not killing another individual), as opposed to the analogous, yet different, international case? In other words, pacifism at the level of the individual—the conscientious objector, for instance—seems much more defensible than advocating that an entire state be geared along pacifist lines. The salience of weak descriptive realism's picture of international relations reveals that state-wide pacifism is a recipe for getting seriously suckered in the international arena. A prudent and moral state ought not to run the sizable risks of adhering to such a view. One of the core functions of the state, after all, is to provide reliable protection from serious, standard threats to our human rights, one of which is armed invasion by an aggressor regime. In light of these realities, it seems plausible to suggest that states ought (both prudentially and morally) to be prepared to enforce that protection, through armed force if necessary.[36]

It seems, therefore, that the combination of both the macro- and the micro-costs of failing to resort to war are sufficient at least to cast doubt regarding whether war-fighting can only result in greater negative, than positive, consequences.

We might also, in our consideration of the cogency of CP, consider the historical record. I am prepared to concede that many—perhaps even most—historical wars can be objected to, very forcefully, by the CP aspect of contemporary pacifism. World War I seems a fitting example of the futility, waste and sheer human tragedy of many wars our ancestors fought. But not all wars seem to fall under this objection. World War II, for instance, seems more controversial. Many thoughtful people, including participants, have argued, appealing to both prudential and moral costs, that defeating ultra-aggressive regimes like Nazi Germany and Imperial Japan was worth the costs of the war-fighting, as enormous as those were. Can we, they ask, imagine and endorse what our world would currently look like had the Nazis been allowed to conquer Europe and rule it, and/or had Imperial Japan been allowed to subdue forcibly most of East Asia?[37]

Perhaps another historical counter-example to CP would be the Persian Gulf War of 1991. Many just war theorists have contended that the Gulf War, on the part of the anti-Iraq coalition, seemed to meet the standard *jus ad bellum* criteria: there was a clear-cut case of international aggression; there was a series of brutal, rights-violative measures taken by the invading Iraqi forces against the victimized Kuwaitis; and there were serious attempts made to resolve the crisis through diplomacy and sanctions. These attempts failed, thereby leaving force as the only measure that seemed to hold out the prospect of an effective solution. The short-term explicit costs of the war-fighting, on both sides (though obviously the Iraqis fared much worse in relative terms), were amongst the lowest ever for a major war, and there were not extensive civilian casualties. This could have been foreseen at the time, given that the unpopulated desert was to be the battlefield. It is hard, in addition, to discern major negative medium-term costs, save perhaps the elusive illness known as "Gulf War Syndrome." While the Iraqi populace, and especially the Kurdish minority, continue to fare very poorly, it is not at all clear that the War was and remains the principal causal factor behind this. The brutalities of the Iraqi regime surely play a substantial role in this as well. The moral benefits of the War, by contrast, were: 1) that an instance of international aggression was repealed and punished; and 2) that such punishment aided, at least to some degree, in the deterrence of similar acts in the future. One major prudential benefit of the War was that half of one of the world's main sources of energy was secured from the threat of control by an aggressive and erratic dictator. It is important to note that enumerating these *jus ad bellum* (and interest-based) arguments is not to be a mindless supporter of the Gulf War action by the international community against Iraq. Questions can, for example, be raised about whether the right intention criterion was fulfilled and whether the various criteria of *jus in bello* were violated and war crimes committed. It is simply to make the case that there seem to be some strong historical counter-examples which at least cast doubt on the bold CP claim that wars are never worth the effort.[38]

A third issue to raise with regard to the CP element within contemporary pacifism focuses on the relationship between consequentialism and the denial of killing, especially on the level that is endemic to warfare. Pacifism places great, perhaps over-riding, value on respecting human life, notably through its injunc-tion against killing. But this core pacifist value seems to rest uneasily with the appeal to consequentialism in the CP aspect of pacifism. For there is nothing to a consequentialist approach to the ethics of war and peace that would object to killing as such. There is here no firm principle or side-constraint that one ought not to kill another person, or that nations ought not to launch military campaigns which kill thousands of enemy soldiers. With consequentialism, it is always a matter of considering the latest costs, benefits and circumstances. When considering whether or not one should kill another human being, consequentialism will typically appeal to the pain and suffering such killing will cause both the victim and his friends and family—not just in terms of the loss of life but also in terms of the loss of further, future life experiences. Appeal will also be made to a more universal, or legislative, point of view, and contention will be made that permitting or mandating killing is a bad precedent that might lead to loss of respect for human life, and thus to serious insecurities within the political community, and so on. These are all excellent and powerful points to be made against killing another human being. The remaining problem is that a consequentialist approach to the injunction against killing and war does not seem to come with the kind of firmness that the pacifist needs to ground his contentions.[39]

Since it is always a matter of choosing the best option amongst feasible alternatives, consequentialism does seem to leave conceptual space open to the claim that under *these* conditions, at *this* time and place, and given *these* possible alternatives, killing and/or war seem(s) permissible. There can be particular counter-examples, some offered above, wherein the calculations may well come out the other way. After all, what if killing x people (say, some members of an invading army) is reasonably deemed necessary to save the lives of x + n people (say, people of one's nation who would die from the rights-violative activities of the unchecked invader, as it sought to consolidate its rule)? It is at least possible to conceive that a quick and decisive resort to war can be employed effectively to prevent even greater suffering, killing and devastation in the future. To put it baldly, it seems rather bizarre for the *consequentialist* pacifist, whose principles exhibit a profound abhorrence for killing people, to be willing in such a scenario to allow an even greater number of people to be killed by acquiescing to the violence of others less scrupulous. Two related points are being made here: 1) the general point that the CP element of pacifism does not, of itself, seem to ground sufficiently the categorical rejection of killing and war which is the very essence of pacifism; and 2) the particular point that the CP aspect of pacifism seems open to counter-examples and thought experiments which question whether consequentialism would even reject killing and war at all in certain conditions.[40]

Before leaving this criticism of CP, it should be pointed out that the core accusations—that pacifism rewards international aggression and fails to protect people who need it—might be responded to by the pacifist in the following fashion: we do not need to resort to war in order to vindicate the ground rules of the international system and to protect our human rights. In the event of an armed invasion by an aggressor nation, an organized and committed campaign of non-violent yet forceful civil disobedience—combined with international diplomatic and economic sanctions—would, in the end, be just as effective as war in expelling the aggressor, with far fewer deaths and destruction of lives and property. After all, the pacifist could say, no invader could possibly maintain its grip over the conquered nation in the face of such systematic isolation, non-cooperation and non-violent resistance. How could it work the factories, or harvest the fields, or run the stores, when everyone would be striking? How could it maintain the will to keep the country in the face of crippling economic sanctions and diplomatic censure from the international community? And so on.[41]

Even though one cannot exactly disprove this pacifist contention—since it is fundamentally a counter-factual thesis—there are powerful reasons to agree with Rawls that such is an "unworldly view" to hold.[42] For, as Walzer points out, such a systematic campaign of civil disobedience would seem to rely much too heavily on the scruples of the invading aggressor. What if, as Walzer asks, the invading regime is extremely brutal and ruthless? What if, faced with an organized campaign of labour strikes, the invading state started to murder the union leaders and the labourers themselves? What if, faced with widespread civil hostility and disobedience, the invader decided to "cleanse" the area of the native population and bring in its own people from back home? What if, faced with economic sanctions and diplomatic censure from a neighbouring country, the invader decided to invade *it*, too? We have some inclination from history, particularly that of the Third Reich, that such brutal tactics are extremely effective at breaking the will of (otherwise principled) people to resist. The defence of our rights may well, against such invaders, require the lethal and organized use of political violence.[43]

Criticizing DP

Having seen that serious doubts can be raised regarding the CP element of contemporary pacifism, attention now needs to be paid to evaluating pacifism's DP element. The core notion here, as we have seen, is that the very activity of war-fighting violates a foremost duty of morality/justice, and thus undertaking such activity can never be justified by appealing to the aims of the war action in question. It is thought that war, as means to an end, is intrinsically unjust; and, since there must be a moral consistency between means and ends, such that unjust means may not be resorted to in order to produce just ends, it follows that the traditional just war criteria can never be fulfilled. War ought never to be resorted to: there is always some vastly superior (moral) option with regard to international dispute resolution, such as diplomacy or sanctions.

Much has been left unsaid in this terse characterization of the DP aspect of the contemporary pacifist's contention. Depth and detail must be added especially to the following consideration: *why* does war-fighting violate *which* foremost duty of morality/justice? In my view, the best pacifist consideration of these matters has been offered by Robert Holmes. Holmes deals with this consideration, first, by stating that the foremost duty of morality/justice which is violated by war-fighting is the duty not to kill other human beings.[44] But the obvious objection to this claim is that such a duty, though crucially important, does not seem to override all other considerations. Consider the most obvious example: A brutally attacks B, thereby posing a serious, lethal threat to B's life. Provided that A attacks without justification, many would respond that B may retaliate in self-defence, with lethal force if needed. Consider another, perhaps more closely related, example: are we not to kill a dangerous terrorist who is credibly threatening the lives of a number of innocent civilians? The answer is by no means straightforward, but it at least seems defensible to assert that we may, so that we protect the lives of the innocent. The essence of this objection has been stated very forcefully by G.E.M. Anscombe, who lambastes pacifism for not distinguishing between "the blood of the innocent" and "the blood of the guilty." The question, as Anscombe would pose it, is:

why should we respect the duty not to kill the terrorist when he seems guilty of a seriously immoral act, namely, credibly threatening and endangering the lives of innocent civilians? Do we not also owe the duty of protection, by lethal force if necessary, to those who are being so seriously threatened? After all, if we do nothing, then serious harm, or even death, will befall these innocents. The terrorist will get his way, even though his way is the morally objectionable one. In short, the claim is that we have weightier moral reasons to side with the civilians instead of the terrorist, even if that means killing him.[45]

There is a raft of complex issues addressed in the rhetorical questions above that requires a much fuller development. The first concerns the permissibility, perhaps even the right, to kill a person who presents a serious threat either to oneself or to others. Why exactly is this permissible? Does it not, for instance, violate the human rights of the person who presents a threat?

It seems cogent to respond that the employment of lethal force against an aggressor is permissible (where it reasonably seems required to defeat the aggression) because the victim of the aggression would lose too much if he were not permitted to kill the aggressor. Indeed, the victim could literally lose everything. But perhaps it will be objected that the aggressor, if killed in response, would also lose everything. So, why may the victim kill the aggressor? The answer seems to be that the aggressor is responsible for forcing the victim to choose between his life and that of the aggressor, and it would be not only unreasonable but unfair to bar the victim from choosing his own life.

An agent A is an aggressor when A violates the human rights of another person, victim V. In violating the human rights of V, A reveals himself to be a very serious threat to V, since human rights serve to protect vital human needs. In short, A aggresses against V when A presents himself as a serious, lethal threat to the reasonable vital needs of V, as detailed in chapter 4.

It is an important claim of this book that the commission of aggression by A against V: 1) justifies V in responding to A with lethal force, if needed; and 2) justifies any third party, T, in employing needed lethal force to A in order to protect V. The key normative principle (NP) at work here is thus: *the commission of aggression by A against V entitles V, and/or any third party T acting on behalf of V, to employ all necessary means to stop A, including lethal force, provided such means do not themselves violate human rights.*[46] Let us analyze this complex principle NP.

Consider the first aspect of NP, namely, the entitlement of either V or T to respond with the required force against aggressor A. Jan Narveson seems to put this point well when he contends that it is a matter of moral logic that if V has a human right HR to x (say, personal security), then V also has title to employ those means necessary to secure x from serious, standard threats, such as the violent aggression of others. This seems required for us to speak of V's truly having HR at all.[47] Thus, if the employment of potentially lethal force against A reasonably seems required to make A desist from aggressing against, or even killing, V, it follows that V is at least permitted to do so. But how does this first-person permission get extended to the third person?

The extension proceeds on the basis of the wrongness of the aggression and the intent of the third party to protect the victim from aggression. Sometimes victims, for whatever reason, lack the wherewithal to defend themselves effectively from aggression. In such cases, are we to say that their factual deficiency undermines their normative claim that the aggressor either stop or be stopped? The answer, clearly, is no. It is crucial to note this last aspect: the normative essence of the victim's claim is that the aggressor stop or be stopped, and not more narrowly that only he (the victim) be allowed to do so. This moral reality suffices to ground a third party's intervention in the case, and to ground the employment of the needed force to make the aggressor stop. It is clear, however, that to be justified, the third party's intent can only be protection of V from A.[48]

Consider now more precisely the second aspect of the principle NP, namely, the permission to employ *lethal* force against A if required. Many thinkers will be quick to pronounce on the need for a proportionality of force in response to a threat from an aggressor.[49] And this claim is undeniable. But it may be worth stressing how we ought not to succumb readily to pious delusions about first trying to disarm the aggressor and then, *only if* that fails, upping the ante, perhaps to the point of killing. In situations where such a measured escalation of violent defence is reasonable, obviously it must be employed. But many situations wherein violent aggression is occurring are ones that practically require a very swift and effective response. We cannot hold victims to excessively stringent interpretations of proportionality in such cases: they are, after all, under an immediate, grievous threat to their lives and rights and they usually only have seconds to respond. Strong natural impulses in favour of survival will exert enormous pressure on their actions. All of this is to say that presumption ought always to be in favour of endorsing the victim's violent response to aggression, including the killing of A—a presumption that can be overturned only by an over-whelming demonstration of disproportion in response.

Let us now turn to the crucial third aspect of the above prin-ciple NP, namely, that the potentially lethal, violent response of V to A's aggression violates no human rights. The obvious, and important, question here is: why would V's killing A in response to A's aggression not violate A's human rights? As the DP pacifist would say: is it not the case that the above principle NP actually compounds the wrongness of the tragic situation by permitting V to kill A if required? Is it not the case that NP is endorsing the claim that two wrongs make a right? The contemporary just war response is no: V does no wrong whatsoever—violates no rights—by responding to A's aggression with lethal force if required.

The reason grounding this just war claim is that the commis-sion of aggression by A causes A to forfeit his human right not to be responded to violently, or even killed. I should like to offer my own understanding of this murky topic, following Judith Thomson's excellent characterization of some of the most promi-nent options in this regard.[50]

One way of claiming that V violates no rights of A's when responding violently to A's aggression is to distinguish between infringing a right and violating it. Essentially, P *infringes* on Q's right R to x if P brings it about that Q loses x or comes not to have it. For example, P infringes Q's right not to be killed if P kills Q. By contrast, P *violates* Q's right to x if P *unjustly* brings it about that Q loses x or comes not to have it. So P would violate Q's right not to be killed only if P killed Q unjustly. Using this distinction, it might be contended that victim V violates none of A's rights in killing A. Presumably, however, V did still infringe on A's rights by killing him.

This "infringement" option seems unsatisfactory because of its suspiciously semantic flavour: we get around the sizable problem by redefining violation and conceding that perhaps the victim is guilty of some lesser offense, such as infringement. This latter aspect seems objectionable in itself: in my view, V is guilty of nothing at all when he violently responds to A's aggression. The only guilt in the situation rests on A's shoulders: guilt for the aggression itself and guilt for forcing V to resort to violence to stop it. So the infringement option should be rejected.

A related option would be to say that V's rights override A's rights in this case and this moral fact is what grounds V's violent response. This "overriding" option is similarly unsatisfactory. The first deficiency this account suffers from is that it demands a very rigorous hierarchical weighting of rights claims and thus would mark a considerable complication in rights theory. Secondly, it is not at all clear *which* of V's rights are overriding which of A's: is the view that the right not to be killed unjustly is weightier than that of not being killed? Such seems implicit—but then we are essentially back to the infringement case. The two accounts share a large flaw in this regard: they both portray V as doing something wrong, even if not ultimately objectionable. In the first account, V infringes A's rights, whereas in the second account it would seem that V straightforwardly violates A's rights but, due to overriding conditions, is permitted to do so.

The forfeiture option is the only one that will enable us to account for the notion that V does nothing wrong at all—is blameworthy of nothing, should feel regret for nothing—in responding to A's aggression with lethal force if necessary. So we should say that A loses his right not to be so treated when he commits aggression. Some theorists have feigned puzzlement over how precisely rights can be lost—and then found. Two comments suggest themselves in response. The first is that the notion of losing your right because you committed some heinous crime is surely no more mysterious and puzzling than the competing notions that: 1) despite your crime, you keep your right, but may still suffer its infringement; or 2) despite your crime, you keep your right, but it may be overridden by someone else's. The second comment is that such puzzlement seems the product of a very contrived and artificial, almost reifying, conception of rights. If rights really were like self-contained properties, inherent in human personhood, it would indeed be quite odd how we could come to lose them, and then regain them as if by magic. But there is no good reason why we should understand rights in this stilted manner.

In the final analysis, rights are reasons.[51] They are not properties of persons; rather, they are reasons to treat persons in certain ways. From this conception, it marks no great conceptual leap to point out that reasons to treat persons in certain ways can change, depending on the circumstances and what they are doing. Provided that one has a non-absolutist and thus reasonable conception of human rights as claims no stronger than their justifying reasons, forfeiture appears to pose no considerable difficulties. It amounts to nothing more than the claim that the weight of reasons in the situation informs us that V does nothing wrong in responding to A's aggression with lethal force if necessary.

Why does V do nothing wrong? What exactly constitutes "the weight of reasons" in this regard? First, it is A who is responsible for forcing V to choose between his own life and rights and those of A. We can hardly blame V for choosing his own. For, if he does not choose his own, he loses an enormous amount, perhaps everything. And it is simply not reasonable to expect creatures like us to intentionally suffer catastrophic loss. Also, consider the question of fairness: if V is not allowed to use lethal force, if necessary, against A in the event of A's aggression, then V loses everything while A loses nothing. Indeed, A seems actually to gain whatever object he desired in violating or killing V. Such would seem a patently unfair reward for deeply objectionable behaviour. Finally, V's having rights at all provides V with an implicit entitlement to those means and measures necessary to secure V's rights, such as the use of force in the face of a serious threat. These powerful considerations of responsibility, reasonableness, fairness and implicit entitlement appear to unite in supporting the claims that V may respond with potentially lethal force to A's aggression, that V does no wrong in doing so, that it would be wrong (i.e., both unreasonable and rewarding of wickedness) to prohibit V's doing so, and that A bears all of the blame in the situation.

Some further aspects of this vexed issue require further comment. The first concerns the following question: would A be justified in violently responding to V's violent response to A's initial aggression? The answer is clearly no. Having committed aggression, A has forfeited his right not to be dealt with harshly in defence, for reasons just offered. So, in violently responding to A's aggression, V violates no rights of A. Since only rights-violation grounds a potentially lethal violent attack, it follows that A would not be justified in violently responding to V's self-defence. A's moral charge and duty is to cease and desist from his aggression against V, not compound his wickedness by stepping up his attack in light of V's resistance.

The second aspect here is that A's forfeiture of some of his rights through aggression is still tied to constraining reasons. By this it is meant, for instance, that A may be violently attacked only by V and/or by a third party T acting to protect V. If another third party, H, were to happen upon the scene of A's aggression against V and take the opportunity to avenge violently some prior disagreement with A and try to claim immunity through A's forfeiture, the claim would be bogus. Once more, A's rights are not "lost," or "given up," in so simplistic a way: it is, rather, the weight of reasons and nothing else that is determinative. If A forfeits HR for a reason, the terms and conditions of the forfeiture are logically tied to the nature of that reason, and it alone.

The third aspect requiring comment is that, once A has stopped his aggression and poses no imminent threat of renewed aggression, his full panoply of rights springs forth intact, save for those still deemed forfeit for defensible reasons of appropriate punishment and restitution for his act of aggression. The notion of "springing forth," once more, is nothing more puzzling than the claim that now the weight of reasons with regard to how we should treat this person has changed. Since he is no longer a clear and present danger to another's vital needs, for example, he may no longer be killed—though he may, perhaps, still be jailed or fined as legitimate punishment.

One related topic which is often mentioned in conjunction with these issues is that of the so-called "innocent aggressor."

George Fletcher and Robert Nozick came up with the first examples in this regard.[52] Say, for instance, that C and D are in an elevator together. Unbeknownst to C, D suffers from a very serious mental disorder, which suddenly causes him to attack C. Is C thereby justified in employing potentially lethal force against D? A number of thinkers—apparently Fletcher, for example—have denied this, claiming that at best C has an excuse. This is to say that C has done something that is not morally permitted (namely, killing an innocent), yet C ought not to be punished for it because he has an excuse. This excuse is the fact that C could in no way be expected to know what was wrong inside of D's head which caused him to attack C.

These very abstract thoughts on this curious figure of the innocent aggressor might be applied to a more relevant case. Sometimes pacifists will contend that soldiers are innocent aggressors—they are not to blame for the wars they fight and many are conscripts in any event—and go further than Fletcher and deny even the excusability of intentionally killing them.[53] At the very least, they will assert, there is no moral permission to kill them: the just war theorist still does not have morality on his side.

The first thing to be crystal clear about, in response, is the uncontested fact that soldiers *are* aggressors, regardless of whether they are conscripts and regardless of their own personal attitude regarding the justice of the war they are fighting. They do indeed present themselves as serious and lethal threats against the lives and rights of those to whom they are opposed. They are armed with deadly force and trained to kill for political reasons.

This first fact establishes, at least, a strong prima facie case in favour of the notion that targeting soldiers with lethal force is morally justified and not merely excusable. After all, it is not as though soldiers can be thought of as being no different from unarmed civilians who do not present themselves as armed threats.

The only plausible objection to this prima facie case is that there can be times when soldiers do disagree profoundly with the cause of their own state in fighting and yet still fight on its behalf for reasons outside of their control. But there are complicated issues to be resolved in this regard: if the soldier in question does have these personal objections, why does he continue to fight? Is the raw fact of his conscription (assuming that were the case) sufficient to exonerate him from his culpability as an aggressor? Or does some further story have to be told about what punishments he would have risked by resisting conscription? I do not pretend to have ready answers to these questions, only to insist that the realities at play in this case are considerably more complex than those in the highly contrived case of C and D in the elevator. I also find it defensible to assert that the burden of proof is on those who would insist that soldiers are innocent aggressors. Innocent in what salient sense? Given that they remain aggressors, what could suffice to undermine the justification of those who target them with force?

My view is that only rarely, if ever, do we come across a genuinely innocent aggressor in the heat of battle. Many soldiers are only too glad to fight on behalf of their own country, for good or ill. Conscription does nothing, one way or the other, to shed evidential light on their interior innocence or guilt. And the external fact remains that *they are aggressors*. Thus, I contend that states possess an on-the-whole justification in responding to aggressive armed forces with forces of their own, for reasons of reasonableness, fairness and implicit entitlement elucidated previously. There may well be exceptional cases where this will mean targeting an innocent aggressor—i.e., a soldier involved in the war, somehow, through no fault of his own—with lethal force. However, states and their military systems have every excuse in so targeting such a figure: there is no way they can be expected to know of his interior innocence, in light of the evidentiary difficulties and the presentation by the soldier of himself as an external threat.[54]

Before moving on to dealing with the next set of challenges levelled by DP, there is one final topic of relevance to handle in this regard. The principles developed thus far—especially NP—ground both self- and other-defence. Is the sense of "defence" here entirely descriptive in nature? More sharply: are self- and other-defence grounded solely reactively? Must a victim actually wait until the first blow has been delivered by the aggressor before being justified in responding with potentially lethal force? The answer seems to be no.

The answer is no because we have defined aggression above as "the posing of a serious, potentially lethal threat to another's life and rights." And a person can present such a threat in at least one of two ways: 1) by actually attacking another person without just cause; or 2) by posing a credible, grave and imminent threat of launching such an attack. Thus, an aggressor can be an aggressor without, empirically, landing the first blow. This must mean that the sense of "defence" employed here is, like that of aggression, *normative* in nature: self-defence is the rights-vindicating repulsion and defeat of rights-violating aggression, by means that may be either empirically offensive or defensive.

The key notion is that forcing victims to wait for the actual blow to be delivered by the aggressor is not a reasonable insistence, since that first blow may well be catastrophic and/or fatal. If the danger the aggressor poses is clear, grave and imminent— i.e., if it is just a matter of time before he delivers the first and perhaps last blow—then the victim's human rights have already been violated. The victim's rational agency has been just as undermined as if the blow had already been struck because the victim is left just waiting for the oncoming attack. The victim's freedom to choose between alternative courses of action has been violated by the aggressor, who effectively eliminates the alternatives, forcing all of the victim's attention and energy to be spent on preparing for his attack. In light of this fact, it seems that the victim ought not to be deprived of the comparative advantage of landing the first blow.

DP pacifists, however, are not at this point out of defensible options. Holmes, for instance, offers another argument which contends that the real foremost duty of morality/justice that is violated by war-fighting is not the duty not to kill aggressive human beings, but rather the duty not to kill *innocent*, non-aggressive human beings. What is the relevant sense of "innocence" here being employed? To be innocent here means to have done nothing that would justify being harmed or killed; in particular, it means not constituting a serious threat or harm to other people. It means not being an aggressor. It is primarily in this sense that civilian populations are thought, by traditional just war theory, to be "innocent" of war and thus morally immune from direct attack during wartime. Even if civilians support the unjust

war effort politically, or even simply in terms of their personal attitude towards the war effort, they clearly are not armed and
dangerous aggressors. Only armed forces, and the political-indus-
trial-technological complexes that guide them, seem to constitute
serious threats against which threatened people may respond in
kind. Civilian populations are morally off-limits as targets.

Holmes contends that this just war criterion of discrimination, with its crucial corollary of non-combatant immunity, can
never be satisfied. For all possible wars in this world—given the
nature of military technology and tactics, the heat of battle and the
limits of human knowledge and self-discipline—involve the
killing of innocents, thus defined. We know this to be true from
history and have no good reason for thinking otherwise. There
simply has never been a war, nor will there ever be a war, without at least some civilian casualties. But the killing of innocent
non-aggressors, Holmes says, is always unjust. Therefore, just war
theory's claim that resort to war can be mandated, or at least
permitted, by justice conflicts with the putative moral fact that the
very acts constitutive of war in our world are unjust. So, for a
pacifist like Holmes, no war can ever be fought justly, regardless
of the ends (such as self- or other-defence) purportedly aimed for;
the just war tradition can, as a result, be seen as a disingenuous
attempt to justify great moral evils. How is a just war theorist to
respond to this pointed pacifist challenge?[55]

A number of thinkers have sought to defeat this pacifist argument by casting doubt on the utility of employing the concept of
innocence in wartime. But a just war theorist subscribing to the
jus in bello criterion of discrimination, with its corollary of non-
combatant immunity, will neither want, nor logically be at liberty,
to argue in this fashion. It seems that, despite all the residual
ambiguities which remain regarding who exactly is "innocent"
during wartime, just war theorists are correct to maintain this
concept. It is hard to see, for example, how young children could
be anything other than innocent during a war, and as such entitled not to be made the object of direct and intentional attack. It
is only those who, in Walzer's phrase, are "involved in harming
us"—i.e. those who are committing aggression against us—that
we can justly target in a direct and intentional fashion during
wartime.[56]

The way in which traditional just war theory has dealt with this pacifist objection has been through the doctrine of double effect (or DDE). The DDE is predicated on the following scenario: assume agent X is considering performing an action A, which foreseeably has both good/moral/just effects G and bad/immoral/unjust effects B. X is permitted to perform A only if: 1) X only intends G and not B; 2) B is not a means to G; and 3) the goodness of G is worth, or is proportionate to, the badness of B.[57] Assume now that X is a country and A is war. The government of X, which is contemplating war in response to an unjustified armed invasion by country Y, knows that, should it embark on war, such activity will foreseeably result in civilian casualties (both in X and Y), even if X manages to vindicate its rights of political sovereignty and territorial integrity. The DDE stipulates that X may launch into such a justified war provided that: 1) X does not intend any resulting civilian casualties (but, rather, aims only at vindicating its rights); 2) that such casualties are not themselves the means whereby X's end (namely, vindicating its rights) is achieved; and 3) the importance of vindicating X's rights is proportionately greater than—or, at least, equal to—the badness of the resulting civilian casualties.

The key notion here is that civilians are not, according to just war theory, entitled to some implausible kind of absolute or fail-safe immunity from attack; rather, they are owed neither more nor less than what Walzer has called "due care" from the belligerent government(s) that they not be made casualties of the war activity in question. Civilians are not entitled to such absolute immunity because the effect of allowing for such absolute immunity would be, essentially, to outlaw warfare altogether—and it is neither reasonable nor fair to require a political community not to resist an aggressive invasion which threatens the lives and rights of its member citizens.[58]

The pacifist might, of course, respond to this by questioning the moral significance of the DDE's distinction between intending the death of Z and "merely" foreseeing that one's actions will result in the death of Z. Many have contended that the DDE is so elastic as to justify anything: all an agent has to do to employ its protective moral cloak is to assert that, "Well, I didn't intend *that*; my aim, rather, was this...." The first point to make in response is that intentions are not infinitely redescribable, nor irreducibly private, as this criticism seems to imply. Agents are not free to claim whatever laudable intention they want in order to justify their actions, however heinous. Intentions must meet minimal criteria of logical coherence and, moreover, must be seen as being connected to patterns of action that are publicly accessible. The criminal justice system of most countries is predicated on this fact: for serious crimes such as murder, the case must be made by the prosecution that the accused had *mens rea*, or the intent to kill. And this is done by offering third-person, publicly accessible evidence tied to the accused's actions, behaviour and assertions leading up to the time of the murder, as well as considering whether he had both incentive and motive to commit the crime. These realities seriously dampen the cogency of the popular claim that the DDE can be used to justify any heinous action, whether in war or peace.

Furthermore, the competing just war contention is that, when states fight in strict adherence to the requirements of *jus in bello*—especially as codified in the positive laws of war—they do not meaningfully intend for innocent civilians to be killed. Which norms are these? They include the following:

JIB 1. Discrimination and non-combatant immunity. Combatant states shall at all times discriminate between the military targets and the civilian population within an enemy state. Morally, states are entitled to respond with lethal force only against the source of the serious and lethal threat that is aimed against them. They are only entitled to target those who are, in Walzer's words, "engaged in harming" them. Thus, they may only aim directly at the legitimate political-military-industrial targets which are the source of the armed threat. Civilian populations may not be targeted.[59]

JIB 2. (Micro-) proportionality. States and their military systems are, when in the midst of war, to weigh the expected universal goods/benefits of each significant military tactic employed within the war against its reasonably expected universal evils/costs. Only if the benefits of the proposed tactic seem at least proportional to the costs may a state and its armed forces employ it.[60]

JIB 3. No intrinsically heinous means or weapons are to be employed during the war. The most frequently mentioned of these are: mass rape campaigns; forcing captured soldiers to fight against their own side; forcing captured soldiers into slave labour, especially when accompanied with torture or medical experimentation; and the use of the NBC (nuclear, biological and chemical) weapons of mass destruction.[61]

Provided that a state X displays evident respect for these rules, JIB 1-3, it will be clear that X intends only to achieve its just aims with regard to the war, and not to produce collateral civilian casualties.

It also seems possible to discern whether a belligerent, such as country X, is employing civilian casualties as a means to its end of victory over Y. If there were greater civilian than military casualties in Y, for example, it would be clear which group of people was bearing the brunt of X's attack. Relatedly, if there were a systemic pattern—as opposed to unavoidable, isolated cases—of civilian bombardment by X on the civilians of Y, it would also be plausible to infer that X was directly targeting the civilian population of Y. From either of these factors it would be reasonable to infer that X was unjustly attempting to use civilian casualties in Y to bring about Y's military capitulation. Conversely, if the systemic pattern of X's war-fighting indicates its targeting of Y's military forces and capabilities, with only incidental civilian casualties resulting, then it would be reasonable to infer that X was not employing civilian casualties to force Y to retreat and admit defeat. X would thus fulfil the DDE's second criterion.

The really difficult aspect of the DDE appears to be the third one: contending that the just cause of X is "worth" the incidental civilian casualties in the war (in both X and Y). Of course the pacifist will object, insisting that the fact that some innocents will foreseeably die renders war the moral equivalent of murder. I simply do not see it this way, though it needs to be admitted that such comparisons and trade-offs are profoundly difficult. My perspective is: how else, in the final analysis, are minimally just states, in our world, to defend themselves, to protect their people, and to vindicate the international system of law and order, save through armed force and the resort to war? And why should states capitulate their rights to political sovereignty and territorial integrity? Above all, why should they fail to protect their own? *Provided* that the other criteria of just war are fulfilled, and *provided* that aspects 1 and 2 of the DDE are fulfilled, then the effective protection of human rights by minimally just states seems worth the cost of incidental civilian casualties resulting from a war in defence of that right.

It is worth it because, as contended above, it is unreasonable and unfair either to require or expect people not to resist an aggressive invasion of their country by force if required—they would lose too much, perhaps everything, if they capitulated. And it is not morally compelling for a government to fail to perform one of its core functions: to protect its citizens, by force if necessary, from serious, standard threats to their lives and their human rights. This hardly constitutes a definitive rejection of this latest pacifist challenge, but we have already commented that such is not to be expected. The best we can do here is to offer powerful competing considerations, such as this version of the DDE, which at least cast serious doubt on the superiority of adhering to pacifism over just war theory.

One final common strategy taken within the DP aspect of contemporary pacifism is to try and use Kantian categories against Kantianism, so to speak. Contention is frequently made that war, as such, treats human beings (both civilian and soldier, combatant and non-combatant) as means to an end and not as ends-in-themselves. War-fighting fails to respect the humanity in the other person, indeed perhaps in one's own person as well. We have seen how Kant would respond to this challenge and can adopt his response as our own. Resort to war can be justified according to principles such as the categorical imperative and the universal principle of justice, which are structured around the notion of human beings as ends-in-themselves. It can be so justified because war, under certain rigorously defined conditions, can plausibly be seen as the only reliable measure we can take to: 1) defend our political communities and protect ourselves and our fellow citizens from aggressive, rights-violative outlaw states; and 2) vindicate the system of international law and order required for progress towards a more just world order. Since propositions 1 and 2 are predicated, above all, on a defence of all our human rights, which stipulate how we ought to be treated as rational beings, they are clearly defensible in terms of the notion of human beings as ends-in-themselves. War-fighting does not necessarily disrespect the humanity in the other person (in the enemy state) because, as Kant says, the justified resort to war treats the regime in the enemy state as being responsible for choosing to commit those unjust actions which ground a violent, even lethal, response. Indeed, this point might be turned around, as it has been by Cheyney Ryan, and the assertion made that adherence to pacifism may amount to failing to respect one's own humanity and dignity, namely, by wilfully succumbing to the rights-violating aggression of outlaw states and by failing to defend oneself and one's people by means deemed reasonably necessary.[62]

The most powerful anti-pacifist argument, from a just war point of view, seems then to be not that it is selfish but that, rather, it is mistaken. It is mistaken because it fails to see how warfare, under rigorously defined conditions, can be *required* in our world to uphold our human rights and to protect ourselves, our states, and the human community from rights-violating aggression. The main task of justice is to structure society, both domestically and internationally, so that every person is treated fairly and equally, and has his reasonable vital needs protected from serious, standard threats, such as violent aggression. The surest way to achieve this, it seems, is to order personal conduct, and to shape social structures, both domestic and international, so that they satisfy everyone's human rights, as contained in the UDHR. But how are we to deal with people who violate human rights and states that violate the system of international law and order necessary to secure human rights fulfilment? Sometimes, it seems, armed force is required for reasonable assurances. We can resort to war to defend ourselves and others, to vindicate an international system of just laws, to punish gross violators of such a system, and, at least to some extent, to deter future violations of it. Such a view is not at odds with humanity and dignity; indeed, it is fundamentally in accord with those praiseworthy values and commitments, given its central concern with human rights and their effective protection from the danger and grit of the real world.

Conclusion

To have a defensible and comprehensive conception of just war, one needs to reject both (strong) realism and pacifism, and to offer compelling grounds for doing so. (Strong) realism and pacifism, it seems, ought to be rejected; neither constitutes the best doctrine on the ethics of war and peace. Just war theory, for all its residual unclarities, seems to be the most appropriate moral (and perhaps even prudential) response to these very difficult and perplexing questions. What needs to be done now is to move from the negative case against competing doctrines to the positive case in favour of contemporary Kantian just war theory. That will be the task of the remaining chapters.

Notes

1. *Jus in bello,* it will be recalled from the Introduction, does not form part of the main object of this work.
2. Notable contemporary realist tracts include the following: H. Morgenthau, *Politics Among Nations* (New York: Knopf, 5th ed., 1973); G. Kennan, *Realities of American Foreign Policy* (Princeton, NJ: Princeton University Press, 1954); R. Niebuhr, *Christianity and Power Politics* (New York: Charles Scribner's Sons, 1940); H. Bull, *The Anarchical Society: A Study of Order in World Politics* (New York: Columbia University Press, 1977); K. Waltz, *Man, The State and War* (Princeton, NJ: Princeton University Press, 1978); R. Keohane, ed., *Neorealism and Its Critics* (New York: Columbia University Press, 1986); and H. Kissinger, *Diplomacy* (New York: Harper Collins, 1995).
3. It should be noted that this diagram is not offered as a logically exhaustive one. The literature on realism is enormous, and often enormously sophisticated, and I do not pretend to have done it full justice. All that is charted, therefore, are my own views about the most important kinds of realism *relevant to the issues here at stake.* Thanks for help on these distinctions is due to Christian Barry and Thomas Pogge. This chart was not employed in connection with the previous Kant exegesis out of fear of committing a serious anachronism: most of these kinds of realism have only recently come to the fore as well-defined doctrines.
4. Waltz, *State,* passim. See also S. Forde, "Classical Realism" (62-84) and J. Donnelly, "Twentieth-Century Realism" (85-111), both in T. Nardin and D. Mapel, eds., *Traditions in International Ethics* (Cambridge: Cambridge University Press, 1992); and R. Holmes, *On War and Morality* (Princeton, NJ: Princeton University Press, 1989), 1-110.
5. I owe this way of putting it to Christian Barry.

6. Forde, "Classical," 62-84; Donnelly, "Twentieth," 85-111; Holmes, *War*, 50-113; M. Walzer, *Just and Unjust Wars* (New York: Basic Books, 1977), 3-21; and C. von Clausewitz, *On War*, trans. A. Rapoport (New York: Penguin, 1994).

7. We can now discern that the exact kind of descriptive realism which Kant probably adhered to was weak descriptive realism.

8. Donnelly, "Twentieth," 85-111.

9. Walzer, *Just*, 3-20.

10. Walzer, *Just*, 3-21.

11. Walzer, *Just*, 3-21 and M. Cohen, "Moral Skepticism and International Relations," in C. Beitz, ed., *International Ethics: A Philosophy and Public Affairs Reader* (Princeton, NJ: Princeton University Press, 1985), 3-50.

12. Thucydides, Machiavelli and perhaps Hobbes all seem to have advocated, or at least entertained, this first form of SPPR. But Morgenthau is probably its most prominent champion.

13. Adherents to this view might well be Kissinger, in *Diplomacy*, and T. Franck, in his *The Power of Legitimacy Among Nations* (Princeton, NJ: Princeton University Press, 1990), especially in the "Appendix."

14. J. McMahan, "Realism, Morality and War" (78-92) and D. Mapel, "Realism and the Ethics of War and Peace" (180-200), both in T. Nardin, ed., *The Ethics of War and Peace: Religious and Secular Perspectives* (Princeton, NJ: Princeton University Press, 1996). See also Walzer, *Just*, 3-21 and Holmes, *War*, 50-113.

15. T. Pogge, *Realizing Rawls* (Ithaca, NY: Cornell University Press, 1989), 211-81; T. Pogge, "Moral Progress," in S. Luper-Foy, ed. *Problems of International Justice* (Boulder, CO: Westview, 1988), 283-304; and J. Rawls, "The Law of Peoples," in S. Shute and S. Hurley, eds. *On Human Rights* (New York: Basic Books, 1993), 41-81.

16. Pogge, *Rawls*, 211–80.

17. Donnelly, "Twentieth," 85-111.

18. Adherents of MPR would include essentially all twentieth-century realists listed earlier. Sharp distinction is usually not made between PPR and MPR, or indeed DR and PR, in many realist tracts—or even in the just war literature. That is why these rigorous distinctions are offered as part of the contribution this book makes to the state of the art. Much more common, in the realist literature, is the scattershot approach: all pro-realist arguments are thrown out, often without much systematic organization, in the belief that it is highly probable that at least some of them will "hit the target" and be found persuasive.

19. Kissinger, in *Diplomacy*, passim, makes one such contention.

20. Kissinger, *Diplomacy*, passim.

21. Kennan, "Morality," 206 and Kennan, *Realities*, 48.

22. Kissinger, *Diplomacy*, passim.

23. Donnelly, "Twentieth," 85-111.

24. This is not to say that a foreign policy animated by more provincial values than human rights satisfaction would not run afoul of this criticism. It may

well—but it is not a claim advanced by this offering of just war theory. See T. Pogge, "How Should Human Rights Be Conceived?," *Jahrbuch fur Recht und Ethik* (1995): 103-20; T. Pogge, "Human Rights as Moral Claims on Global Institutions," (forthcoming paper); Rawls, "Law," 41-81; and T. Scanlon, "Human Rights as a Neutral Concern" in P. Brown and D. MacLean, eds. *Human Rights and U.S. Foreign Policy* (Lexington, MA: Lexington Books, 1977), 83-92.

25. H. Shue, *Basic Rights: Subsistence, Affluence and U.S. Foreign Policy* (Princeton, NJ: Princeton University Press, 1980), passim; T. Pogge, "The Bounds of Nationalism," in J. Couture, et al., eds., *Rethinking Nationalism* (Calgary, AB: University of Calgary Press, 1998), 463-504; and Rawls, "Law," 45-50.

26. Rawls, "Law," 45–50.

27. W. Kymlicka, *Liberalism, Community and Culture* (Oxford: Clarendon, 1988) and W. Kymlicka, *Multiculturalism and Citizenship* (Oxford: Oxford University Press, 1995).

28. Pogge, "Bounds," 463-504. Of course, many will point out the relevant disanalogy here: that the family presupposes a secure context provided by the state whereas the state itself cannot count on any larger authority in the international context and thus should enjoy larger prerogatives. Fine. But this does not speak to the present argument. For this argument is designed to show that the appeal to national priority on grounds of identity—not security—is undermined by the family counter-examples.

29. C. Beitz, "Cosmopolitan Ideals and National Sentiment," *Journal of Philosophy* (1983): 591-600. A recent collection of essays on communitarianism versus cosmopolitanism, by a number of top American scholars, is M. Nussbaum, *For Love of Country: Debating the Limits of Patriotism*, ed. J. Cohen (Boston: Beacon Press, 1996).

30. M. Gelven, in his eloquent and fascinating, yet ominous and disturbing, study, *War and Existence* (Notre Dame, IN: University of Notre Dame Press, 1994), 12.

31. J. Teichman, *Pacifism and the Just War* (Oxford: Basil Blackwell, 1986), passim. For more on defining pacifism, see Holmes, *War*, 19-49; J. Narveson, "Pacifism: A Philosophical Analysis," (originally in *Ethics*, 1967), in R. Wasserstrom, ed., *Morality and War* (Belmont, CA: Wadsworth, 1970), 63-77 and J. Narveson, "Violence and War," in T. Regan, ed., *Matters of Life and Death* (Philadelphia, PA: Temple University Press, 1980), 109-47; J.B. Brady and N. Garver, eds., *Justice, Law and Violence* (Philadelphia, PA: Temple University Press, 1991); R.G. Frey and C.W. Morris, eds., *Violence, Terrorism and Justice* (Cambridge: Cambridge University Press, 1991); and H. Arendt, *On Violence* (New York: Harcourt Brace Jovanovich, 1970).

32. The works of John Howard Yoder (e.g., *When War Is Unjust: Being Honest in Just-War Thinking* [Minneapolis, MI: Augsburg, 1984]) offer a good example of such a religious justification for pacifism. There are many other sources relevant here, including the following: J.P. Burns, *War and Its Discontents:*

Pacifism and Quietism in the Abrahamic Traditions (Washington, DC: Georgetown University Press, 1986); L.S. Cahill, *Love Your Enemies: Discipleship, Pacifism and Just War Theory* (Minneapolis, MI: Fortress, 1994); M.C. Cartwright, "Conflicting Interpretations of Christian Pacifism," 197-213, and T.J. Koontz, "Christian Nonviolence: An Interpretation," 169-96, both in T. Nardin, ed., *The Ethics of War and Peace: Religious and Secular Perspectives* (Princeton, NJ: Princeton University Press, 1996); D. Dombrowski, *Christian Pacifism* (Philadelphia, PA: Temple University Press, 1991); and S. Hauerwas, *Should War Be Eliminated? Philosophical and Theological Investigations* (Milwaukee, WI: Marquette University Press, 1984).

33. It ought to be noted that this CP/DP distinction is only intended as one of degree and not necessarily one in kind. There are many well-known problems with regard to distinguishing clearly and steadfastly between the two. Some comment on this was previously made in chapter 1 of this book.

34. Holmes, *War*, and R. Norman, *Ethics, Killing and War* (Cambridge: Cambridge University Press, 1995).

35. One attempt to offer a more precise accounting, from a just war point of view, will be offered next chapter in the section on proportionality.

36. Walzer, *Wars*, passim; M. Walzer, "The Moral Standing of States: A Response to Four Critics," *Philosophy and Public Affairs* (1979/80): 209-29; and T. Nagel, "Ruthlessness in Public Life," in his *Mortal Questions* (Cambridge: Cambridge University Press, 1979) 75-90.

37. M. Walzer, "World War II: Why Was This War Different?" *Philosophy and Public Affairs* (1970/71): 3-21; and W.V. O'Brien, *The Conduct of Just and Limited War* (New York: Praeger, 1981), 35-65.

38. On the Gulf War and just war theory, see M. Walzer, "Preface" to the second edition of *Just and Unjust Wars* (New York: Basic Books, 1991); J.B. Elshtain, et al., *But Was It Just? Reflections on the Morality of the Persian Gulf War*, D. DeCosse, ed. (New York: Doubleday, 1992); A. Geyer, *Lines in the Sand: Justice and the Gulf War* (Louisville, KY: John Knox Press, 1992); B. Hallett, ed., *Engulfed in War: Just War and the Persian Gulf* (Honolulu: University of Hawaii Press, 1991); J.N. Moore, *Crisis in the Gulf: Enforcing the Rule of Law* (Dobbs Ferry, NY: Oceana, 1992); K. Vaux, *Ethics and the Gulf War* (Boulder, CO: Westview, 1992); and James T. Johnson and G. Weigel, eds., *Just War and Gulf War* (Washington, DC: Ethics and Public Policy, 1991).

39. Norman, *Ethics*, 80-93.

40. Norman, *Ethics*, 290-93 and Narveson, "Pacifism," 62-77.

41. This pacifist argument is developed, as a foil, by Walzer, in *Just*, 329-36. It is also defended in Holmes, *War*, 260-96 and in Norman, *Ethics*, 210-15.

42. J. Rawls, *A Theory of Justice* (Cambridge, MA: harvard University Press, 1971), 370-82.

43. Walzer, *Just*, 329-36.

44. Holmes, *War*, 146-213, esp. 183-213.

45. G.E.M. Anscombe, "War and Murder," in R. Wasserstrom, ed., *War and Morality* (Belmont, CA: Wadsworth, 1970), 41-53.

46. NP is offered as another advance on current just war theory. No contemporary work offers a comparative general principle on aggression which is as clearly or rigorously defined.

47. Narveson, "Pacifism," 63-78, and J. Narveson, "Violence and War," in T. Regan, ed., *Matters of Life and Death* (Philadelphia, PA: Temple University Press, 1980), 109-47. Similar notions are expressed in Shue, *Basic*, passim, and A. Gewirth, *Human Rights: Essays in Justification and Application* (Chicago: University of Chicago Press, 1982), passim.

48. Walzer, *Wars*, 50-75.

49. See, for example, G. Fletcher, "Proportionality and the Psychotic Aggressor," *Israel Law Review* (1973): 367-90.

50. H. Bedau, "The Precarious Sovereignty of Rights," (forthcoming paper); J. Thomson, "Self-Defence and Rights," in her *Rights, Risk and Restitution* (Cambridge, MA: Harvard University Press, 1986), 33-50; J. Thomson, "Self-Defence," *Philosophy and Public Affairs* (1991): 283-310. The first of Thomson's essays displays a marked hostility to the notion of forfeiture, whereas the second one appears to offer a rather muted, uneasy support of the concept.

51. As we have seen last chapter.

52. See Fletcher, "Psychotic," 367-90; and R. Nozick, *Anarchy, State and Utopia* (New York: Basic Books, 1974), passim.

53. M. Otsuka appears to support this claim in his "Killing the Innocent in Self-Defense," *Philosophy and Public Affairs* (1992): 74-94. It is also present in Holmes, *War*, passim.

54. Walzer, *Wars*, 34-50 and 138-43; Holmes, *War*, 114-213; R. Fullinwinder, "War and Innocence," *Philosophy and Public Affairs* (1975): 90-97; G. Malvrodes, "Conventions and the Laws of War," *Philosophy and Public Affairs* (1975): 117-31; L.A. Alexander, "Self-Defence and the Killing of Noncombatants: A Reply to Fullinwinder," *Philosophy and Public Affairs* (1975/76): 408-15; and J.M. Dubik, "Human Rights, Command Responsibility and Walzer's Just War Theory," *Philosophy and Public Affairs* (1982): 354-71.

55. Holmes, *War*, 146-213.

56. Walzer, *Just*, passim.

57. We should now realize how the DDE, thus defined, could not have been employed earlier in the case of the innocent aggressor. Say soldier S is considering shooting soldier T, who under some description is an innocent aggressor. S cannot appeal to the DDE here because, while he might say that he intends only to defeat the aggression and not kill an innocent, and while he might contend that the defeat of the aggression is worth the price, he cannot plausibly contend that killing the innocent is not means to his end of defeating the aggression, since the innocent and the aggressor are (by hypothesis) one and the same person. Innocent aggressors, if such there be, must thus be dealt with differently than innocent non-aggressors.

58. Walzer, *Just*, 152-59, 257, 277-83 and 317-21 and Norman, *Killing*, 73-118 and 159-200.

59. Reisman and Antoniou, eds., *Laws*, 43-48. Discrimination and non-combatant immunity is a complex norm codified in Articles 22-28 of the Hague Convention (IV), and emphatically in Article 48 of the First Protocol to the Geneva Convention.

60. Reisman and Antoniou, eds., Laws, 47. Proportionality is codified in international law in Articles 22-23 of the Hague Convention (IV).

61. Reisman and Antoniou, *Laws*, 49-68, 84-87 and 149-230. The just war rule of no intrinsically heinous means (also called means *mala in se*) is codified throughout a number of specific international law conventions, such as those banning the use of chemical (1925), biological (1972) and "excessively injurious weapons" (1980). Also relevant is the convention against genocide, 1948.

As mentioned previously, it is not one of the aims of this work to offer a detailed justification of these *jus in bello* norms. Existing works of just war theory already do a compelling job of this. See, for example, Walzer, *Wars*, 34-50 and 127-224; O'Brien, *Conduct*, 37-70; Regan, *Cases*, 96-100; Wasserstrom, *Morality*, passim; Elshtain, *Theory*, passim; T. Nagel, "War and Massacre," *Philosophy and Public Affairs* (1971/72): 123-45); and R.K. Fullinwinder, "War and Innocence," *Philosophy and Public Affairs* (1975): 90-97.

62. Norman, *Ethics*, 37-118 and Cheyney Ryan, "Self-Defence, Pacifism and Killing," *Ethics* 93 (1983): 518-20. Shades of this self-respect argument also appear in Narveson, "Pacifism," 63-78. I deal with these, and related, issues in my forthcoming articles "A Just War Critique of Realism and Pacifism," *Journal of Philosophical Research*; and "Evaluating Pacifism," *Dialogue.*

CHAPTER 6

Jus ad Bellum

In the previous two chapters, we have: 1) detailed the core elements of a contemporary Kantian internationalism, notably human rights; 2) expounded more fully on the meaning, justification and specification of these human rights, from a contemporary Kantian point of view; and 3) given powerful reasons for rejecting both (strong) realism and pacifism as adequate conceptions of the ethics of war and peace between nations. The goal of this chapter is to begin the positive task of constructing a contemporary Kantian just war theory by fashioning a theory of *jus ad bellum*—the justice of the resort to war.

We have seen, in previous chapters and notably in proposition KI 7,[1] that contemporary Kantian grounds for resorting to armed force in international relations most centrally involve the need to vindicate, enforce and realize universal principles of justice—namely, state rights SRs 1-9 and state duties SDs 1-9[2]—whose aim is to procure, for all, a secure condition of peace-with-rights. A state may resort to war if, in the absence of an effective global authority, such is reasonably deemed required to uphold its rights, and those of the international community, on behalf of

---

Notes to chapter 6 are on pp. 212–16.

the human rights of its individual citizens. We have already listed those rights and principles and offered at least some explanation as to their rationale and normative purchase on our attention. The main task of this chapter is to examine, in much greater detail, those particular contemporary Kantian just war principles of *jus ad bellum* that collectively justify the resort to war. A secondary goal of this chapter will be to compare and contrast the proffered contemporary Kantian norms with the current international laws of armed conflict.

Groundwork

It must be stressed, straightaway, that all the *jus ad bellum* criteria endorsed below are endorsed holistically—i.e., all of the criteria must be fulfilled, and jointly satisfied, to justify the resort to war. Each *jus ad bellum* criterion is necessary, but only all together are they sufficient, to justify resorting to war. This means, importantly, that having a just cause (for example) for launching a war does not, of itself, justify the actual resort to war. The other criteria must also be satisfied.

Jus ad bellum, we have already seen,[3] is the preserve of political leaders. It is first and foremost the leaders of the state in question who are to consider whether or not they should resort to armed force. It is they who bear the primary responsibility for the choices they make in this regard. An important corollary to this principle is that, *ceteris paribus*, ordinary soldiers ought not to be held responsible for the (in)justice of the wars they are ordered to fight by their political leaders. Furthermore, to the extent to which the state in question is democratic, moral responsibility for resorting to war might reasonably be seen as being diffused throughout the citizenry. In such an instance, the general principle of moral responsibility would be: the stronger a person's ability to affect the resort to war, the greater the moral responsibility that he bears with regard to the adequacy with which his state fulfils the criteria of *jus ad bellum*.[4]

It is of the utmost importance to recall a point made in the Introduction: all claims of states, with regard to how well they fulfil just war criteria, must be held to public scrutiny and to standards of evidence and reasonableness. *States ought not to be allowed a subjectivist, or utterly self-applying, use of just war criteria*. States cannot simply proclaim that they have a just cause, and that it is proportional to the costs required to achieve it, and expect to have such a claim accepted at face value by the international community. Such laxity would result in the hollowing out of all just war norms. Just war theory would, under such circumstances, be completely vacuous. It is crucial, therefore, to understand that such cannot be the case and that the criteria make sense and have normative purchase on our attention only when viewed in light of their proper function as standards against which (state) behaviour can, and ought, to be publicly evaluated according to standards of evidence and cogency.[5]

Finally, by way of preliminaries, it should be considered whether a just war is merely permissible or fully obligatory. All that is here being claimed, on behalf of Kantian internationalism, is that, provided all the relevant criteria are fulfilled, resort to armed force is morally permissible. As Frances Kamm has said, "[t]o say a war is justified is to show that it is morally permissible, though not necessarily obligatory."[6] Peoples, as represented by their states, have the choice whether to resort to force (so justified) or not.[7]

Having stipulated the nature and function of *jus ad bellum* criteria, how they jointly stipulate conditions of permissible resort to war, and having considered who bears responsibility for meeting such criteria, and how this ought to be determined, we can turn directly to the question of which *jus ad bellum* (JAB) criteria precisely ought to be endorsed by a contemporary Kantian. The following principles, JAB 1-6, seem reasonable.

Just Cause

JAB 1. Just cause. A state may resort to armed force against another state if, in the absence of an international authority to deal effectively with the problem, such action is reasonably deemed required to vindicate universal principles of justice, notably human rights and those state rights and duties (enumerated previously as SRs 1-9 and SDs 1-9) which are compatible with, and/or necessary for, them. The key principle here is the defence and vindication of fundamental rights and the protection of those who bear such rights from serious harm. From these general reflections, three just causes, in particular, can be deduced: 1) self-defence from aggression; 2) the defence of others from aggression; and 3) armed intervention in a non-aggressive country wherein grievous human rights violations are occurring.[8]

The key question, at least with regard to 1 and 2, is: what is "aggression"? Aggression is here defined normatively, as it was in chapter 5; it is the violation of those universal principles of justice listed previously as SRs 1-9 and SDs 1-9, especially as done through the use of armed force.[9] Aggression is the violation of rights, which is done by presenting a serious and lethal threat, based on compelling evidence, to another's life and liberties or, in this interstate case, to another's sovereignty and integrity. A similar view is encapsulated in Article I of the UN General Assembly's 1974 "Definition of Aggression": aggression is "the use of armed force by a State against the sovereignty, territorial integrity or political independence of another State, or in any other manner inconsistent with the Charter of the United Nations." It should be noted here that the most basic and important principles of the UN Charter are twofold: 1) international peace and security; and 2) human rights satisfaction.

So we might concur with Michael Walzer when he says that "aggression is a crime," because it violates critically important rights and because it forces the victims to risk their lives and liberties fighting for the defence of these rights.[10] And, as Walzer infers: "Aggression justifies two kinds of violent response: a war of self-defense by the victim and a war of law enforcement by the victim and any other members of international society."[11] Indeed, Article 51 of the UN Charter echoes this reasoning: "Nothing in the present Charter shall impair the inherent right of individual or collective self-defence if an armed attack occurs against a member of the United Nations." Indeed, the Security Council of the UN is explicitly empowered to determine whether an instance of aggression has occurred and, if so, to take whatever measures it deems reasonable and effective (including "such action by air, sea or land forces as may be necessary") to maintain or restore international peace and security.[12]

Turning from the current international law on just cause back towards reflective philosophical consideration, we recall from chapter 5 what is grounded by the commission of aggression, *via* normative principle NP. NP stipulates that the commission of aggression by the aggressor A against the victim V entitles V, and/or any third-party vindicator T, acting on behalf of V, to employ all necessary means to stop A, including lethal force, *provided* that such means do not themselves violate human rights. Let us now understand the relevant agents A, V and T as states and not persons. And let us consider first the normative grounds for why V possesses such an entitlement: reasonableness; fairness; responsibility; and implicit entitlement.

First, it would be unreasonable to deny V permission to take effective measures to protect its people from serious harm or lethal attack at the hands of A. Simply put, it is not reasonable, given the kinds of creatures we are and the kind of world in which we live, to expect a state charged with the responsibility to protect its member citizens to capitulate utterly in the face of aggression.

The fairness argument stipulates that it would be not only unreasonable but unfair to deny V the permission to resist A with force because, in the absence of such measures, V will suffer catastrophic loss of life and liberty while A will actually gain whatever object it had in mind in attacking V. And it seems clear that aggression and rights-violation ought not to be unfairly rewarded in this way, both in the particular case and for the sake of not eliciting such behaviour in the future.

Not only would denying V permission to resist forcibly the aggression of A be both unreasonable and unfair, it would also ignore the fundamental issue of who bears responsibility for the choice situation. It is the aggressor A who is responsible for placing V in a situation where V must choose between its rights and those of the aggressor A. (And this point ties neatly into the reasonableness claim, since it is only reasonable to expect V, in such a situation, to choose its own rights.) The aggressor A, if it does not wish to subject itself to the consequences of the resort to defensive force by V, can always cease and desist from its aggression. So if A does not cease and desist, it is hardly in a position to cry foul should V decide to do the reasonable and fair thing and defend itself and its citizens with the needed force.

Finally, any victim V has the implicit entitlement to use whatever measures are necessary to achieve reasonably secure access to the objects of its rights and those of its citizens. The relevant argument has the following form:

1. Minimally just states have moral rights, SRs 1-9, and duties, SDs 1-9, vis-à-vis other states. These rights and duties constitute the ideal Kantian system of international law, designed to realize the fundamental priority of international justice: the human rights of persons.

2. These rights, SRs 1-9, entitle states to employ reliable measures necessary to secure the objects of these rights and to protect them from serious standard threats to them, such as the violent aggression of others. (This follows as a matter of moral logic: if P has the right R to Q and M is a means necessary to secure Q, then P must also have a right to M. Otherwise, to what extent could we speak of P's original right to Q?)

3. There is no reliable or effective international authority that can currently assure states in the possession of (the objects of) their rights. Thus, states are, in the final analysis, on their own with regard to such assurance.

4. Currently, the most effective and reliable form of such self-help assurance with regard to rights-protection, at least in the last resort, is the use of armed force.

5. Thus, faced with violation of their rights SRs 1-9 (i.e., with aggression), states are entitled to employ armed force and war in order to punish the rights-violator, vindicate their rights and resecure their objects and those of their citizens' human rights.

This brings us to the second core aspect of principle NP: granted that V possesses entitlement to respond to A's aggression with armed force, how is V to do so without violating rights? There are two elements to note in response: 1) state A, through the commission of aggression against V, forfeits its state rights not to be attacked with lethal force in return; and 2) provided that V adheres strictly to norms of *jus in bello* during its just war against A, it will succeed in offering the required "due care" to innocent civilians in both states, and thereby avoid violating their rights. It will therefore fully satisfy NP. Let us deal with each one of these elements in turn.

Why and how does A forfeit its right as a state not to be subject to armed attack by committing aggression against V? A forfeits its rights because, as we saw in chapter 5, the weight of reasons in the case indicates that no wrong is done to A in the event that victim V resists A's aggression with means of war. And the weight of reasons in this case must draw on those just offered in defence of V's entitlement to resort to force in the first place: it would be unreasonable, unfair, oblivious of responsibility and at odds with implicit entitlement to declare that V would do wrong in resisting A's aggression with armed force. And if V would do no wrong in violently resisting A, then A must fail to have moral rights that such not be done. It must thus have forfeited its rights; it must have violated the minimal requirements of a just state and so lost its title to the full panoply of state rights.

And since A forfeits its state rights in this regard, this permits any third party T (or group of third-party states G) to intervene forcibly on behalf of victim V. We saw in chapter 5 that this legitimacy of other-defence is grounded in the normative core of the victim's claim that the aggressor either stop or be stopped, regardless of which is the agent bringing about the stopping. Provided that the demonstrable aim is the protection of the victim and its citizens from rights-violation, armed resistance is permitted to any state willing to take on its associated burdens.

So V's (or T's) resisting A's aggression against V with armed force will not violate A's state rights because, by committing aggression, A has forfeited its state rights. But what of the human rights of the persons in both A and V (or T)? Why and how will launching a just war at the state level not violate these individual rights? We have already encountered the answer towards the end of chapter 5: these rights will not be violated *provided* that V (or T) fully adheres to the other criteria of *jus ad bellum* and *jus in bello*.[13]

The human rights of persons are entitlements to reasonably secure access to those things persons vitally need and which they can reasonably request from others and from social institutions. During the course of an otherwise justified war, such a threshold of "reasonably secure access" is equivalent to that of "due care" provided by the belligerent victim/vindicator. And the giving of due care is fulfilled by state adherence to the norms of *jus ad bellum* and *jus in bello*. Thus, states considering resort to armed force in defence of their rights need not only to fulfil all of the *jus ad bellum* criteria but also to commit themselves at the outset to adhering, to the best of their ability, to the three norms of *jus in bello*: non-combatant immunity from intentional targeting; (micro-) proportionality; and complete avoidance of intrinsically heinous means.

So, a state has a just cause for resorting to war in terms of self- and other-defence if and only if: 1) it is the victim of aggression or is coming to the aid of a victim of aggression; and 2) its resort to armed force fulfils all aspects of the core principle NP. Both 1 and 2 revolve, most centrally, around the general norm of protecting and defending minimally just communities and the lives and rights of their citizen members.

Further comment needs to be made on a relevant issue mentioned in chapter 5: whether "defence" is being employed descriptively or normatively. The answer, we have seen, is the latter. A just war is one that is *normatively* defensive—it defends people from aggression and seeks, in response, to resist and repeal it—whereas the tactics that can be employed within the context of such a just war may be either empirically defensive or offensive. It will be recalled that aggression has been defined as the violation of state rights SRs 1-9 and that this violation occurs when a state presents itself as a serious and potentially lethal threat to another state and its people. And a state can present itself as such a threat in at least one of two ways: 1) by actually attacking another state without just cause; or 2) by posing a credible, grave and imminent threat, based on compelling evidence, of launching such an attack. So a just war of self- or other-defence need not be wholly reactive: there is room here, as Kant suggested (but did not explain), for anticipatory attack as well.

The notion, with regard to anticipatory attack, is that forcing states to wait for the actual attack, despite its evident and imminent coming, is not a reasonable insistence. This is especially the case if there are compelling and public grounds for believing that the coming attack is going to be of some considerable force and destruction. A state would be derelict in its duty to protect its members if it did not reserve the right to make well-grounded anticipatory attacks in this regard. It is no less a violation of fundamental rights to pose a credible and imminent serious threat—i.e., a clear and present danger—to another person or state. Such interferes with the lives and liberties of states and peoples as readily as does an explicit and actual invasion because it leaves them just waiting for the oncoming attack. The threat functions, and is intended to function, in the same manner as the actual attack: to bring about the capitulation of the other country. From a just war point of view, the resort to arms by the victim is hence equally justified in either event.

Perhaps it should be noted how this Kantian conception of defence from aggression seems not radically at odds with the above General Assembly view of aggression, nor with Article 51 of the UN Charter, since there is considerable ambiguity with regard to whether a descriptive or prescriptive use of the terms is being employed in those sources. For instance, aggression in the General Assembly resolution is seen as the use of armed force "against" another state. We might ask: "against," how? Literally, such that only an actual attack grounds a violent response? Or is it also the case that the imminent threat of such an attack works "against" the purposes of the Charter? Furthermore, "defence" in Article 51 is wholly unspecified as to its descriptive or prescriptive intent. Perhaps, indeed, the ambiguity was deliberate. The contention here, with regard to international law, is thus that, as stated, there is no clear dissonance between the contemporary Kantian view and the substance of the current laws of war on the topic of just cause.[14]

It would seem quite helpful to devise three thought-experiment cases to illustrate more precisely these three just causes: one where resort to war is justified and (empirically) defensive; one where the resort to war is justified and (empirically) offensive; and one where the resort to war in unjustified.

Case #1. State A is a bellicose and militaristic regime. It is a big, rich and powerful country surrounded by a collection of smaller, weaker states. A decides that, given this power imbalance, it can easily afford the explicit prudential costs involved in invading and conquering some of its neighbours. And it wants more territory for the sake of demonstrating its power and for the economic gains involved from having more land and resources. A believes that such is only proper: like a strong realist, A subscribes to the notion that such aggrandizement is what powerful states have always done, will always do, and, moreover, that this is what they ought to do. A proceeds to launch an attack on one of those smaller, weaker neighbouring countries B. B is caught unawares by A's attack, given A's superior preparedness, resources and cunning. A makes clear its aim of overthrowing the existing, democratically elected government in B and replacing it with an unelected puppet regime which will regulate and oversee its takeover and resource exploitation of B. And who knows what will happen to the citizens of B after that new structure is in place?

In this case it seems clear, given our just war principles, that B has at least a just cause in going to war against A and resisting A's aggression with lethal armed force. Indeed, it is crucial to note that, *even without* substantive and detailed knowledge of A's goals or aims in attacking, B's armed response is justified simply given the act of A's armed invasion itself. Given *that* kind of force, and *that* kind of brutal invasion, A's declared goals verge on irrelevancy. Truly, the thrust of A's intentions is made sufficiently clear through the raw act of aggression itself. As such— i.e., with no further information being required—we can see that A poses an unjust, serious and lethal threat to the lives and rights of those in B. And that reality alone grounds B's armed response, with lethal force if that reasonably seems required. Since, in this case, A has attacked first and caught B unawares, B's justified war against A would be defensive in both senses: 1) normatively, because it is aimed at protecting its own citizens from the ravages of aggression; and 2) empirically, because it is carried out in factual response to a first attack by the aggressor.

Case #2. Assume that the particulars of Case #1 are still in play: A is a large, powerful, ambitious and bellicose state and B is a smaller, neighbouring state with no such ambitions for greater influence. The relevant question in this case is: when may B justifiably launch an anticipatory attack (i.e., an empirically offensive strike) in (normative) defence from the aggression of A? It has been contended that B may do so *only* when A poses, to B, a clear and present danger to its sovereignty and integrity as a state, based on compelling evidence. When would A count as such? It seems that a justified resort to force in this case, on B's part, will have to rely much more heavily on a substantive knowledge of

A's goals and intentions. And such knowledge must, as always in just war theory, be based on cogent, publicly accessible evidence. Say, for instance, the leader of A declares repeatedly his wish that B be incorporated into a "Greater A." And say that A's diplomacy with B becomes rancorous, calling for materially unreasonable concessions from B in lieu of attack (like voluntarily ceding a long-held border province to A, regardless of the wishes of the people there). And, finally, say A sets into motion a recognizable and demonstrable military buildup, near the border with B, and one with clear offensive potential. In light of these phenomena, it would seem as if it were just a matter of time before A attacks: the threat is serving to function in an identical manner to that of an actual attack, namely, by trying to force the capitulation of B to A. Here it seems quite manifest that A constitutes a clear and present danger to the lives and rights of those in B. And as such A has already committed aggression, in our normative sense. Since it is just a matter of time until A attacks B, and since the threat functions identically to an attack, it would be unreasonable and unjust to refuse to permit B from depriving A of the element of surprise by attacking first. So, the grounds for launching an anticipatory attack are quite stringent—as they ought to be, in order to block abuse of the principle. Anticipatory attacks by any X are justified if and only if failure to launch them shall demonstrably run grave risk of an unjust, serious and lethal attack on X and its people.

Case #3. This final case also assumes the basic particulars of Cases #1 and #2: A is a large, wealthy, powerful and bellicose country while B is one of A's smaller, weaker and more quiescent neighbours. Let us add the assumption that A and B have a history of military conflict between them. Let us assume further that there is a noticeable military buildup in A, or that A develops a new weapons system. It seems that, in light of these realities alone, B would not be justified in launching an anticipatory strike against A. A military buildup, or a new weapons system, does not of itself constitute aggression. After all, the buildup, or weapons innovation, even in bellicose country A, and even considering the history between A and B, might be animated out of a sense of fear of another country C (which also has interests in the region) and not out of a desire for aggrandizement vis-à-vis B. There are here no complementary political grounds for believing that A is imminently about to attack B. Thus, it seems that there are two broad criteria that must be fulfilled, and to a threshold level of clear and present danger, for aggression to have occurred and thus for an anticipatory strike to be grounded: 1) the existence of a strong and potent offensive military capability; and 2) a recent and escalating pattern of behaviour and declaration indicating political willingness to use that military threat unjustly. The obtaining of the one without the other does not justify anticipatory attack, and a country acting on that basis would itself be committing an act of aggression. The threshold for anticipatory strike, once more, must be thusly stringent—i.e., both 1 and 2 met, and to the degree of clear and present danger—in order to give real substance and meaning to the doctrine, as well as to prevent its misuse by unscrupulous regimes.

So, aggression—i.e., the presentation of an unjust, serious and potentially lethal threat to another's vital needs, either by actual attack or by posing a clear and present danger of such an attack—justifies the resort to armed force and war on the part of the victim of the aggression and/or any third party out to defend the victim.

But, having dealt with self- and other-defence from aggression as just causes for resorting to interstate armed conflict, what of the third just cause enumerated above, namely, armed intervention in a country that did not commit aggression against any other state? This is a hotly disputed topic, and the body of positive international law is nowhere near as settled as it is when it comes to individual and collective self-defence. In general, there is an very strong presumption in positive international law against outside interference with the domestic situation of any country, especially interference backed up with the force of arms. But it should, perhaps, be noted that a considerable number of such interventions have been authorized by the UN Security Council, most recently in Somalia in 1992-94 and, in a more complex fashion, in the former Yugoslavia in 1992-95.[15]

It seems that a contemporary Kantian internationalist ought to recognize the permissibility of the world community intervening in a state in which the MJ 1-4 criteria of a minimally just state are not met: domestic law and order; human rights satisfaction;

ability to protect its people; and adherence to basic rules of international conduct, notably non-aggression. One thinks here in particular of a state committing gross human rights violations in violation of MJ 2. Such a state has no right not to be interfered with. And the people suffering from such a condition have the right to request rescue from it, from whatever source is willing and able. The object of such intervention, as Walzer says, must be just that: rescue, and not rule.[16]

The intervenor is only to vindicate the people's right to political sovereignty, under a state mechanism of their choosing—and one that can reliably meet the MJ 1-4 criteria. Once that has been achieved, the grounds for continued occupation dissolve. So, we ought to endorse, from a moral point of view, the positive international law's conventions stipulating that any would-be intervenor N faces a very heavy burden of proof regarding the grounds for its intervention in target country T. Just cause in this case means, in particular, there being very serious and publicly evident violations of human rights on a mass scale in T.

But the different kind of just cause is not the only thing that sets armed intervention in a non-aggressive outlaw country apart from the paradigmatic cases of self- and other-defence against aggression. There are other normative criteria, *in addition to* those of just war theory enumerated this chapter, which must be fulfilled in order for such an intervention to be justified. These are: 1) the would-be intervenor N must be freely invited to intervene by the people in target country T who require rescue; and 2) N must commit itself, in advance, to meaningful participation in the reconstruction of T, after the intervention has achieved its aim. It follows that the normative criteria grounding armed intervention in a non-aggressive outlaw country are more stringent than those grounding war against an aggressive outlaw country: not only does the prospective intervention have to satisfy all other just war criteria (as enumerated in this chapter), it must also satisfy these two additional criteria. It seems that this theoretical conclusion about armed intervention accords perfectly with our reflective intuitions about, as well as with current international law regarding, this very delicate and difficult topic.[17]

Consider a thought-experiment case applying these abstract principles of justified armed intervention. State C is composed of three distinct peoples: D, E and F. There has been a complicated and conflictual history between these three groups, though they have managed for some time to retain a unified state structure. However, in recent years, two demagogues have risen to rival positions of power: one is a self-styled representative of D, the other of E, the two largest groups with a conflictual history between them. The demagogues have whipped up communal sentiment within their respective groups and have used their respective powers in such a way as to favour blatantly their own people. Some kind of confrontation between them seems inevitable. However, given the relative parity of power and influence between the groups D and E, it looks as though such a conflict will offer few gains—that is, unless F had a much diminished share of power, influence and goods. The demagogues of D and E come to a tacit understanding that they will give vent to the communal passions of their peoples on the back of the minority F. F has, in fact, been a much maligned and marginalized community since the founding of state C and has suffered considerably for this, in terms of rates of poverty, illness, crime and so on. But the new campaign against F, led by the demagogues in D and E, quickly takes on darker overtones and serious persecution. Citizens begin to be categorized in terms of their nationality, and those of F-heritage are summarily stripped of many of their civil rights: they are blocked from the national vote and from running for national public office, deprived of many due process rights, forbidden to own property and the like. Members of F have also been territorially concentrated in a certain province P within C for generations. The new national government, led by D and E, unilaterally contracts the borders of P, forcing mass migration and dislocation within the F-community. It then carves up the territorial and resource gains from the border contraction between D and E.

This process of systematically persecuting members of F begins to take on a depraved logic of its own, and the ethnic frenzy whipped up by the new national government spurs some private "citizens' groups" to foment conflicts between themselves and members of F. Members of F begin to suffer serious physical violence at the hands of people from D and E. The national government does nothing to stop such attacks, despite the fact that dozens in F are killed and hundreds are injured. Fearing for their own safety and well-being, the people of F start to organize something like a defensive militia to protect themselves from such attacks. The demagogues in D and E pounce, proclaiming that the formation of the defensive militia is tantamount to a declaration of secession of the province P from C. National security demands, they contend, the violent suppression of this "rebellion." So, they order in the national army. The national army is dominated by members of D and E, and is infinitely better trained and more resourceful than the rag-tag defensive militia of F. The army sweeps into P, rolls over the defensive militia and is now poised to conquer the province entirely.

The principles defended above would clearly ground an armed intervention by a foreign power—preferably the world community as a whole—at this point, provided that: 1) legitimate representatives of F (say, the provincial government of P) have requested such assistance; and 2) the intervening force committed itself to assistance with regard to the costs of reconstruction in P following the intervention. Let us say these two criteria are also the case. At this point, and presuming the other *jus ad bellum* criteria (to be discussed below) are met, the intervenor N would be justified in sending a rapid reaction force into P to protect the people of F from wholesale massacre and perhaps genocide at the hands of the army of C, with lethal armed force if necessary. C has proved itself an outlaw regime, devoid of rights to non-interference, through its systematic "internal aggression," and grievous rights-violation, against some of its own citizens. N would, of course, also have to abide by the norms of *jus in bello* during the course of its intervention: the central point here has simply been to detail a more concrete case where such intervention seems clearly permitted by the principles of human rights protection we have contended ground the resort to war in the first place.

This extended section on just cause has dealt with only the first criterion of *jus ad bellum*. Recourse must still be made to elucidating and explaining the remaining criteria, as follow below.

Right Intention

JAB 2. Right intention. This criterion should be more prominent and important than it traditionally appears in just war theory. Two relevant aspects of the right intention criterion, from a Kantian point of view, need to be stressed:

1) A state resorting to war must do so only for the sake of vindicating those rights whose violation grounds its just cause in fighting. A state may not employ the cloak of a just cause to prosecute a war for the sake, for instance, of ethnic hatred or national glory. The vindication of state rights SRs 1-9, and human rights in general, remains the sole just cause grounding resort to warfare.

2) A state resorting to war must, in advance, commit itself to upholding, to the best of its ability, the norms of *jus in bello* and *jus post bellum*. It seems that this is the most appropriate spot for something similar to Kant's earlier criterion of comparative justice. It will be recalled that the criterion of comparative justice contended that all belligerents ought, self-critically, to acknowledge limits to the justice of their own cause in prosecuting a war. They ought to acknowledge the possibility that the justice of their cause is only comparative, and that the opposing side may also have some defensible rationale for fighting. In the absence of a totally determinate theory of justice and/or international juridical authority, it was thought only reasonable to acknowledge that one's cause or end is not absolute and overriding, and thus that the means which one may employ to realize that end may not be unlimited.

This old principle ought *not* to be included in a contemporary criterion of comparative justice because it seems open to devastating counter-examples. For instance, what was the comparative justice of Nazi Germany's cause in resorting to war in 1939? Or the comparative justice of state A in Case #1 above? It seems that, in both cases, the aggressor had absolutely none. At the very least, we can imagine scenarios in which an especially brutal outlaw regime prosecutes a war for no just cause whatsoever. But if that is the case, then it would be inaccurate to talk about comparative justice in such an instance. Any victim resorting to armed force to defend itself against such a regime would not have merely comparative justice in doing so, it would have justice plain and simple. It would not be a matter of degree: the aggressor would be unjust (period) in attacking and the victim would be just (period) in defending itself with force. For this reason, I prefer the maintenance of this binary way of thinking about judgments of the resort to war in all possible cases. In the absence of deeply conflicting data and competing considerations—which would lead us *not* to considerations of comparative justice but, rather, to the conclusion that we could not pronounce on the justice of the resort to war on either side—there will always be one side that commits aggression and is therefore unjust (period), against which the victim and/or its defender is justified (period) in responding with armed force and warfare. Thus, it is not the case that two states can go to war with each other, each in self-defence. Either one is the all-things-considered aggressor or the case is so indeterminate that pronouncement cannot be made with regard to the justice of the resort to war on either side—i.e., in the absence of clear justification to go to war, no partial justification is to be extended.[18]

It cannot be stressed enough that, on this binary conception, the victim's having justice, *tout court*, on its side in terms of *jus ad bellum* would not thereby ground prosecuting its just cause in any fashion it desired. It would still have to face the tribunal of the norms of *jus in bello*. Indeed, that is why it makes such compelling sense to have at least two separate categories of evaluation in just war theory, precisely to avoid such problematic linkages between *jus ad bellum* and *jus in bello* as are implied by comparative justice. Hence the rationale for doing away with that criterion, and replacing it with what seems a more accurate one, namely, a requirement of right intention that a state commit itself in advance to prosecuting a just war (as defined by *jus ad bellum*) in accord with the norms of *jus in bello* and *jus post bellum*.

Perhaps it requires reiteration at this point that intentions are seen as having necessary linkages to norms of logical coherence, as well as to patterns of action and behaviour. Intentions can be, and ought to be, discerned through a reasoned examination of such publicly accessible evidence, in addition to reliance on explicit avowals of intent. Intentions are thus neither infinitely redescribable nor irreducibly private, and so right intention is not a vacuous normative criterion for moral judgment during war. It is possible to tell whether a state is prosecuting a war out of ethnic hatred, as opposed to vindicating its rights. That kind of dark motivation produces distinctive and noticeable results. We have the case of the very recent war in former Yugoslavia to offer as historical evidence, and the instance of country C above, as cases in point. It is also possible to tell whether a state has violated the requirements of *jus in bello*, for instance by systematically targeting and striking civilian population centres, by employing mass rape campaigns or by using weapons of mass destruction.

Proper Authority, Public Declaration and Domestic Rights Protection

JAB 3. Proper authority, public declaration and domestic rights protection during war. Wars may be declared only by the legitimate authority in the state—i.e., the national level of government which fulfils MJ 1-4. This declaration must be public and commitment to domestic human rights satisfaction must be made at the same time.

This criterion has tended to fall by the wayside, so to speak, in contemporary just war theory. On the one hand, this is understandable, since the requirement that only legitimate public authorities, and not private groups with their own vendettas, may authorize the launching of an armed attack upon another political community seems so obvious as to be rather trite.[19] On the other hand, the relative disuse of the proper authority criterion is regrettable and requires rectification. For this criterion also represents an important constraint on the power and authority of heads of state, and state mechanisms in general, to risk the lives and liberties of their citizen members in such a dangerous enterprise as war. If state prerogatives in times of war are to be kept reasonably in line with the human rights of their member citizens— which ground such state rights in the first place—we cannot lose sight of this just war criterion. The people must, in some public procedure, meaningfully consent to the launching of a war on their behalf.

This consent requirement need not preclude a rapid and effective response to some "blitzkrieg" instance of aggression—

usually there are defensible constitutional procedures designed to deal with such scenarios. (One such procedure would be authorizing the executive branch to deal militarily with such "blitzkrieg" scenarios as it deems fit and then, should it seem as though a more lengthy armed response to the incident of aggression is required, that such be authorized through a more deliberative process, for instance in the legislature.) Furthermore, the enemy state and its member citizens are entitled to receive a public declaration of war so that there can be no room for duplicitous manoeuvring; so that, in short, they are apprised that they are facing war, and all it entails, as a result of their aggressive actions. Such entitlement to public notification is codified in the Hague Convention (III).[20]

The further aspect that I have added to this criterion, rights protection on the domestic front during wartime, requires some comment and defence. It seems an important aspect of the decision of a state to go to war to consider whether the measures which seem reasonably required to realize the end of a just victory do not themselves seriously violate or jeopardize the human rights of *its own member citizens*. A state, once more, may not violate any human rights, whether foreign or domestic, either in peace or war.

This is not an idle thought experiment: as we have seen, rights-protection and satisfaction come at a price. During a serious and protracted war, there will be strong incentive for governments to use as many resources as they can, including some previously devoted to domestic rights satisfaction, in order to fight the war as best they can. In fact, this consideration of rights protection on the domestic front is an especially important aspect of just war thinking, since some of the most gruesome human rights violations in wartime (for instance, the Holocaust of the European Jews in wartime Nazi Germany) have occurred within, and not between, national borders. Belligerent governments, to be justified in resorting to armed force, are not entitled to use the cloak of war with foreign powers in order to commit massive human rights violations domestically, usually vis-à-vis some disfavoured racial, ethnic, linguistic and/or religious minority. This just war norm of domestic human rights protection is codified in the Second Amendment to the Geneva Convention.[21]

By far and away the most written-about aspect of domestic rights fulfilment during wartime is the issue of conscription. It seems that Walzer has come up with at least the suggestions of a satisfactory doctrine in this regard. A just, rights-respecting society ought, on the basis of the human right to freedom of conscience, to abide by the good-faith claims of conscientious objectors, and/or pacifists to be exempt from military service. A just state in the midst of a serious and justified war may, however, reasonably ask for some assistance from conscientious objectors, such as clerical or administrative work, in return for respecting their personal beliefs that they ought not to kill (much less be forced to kill) for political reasons. So, a state ought to meet its military needs through voluntary enlistment, where possible. There are many incentives that armed forces can, and do, employ to keep enlistments at the desired levels. As most military experts agree, very rarely is there a credible military case for universal conscription. Such would seem defensible perhaps only in those so-called "supreme emergencies" wherein the entire state in question is credibly threatened with destruction and genocide.[22]

No Precipitate Resort to Force

JAB 4. No precipitate force. This *jus ad bellum* criterion is the contemporary Kantian substitute for the traditional criterion of last resort. The reasons for this substitution are as follows. First, Walzer seems right when he contends that, strictly speaking, there is no such thing as a last resort. No matter how fearful the situation, there is always something else that can be tried—yet another round of diplomatic negotiations, for instance—prior to the resort to war. So it would be quite absurd, in this sense, to say that states may only turn to war as a last resort.[23]

Second, negotiations, threats and economic sanctions are frequently offered as morally more compelling means of international problem solving than the use of force. At face value, this claim seems indisputable: if a reasonable resolution to the crisis in question can be had through a credible threat (of what it would otherwise be permissible to do), or through a negotiating session, or perhaps through sanctions, then surely that appears preferable to running the sizable risks of war. Articles 33-40 of the UN

Charter enumerate and commend such mechanisms as peaceful dispute-resolution alternatives to the resort to force. Upon closer inspection, however, much depends on the nature of the particular act of aggression and the nature of the aggressive regime itself. Sometimes threats, diplomacy and sanctions will not work. The incidents leading up to the Persian Gulf War form a particularly apt instance in this regard.[24] Foreign policy experts concur that, given the salience of weak descriptive realism, armed force is the only means, in the current state of international affairs, which offers a reasonable assurance of being able to roll back an instance of armed aggression. Other times, aggressors will employ diplomacy as a bad-faith cloak or stalling tactic, enabling them to consolidate their military gains and thereby improve their bargaining position during any settlement talks. So care must be taken that appeals to last resort or no precipitate force do not end up rewarding aggression. Finally, a number of theorists, such as Walzer, Albert Pierce and Lori Damrosch, have pointed out that the levelling of systematic economic sanctions often violates the *jus in bello* principle of discrimination, since it is most often innocent civilians (often the poorest and most vulnerable) who bear the brunt of economic embargoes. In the absence of force directed against them, outlaw regimes always seem to find a way, within their own borders, to take care of themselves; the regime of Saddam Hussein in Iraq, once more, is a very instructive case study of the complexities involved in this regard.[25]

As a result of these reflections, it seems much more plausible to contend *not* that war be the last resort after all other means have been exhausted but, rather, that states ought not to be precipitate in their resort to force. There ought to be a strong presumption against the resort to force. And Article 2(4) of the UN Charter does indeed enshrine such a presumption, very forcefully, in international law. But beyond this general principle, so much here depends on the concrete details of the actual situation in question. It is critically important, for example, when the aggressor is mounting a very swift and brutal invasion, to respond effectively before all is lost. It is also relevant to consider the nature of the territory of the victim of aggression; if it is a tiny country, like Israel, the need for a speedy and effective response against aggression will likely be much greater than that required by a country the size and strength of the United States. Furthermore, the response of the international community and allied nations is also relevant. But here too the attention must always be focused, in terms of this criterion, on the nature and severity of the aggressor and its actions, for often the international community is quite slow in mounting an effective response to aggression. Indeed, this is one of the things that grounds the right of armed self-help in the first place. The key question this criterion demands always be asked is: is the proposed use of force reasonable, given the situation and the nature of the aggression?

Probability of Success

JAB 5. Probability of success. This is another elusive just war criterion for which only very general principles can be convincingly conveyed. Indeed, its consequentialist and/or prudentialist flavour explains this: it is always a matter of circumstances and of taking reasonable options within the constraints and opportunities they present. Traditionally, the probability of success criterion stipulates that a state may not resort to war if it can reasonably foresee that doing so will have no measurable impact upon the situation. The aim of this criterion is to block violence, killing and destruction which is going to be futile; and, as such, the principle is quite laudable and necessary as an aspect of any comprehensive just war theory. Great care, however, needs to be exercised that this criterion, like JAB 4, does not amount to rewarding aggression, and especially that by larger and more powerful nations. This is so because otherwise smaller and weaker nations will face a comparatively greater task when it comes to fulfilling this particular criterion. Neither a particular state, nor the community of nations, ought to acquiesce to a grave crime such as aggression. And the calculation of expected probability of success for resorting to war, after all, is incredibly difficult. The vicissitudes of war are, as we know from history, among the most difficult phenomena to predict reliably. Even when the odds have seemed incredibly long, remarkable successes have sometimes and somehow been achieved. Such are the stuff of military legend.[26] There may also be considerations of self-respect that come into play in this criterion, according to which victims of aggression ought to be permitted at least some resistance, should they decide to do so, as an expression of their strong objection to the aggression and as an affirmation of their rights.

In light of these reflections, it seems reasonable to claim that, given an incidence of aggression and given that the other just war criteria can be met, there is a presumption in favour of permitting some kind of armed response, even when the odds of military success (however defined) seem long. At the same time, this criterion is not idle: it remains important that communities contemplating war in response to aggression still consider whether such an extreme measure has any reasonable probability of success. That is the least, we might say, that they owe themselves. We should also note the very important role played by other states in the determination of probability of success. Were there some more effective mechanism for interstate cooperation regarding the punishment of aggression and grievous human rights violation, states (especially small ones) would face lessened pressure in terms of considering whether or not their own response would be likely to have the desired effect.

(Macro-) Proportionality

JAB 6. (Macro-) Proportionality. A state must, prior to initiating a war, weigh the expected good to accrue from its prosecuting the (otherwise just) war against the expected evils that will result. Only if the benefits seem reasonably proportional to the costs may the war action proceed. This norm is codified in international law, at Articles 22-23 of the Hague Convention (III).[27] It is very important to note that it is only reasonable to require a state to consider the expected costs and benefits of its own participation in the war. And by costs and benefits, a contemporary Kantian must mean not just costs and benefits to one's own state and people, but costs and benefits to all, from a universal or agent-neutral point of view.

As should be clear, given repeated discussion previously offered in this work, proportionality is one of the most contentious, difficult and challenging *jus ad bellum* criteria.[28] Kant and Walzer, in particular, offer strong cases against proportionality, focusing largely on the malleability of its recommendations.[29]

And yet its difficulty vitiates neither its cogency nor its moral desirability. Judgments about the worth of desired ends, and the costs of the means of achieving those ends, are of the very essence of practical rationality. And proportionality plays a very prominent role in the positive international law regarding warfare, such as at those Articles just mentioned. As Richard Regan points out, consideration of (macro-) proportionality, however difficult, must involve at least three elements: 1) a value judgment about the worth of the cause that grounds the resort to war; 2) factual judgments about the war's likely casualties and costs; and 3) another value judgment about the relative, or proportional, worth of the war's cause in relation to its likely casualties and costs.[30]

In terms of the first of Regan's elements of (macro-) proportionality, we have seen that a contemporary Kantian internationalist will ground war in a defence of rights. The objects of these rights—both state and human—are of the utmost importance to the quality and fabric of our lives as rational agents. Thus, should a country truly have a just cause in resorting to war, and presuming the other just war criteria to be satisfied, it follows that the reasonably predicted costs, both explicit and implicit, both prudential and moral, of fighting the war would have to be very considerable in order to defeat the justification for that country's resort to war. As Kamm reminds us, the most relevant and instructive question in terms of considering, and cashing out, (macro-) proportionality is: what would a state and its people lose by not being permitted to resort to war?[31] If they would lose the objects of their human rights, and if those objects are synonymous with those of their reasonable vital needs, then resort to war would indeed seem proportional to the price exacted for waging it, unless such were expected to be apocalyptic.

Perhaps an attempt should be made to offer a more rigorous and organized accounting of the relevant universal costs and benefits of war-fighting in this regard.[32] The main benefits (B) of fighting an otherwise just war are: B1) its general end is the vindication of human rights and the core norms of international justice, which constitute the baseline of political reasonableness in our era; B2) its particular end is to protect specific people from aggression and to save them from the enormous sufferings of life under a rights-violative regime; B3) it punishes aggression and represents the currently most forceful and effective objection to it; and B4) it could act as a possible deterrent to future, would-be aggressors and thus strengthen, in the long term, the system of peacefully resolving serious international disputes. The main costs of war-fighting are both explicit (EC) and implicit (IC): EC 1) the immediate costs of mobilization and deployment (without which the war-activity cannot be sustained); EC 2) the secondary costs (not necessary to sustain the activity) of casualties, both military and civilian, and all the suffering they imply; EC 3) secondary costs of infrastructure and property damage; IC 1) the diversion of resources—human, natural, technological—away from peaceful pursuits to war-time activity; IC 2) possible strain on the resources devoted to domestic rights fulfilment; and IC 3) perhaps the raw fact that war had to be resorted to at all, given our rational preference for peaceable solutions.

In terms of the relative weighting of these costs, contemporary Kantianism, as stated above, stipulates that B 1-3 are of the foremost importance in considering (macro-) proportionality. If fulfilled, they can be overthrown only by a cogent demonstration that the costs of seeking them, in particular EC 1-2 and IC 2, shall be universally ruinous—for instance, that the result of resorting to war will be destruction of such magnitude that none of the state participants will be able to fulfil MJ 1-4 after its conclusion.

It should be noted how it is that consequentialist and/or prudentialist appeals to probability of success and (macro-) proportionality seem consistent with the core elements of a contemporary Kantian internationalism. The first thing to note is how it was established in earlier chapters that prudential elements of weak realism, both descriptive and prescriptive, seem at least partially consonant with an emphasis on Kantian morality. The grounds of prudence and those of morality may well be complementary in certain cases like these, even if a recognizably Kantian theory will have to stress and emphasize the importance of morality and justice. It will also be recalled that Kantian internationalism is centrally concerned with human rights and their actual fulfilment, notably as they are conceived within the Universal Declaration of Human Rights (UDHR). The actual fulfilment of human rights has been at least partially conceptualized in terms of ordering state interactions and shared institutions in accord with those ground rules that are expressive of human rights. War is one such interaction and the criteria of just war theory seek to protect and provide for the objects of human rights as best as possible, given the extreme circumstances of war. Just war theory seeks to stipulate the ground rules that ought to govern the institution of warfare. But as agents who are both moral and rational, we ought not to restrict ourselves, when evaluating ground rules, to considering solely those actions and patterns of behaviour that are direct or established results of adhering to a certain set of ground rules. We ought, additionally, to concern ourselves with considering the indirect effects that are engendered by ground rules. We ought, in short, to be concerned with how a system of ground rules regulating certain aspects of interstate interaction actually gets instantiated in the world, and with what concrete results. We ought to be concerned not only with that system's core principles and their intrinsic moral rationale but also with their concrete consequences in the real world.

One of the biggest concrete consequences of war, whether just or not, is immense human suffering. A contemporary Kantian will object to human suffering—where it arises out of intentional action that is both destructive and preventable—as it tends, quite clearly, to weaken and undermine rational agency. A seriously pained and wounded human being is one whose capacity for autonomous action, according to rationally defensible principles, has been gravely weakened. Preserving, protecting and enhancing rational agency will thus involve materially constraining human suffering. It will, at least, call for ground rules governing social interaction which do not allow for (otherwise preventable) human suffering that is excessive, unnecessary and seriously debilitating. In terms of war, the criteria of probability of success and proportionality play a crucial role in fulfilling this contemporary Kantian value. A Kantian, if not Kant himself, need have no qualms about endorsing both of them as legitimate, even necessary, elements of contemporary just war theory.[33]

Two Real-World Cases for Applying **Jus ad Bellum**

It would be helpful and illustrative to apply the above contemporary Kantian criteria of *jus ad bellum*, JAB 1-6, to two real-world cases. The argument will here be made that: 1) World War II, on the part of the Allies, was a just war (falling into the category of self- and other-defence); and 2) armed intervention in Rwanda, in 1994-95, by the world community, would have been justified. For the sake of greater clarity and specificity, I shall focus mostly on the United States as the relevant "addressee" of these remarks. Of course, given the deep complexities of these real-world cases, attention cannot be paid to every element: the aim in this section is hence to give a rather brief application of the Kantian principles JAB 1-6 to these real historical cases, in order to give a flavour of their real-world life, vitality and relevance.

Perhaps it will be asked: why these two cases as opposed to others? The answer is that they seem the strongest real-world examples in favour of the abstract Kantian just war principles defended here. They simply serve as the most supportive illustrations. That is why reliance is made on a rather dated case in World War II[34] and a case that only could-have-been, with reference to intervention in Rwanda.[35]

World War II

JAB 1. Just Cause. Did the Allies, and particularly the United States, have just cause in resorting to war between 1939 and 1941? It seems clear to contend that, in the European theatre, Nazi Germany was the embodiment of precisely that kind of ultra-aggressive, totalitarian, outlaw state which just war theory holds up as the kind of threat against which the resort to armed self- and other-defence seems most plausibly grounded. Imperial Japan was likewise by all accounts an ultra-aggressive totalitarian regime. Both of these powers were blatant aggressors: Nazi Germany first in Poland in 1939 and then in 1940 through the Low Countries into France; and Imperial Japan first in China in the mid-1930s and then also into Korea and the surrounding areas. There was no just cause whatsoever grounding the actions of these regimes: they were animated solely by desires for more territory, resources, power, glory and perhaps even darker motives related to their beliefs in their own ethnic superiority. Germany and Japan posed serious and lethal threats to those countries they invaded and, once they conquered these latter, subjected them to brutalizing rights-violative measures that still rank amongst the grossest in history. The commission of aggression caused both of these regimes to forfeit their state rights to non-interference and not to be attacked in return. So the Allies, as a matter of self- and other-defence, general rights-vindication and punishment for rights-violation, did no wrong—violated no rights—in responding in kind. So the resort to war by England and its Commonwealth, for instance, and eventually by the United States, was justifiable on this basis. Indeed, in the case of the United States, resort to war was made (explicitly) only after the Pearl Harbour aggression by Japan, and Germany's accompanying declaration of war on America. The moral requirement to defeat such regimes stands out as one of history's most compelling causes for ever unleashing the black dogs of war.

JAB 2. Right Intention. The Allies, in particular the United States, seemed to undertake World War II with the right intention, namely, the defence of their own nation and those of others, the defeat and punishment of aggression, and the repeal of its gains. Did the Allies display a reasonable commitment, prior to launching into war, to upholding the norms of *jus in bello* during its course and *jus post bellum* following its end? This is less clear, given the immense destruction that was carried out during the war, and indeed has been one of the reasons why the contention was made above that such ought to be newly incorporated into the right intention criterion. In fairness, the postwar actions and activities of the Allies—restoration of most of the previously existing borders (albeit under the auspices of the new Cold War dynamic), meaningful reconstruction of the defeated enemies, the Nuremburg and Far East War Crimes tribunals, the formation of the United Nations, the passage of the UDHR—might, in retrospect, reveal some of the laudableness of their pro-rights intentions. In light of this conflicting data, perhaps all that can be said firmly with regard to this criterion is that the Allies really did seem to undertake the war with at least the proper *jus ad bellum* orientation of rights-vindication.

JAB 3. Proper authority, public declaration and domestic rights protection. Let us here take the case of the United States. America's explicit entry into World War II in 1941 was indeed declared through the appropriate constitutional channels, with both the executive and the legislative branches concurring. The declaration, on both Japan and Germany, was indeed publicly declared. Did America commit itself to domestic rights-protection during the war, prior to embarking on it? It seems that a reasonable commitment to such domestic protection was made through the emergency measures, save perhaps with regard to Japanese Americans and their internment.

JAB 4. No precipitate force. It seems that the Allies did not resort to war in the 1939-41 period with precipitate force. England and France, the major Allied powers in Western Europe, made a serious diplomatic effort to placate Hitler with the Munich accords in 1938. Hitler disregarded any such aspirations for peace; in fact, he seemed to use the Munich process as a bad-faith cloak with which he could legitimize his past actions and disguise his future ambitions. He then launched his ultra-aggressive attempt to conquer Europe on behalf of the Aryan race. Similarly, the Soviet Union signed the Molotov-Ribbentrop pact of mutual non-aggression with Germany in 1939. The Soviet Union clearly wanted to avoid war. However, that pact was rendered asunder when Hitler, having conquered continental Western Europe, proceeded to turn his sights eastward in 1940-41. Indeed, it seems clear that, as of 1939-40 in Western Europe, and as of 1940-41 in Eastern Europe, there was no other feasible alternative to halting the aggression of Hitler than through the use of armed force. As such, the resort to war on the part of the Allies was not precipitate.

It also seems that the United States' resort to war against Japan was not precipitate. After all, Japan had been committing aggression throughout East Asia, particularly in northern China and Korea, for several years prior to the outbreak of World War II. Secondly, Japan itself launched the armed attack on Pearl Harbour in 1941. Once Japan launched such a large-scale, violent attack, its intentions were clear and manifest. America was not hasty in resorting to force in light of that attack.

JAB 5. Probability of success. This criterion is less clearly fulfilled in the case of Allied countries like Poland and France, and perhaps even England, but it seems that the United States clearly fulfilled it. Even though it was to fight enemies on opposite sides of the world at the same time, the United States could reasonably have foreseen, in 1941, that its manpower, industrial sophistication and productive capacity, to say nothing of its military might, were second to none. It had every reason to believe, at the time, that it could outproduce, outfight and overwhelm both of its enemies. And this would have been a compelling contention even if those enemies were at the prime of their fighting capacity, which they were not: their earlier campaigns had drained considerable military resources. With regard to Hitler, he was just beginning to be sucked into the endless morass of the campaign in Russia and was inordinately distracted, on the domestic front, by setting into motion the madness of the Holocaust. It was very predictable in 1941 to see that Hitler, faced with the might of the Soviet Union on one front, and the nexus between England, her Commonwealth (notably Canada and Australia) and the United States on the other, was outmatched. At the very least, it seems that the United States entered the European war with a considerable probability of success.

JAB 6. (Macro-) Proportionality. It is very important to consider the extent of Allied, and especially American, fulfilment of this category solely in terms of the time of the decision to resort to war. It seems quite reasonable to contend that no one could have foreseen, in 1939-41, the full and total extent of the immense costs and casualties of World War II, much of which was tallied up in the final few months of the war. At the time, say, of the American entry, it seemed reasonable to contend that the defeat of these two ultra-aggressive regimes was worth the projected prudential and moral costs of doing so. Given that Hitler was going to be so clearly outgunned on both fronts, it would have been reasonable to contend at the time that the military casualties in Europe would be absorbable, and that damage to the United States itself would be negligible.

One thing that would have weighed on the conscience at the time was the quite foreseeable notion that, given Europe's population density, there would be considerable civilian casualties from stepping up the war effort, and moving onto the continent itself to roll Hitler back within his own borders. As we have seen, there is no uncontroversial calculus for balancing foreseen but unintended civilian deaths and the great importance of defeating regimes the likes of Nazi Germany. Based on previous reasoning, I concur with theorists like Walzer and Rawls when they contend that the latter was an immensely pressing task of morality and justice, and was perhaps even worth the total costs racked up in World War II. And since there was no way America could have predicted the scale of those total costs at the time of its entry, it seems at least plausible to contend that its resort to war in 1941 seemed a measure whose expected benefits—crushing ultra-aggression and fascism for the sake of rights vindication—were proportional to the costs expected at the time to be required to do so.[36]

Rwanda

Let us turn now to the case of Rwanda in 1994-95. The argument will be made that the world community would have been justified, on the above just war grounds, in intervening in the midst of the dreadful communal conflict that consumed that unfortunate republic. So, this is not an example of a justified war of self- or other-defence against an aggressor regime; rather, it is an example of the third kind of just cause for resorting to armed force defended above in JAB 1, namely, armed intervention in a non-aggressive country.

In 1994-95, between 500,000 and 800,000 people were massacred in Rwanda as a result of ethnic clashes between the Hutu and Tutsi peoples, who together compose the Rwandan population. The killing resulted from a deepening intercommunal crisis that was several years in the making. The government of Rwanda was for some time coming under the increasing domination of the Tutsi minority. The Tutsis began to rule in a manner like that of a privileged ethnic elite, entitled to all of the plum positions of power. The military, in particular, became a critically important site of Tutsi ascendancy. Spurred on by a rising sense of ethnic privilege and prerogative, the Tutsis and their government began issuing official documents that classified people not as citizens and non-citizens but, rather, as members of their respective ethnic community. Then, some extremist elements within the Tutsi population—both in and out of government—wanted to capitalize on the recent turn of events and began to promulgate venomous ideological attacks against the Hutu majority. Some members of the Hutu population took these ideological campaigns quite seriously, and began to organize small demonstrations and counter-intimidation tactics. Small skirmishes, some resulting in murder, occurred. A profound crisis of intercommunal confidence followed and systematic, murderous intercommunal raids became commonplace. The Tutsis turned to their army to gain the advantage and, under its auspices, wholesale slaughter began in earnest, and the Hutus reciprocated to the best of their ability. Hundreds of thousands, from both groups, were massacred and/or uprooted and sent fleeing into neighbouring countries. All told, between half a million and 800,000 people were murdered. It was only when the Hutus prevailed, apparently through sheer force of numbers, that an eventual end was brought to the murder and mayhem.

The international community failed to intervene decisively during these events, with the UN Security Council labelling the event either a "domestic upheaval" (perhaps even a "civil war") or, at best, "a central African, regional concern."[37] Would it have been justifiable for the international community to intervene after the first few massacres made clear, to all informed observers, the depth and breadth of the oncoming tragedy? Let us consider whether the situation could have met the above just war criteria for a well-grounded armed intervention in an externally non-aggressive regime.

JAB 1. Just cause. We saw previously that the most powerful just cause for armed intervention in a state that has not committed interstate aggression is massive human rights violations within its own borders. It seems clear that, if anything in this area counts as a massive domestic human rights violation, it is the ethnically inspired mass murder that occurred in this case. Indeed, the Tutsi-dominated Rwandan state revealed itself to be an ill-ordered, or not minimally just, regime in two senses during this period: 1) by initially committing, and/or acquiescing, to the mass slaughter of its citizens (particularly that of one ethnic group, the Hutus); and 2) by failing to provide, in the midst of the crisis, the rudiments of effective governance for any of its people, since the escalating spiral of mass killings had by then completely undone the socio-political glue holding Rwanda together. As such, the Rwandan state was not at that time entitled to the full panoply of state rights, especially that of non-intervention. Having committed internal aggression, and then having lost control of the process begun by that aggression, the Rwandan regime forfeited its rights against foreign intervention. Hence, foreign intervention—for instance, by the United States—would have violated no rights and thus would have been at least permissible in terms of just cause.

JAB 2. Right intention. It seems quite plausible to contend that the United States could have fulfilled the requirements of this criterion. It could have intended to launch into military action only to rescue the people of Rwanda from mass slaughter and quite easily avoided the temptations of aggrandizement and political tinkering. Indeed, one of the reasons cited for United States non-interference at the time seems to ground this contention: the fact that the United States has no vital national interests (from a purely prudential or realist foreign policy perspective) in the central African region. In the absence of such interests, there would have been little temptation to be motivated by anything other than armed rescue.

In terms of the second aspect of the right intention criterion, it also seems plausible to contend that the United States could have committed itself quite sincerely to upholding the norms of *jus in bello* during its intervention. Given the fact that the vast majority of the killings in Rwanda were caused with small hand-held weapons, particularly machetes and handguns, it seems that an American force of overwhelmingly superior capability would have faced little serious temptation of violating the rules of war-fighting. Empirically, *jus in bello* violations tend to be committed most often when the army in question is faced with an enemy perceived to be of roughly equivalent strength and ingenuity. This was manifestly not the case in the Rwanda of 1994-95. Furthermore, in light of some unfortunate experiences in the Vietnam War,[38] the United States has, since that time, been one of the most diligent and rigorous instructors of its troops in the laws of armed combat and the norms of *jus in bello*. This is another reason for believing that the armed forces of the United States could have successfully committed themselves, in advance, to adhering to the norms of *jus in bello* during the posited intervention in Rwanda.

We have seen that an additional requirement of right intention in the case of armed intervention is a firm commitment on the part of the would-be intervenor to some kind of meaningful assistance to the objects of rescue following the intervention, in order to repair infrastructure damage, and the like, caused by the intervention. It seems clear that there could easily have been such a firm commitment on the part of the United States, perhaps in conjunction with other nations.

JAB 3. Proper authority, public declaration and domestic rights-protection. It seems obvious that this criterion could have been met by any contemplated United States intervention: the President and Congress, had the will been there, could have authorized the participation of the force, and could have publicly declared its terms of engagement to the world community and the Rwandan people. Clearly, given the distance and the serious power imbalance between the two countries, there would have been no incentive or threat whatsoever of the intervention requiring domestic rights-curtailment in America.

But perhaps this is too quick. Two things, at least, need to be considered. One is whether the Rwandan people would have consented to such intervention, which is another required criterion for armed intervention according to contemporary Kantian just war theory. The answer to this concern is that not only would they have, they did. The Hutu community, the main object of the original violence, repeatedly asked for international assistance, even prior to the first outbreak of serious violence. Indeed, even the Tutsi people, once the killing started to escalate on both sides, began to call for some foreign assistance. So, not only did the main target population of the original massacres repeatedly request foreign intervention, the other group (in the end) also appealed for foreign help. The consent criterion was fulfilled.

The other thing to consider is whether the "proper authority" in question ought to have been the UN. The UN Security Council, admittedly, did not authorize any intervention in Rwanda beyond an observer force. But this was so because none of the major powers—the permanent members of the Council—thought they had any national interest in doing so. The Council also decided to interpret its mandate very narrowly, contending that its charge to look after interstate peace and security would not permit it to rule and intervene in cases of intrastate conflict or civil war. But this was less principled and more ad hoc than it might originally seem, especially given the fact that in 1993 the Security Council authorized intervention in Somalia, despite the fact that no demonstrable cross-border security issue was involved.[39] So, it seems that lack of UN Security Council authorization would not be an insurmountable obstacle to the moral case being made here for intervention: such lack of action was clearly based on prudentialist considerations of national interest and not upon any deeply principled conception of justice. In fact, we might say that it was precisely the lack of UN action that would have made purely domestic authorization in the would-be intervenor, for instance the United States, the appropriate site for obtaining proper authority, provided the consent of the object of rescue was there. And it was.

JAB 4. No precipitate force. In order to fulfil this criterion, the United States would have had to wait until there was compelling evidence, from the first few massacres, that events were quickly spinning out of control and that the Rwandan regime was both unwilling and incapable of governing in even a minimally just fashion. There *was* such credible evidence available, largely from the non-governmental (NGO) human rights community, which has in recent years developed very sophisticated "early warning systems" of imminent mass rights violations. The United States, to fulfil this criterion, could also have organized quick administrative and/or congressional fact-finding missions to Rwanda, made clear to the parties to the slaughter that, unless some viable political solution were soon sought, it would intervene, and so on. It would seem, however, that after the first set of massacres, any United States intervention would not have been precipitate: it would, in fact, likely have saved hundreds of thousands of lives.

JAB 5. Probability of success. There is considerable evidence from other interventions (e.g., the UN's in Cyprus) that poorly armed fighting factions stop fighting when there are well-trained, heavily armed peacekeepers, from developed countries, separating them. The "factions" in Rwanda were indeed poorly armed—again, most of the killing was done by machete. Thus, in terms of stopping the killing and separating the rival groups, it seems that the probability of success of a well-conceived and timely American intervention in Rwanda would have been extremely high.

JAB 6. (Macro-) Proportionality. What would have been the likely benefits and costs of the posited United States intervention in Rwanda? The benefits seem clear: an end to the savage slaughter campaigns, resulting in hundreds of thousands of lives saved; the probable prevention of the concomitant mass uprooting and migration, with its enormous humanitarian costs; and the much greater stability engendered from having a relative peace brokered and enforced by a major power, which would have greatly improved the climate for beginning to find a political solution to the tribal differences.

The costs of the intervention would have included the explicit casualties resulting from it. However, due to the deep power imbalance, it seems to me that these would, for that kind of operation, have been quite low. The Rwandans, after all, lacked substantial means for killing American soldiers in considerable numbers and the Americans thereby lacked incentive to violate *jus in bello* norms and engage in disproportionate killing.

Of course, a mediated and difficult political solution would then have had to be sought, which would have increased the costs of the continued deployment, would certainly have called for painful concessions from both sides to the conflict and so on. Such a process may well have continued up to the present day and beyond. But, it seems that if one weighs these costs against the above expected benefits, notably of saving hundreds of thousands of lives, then it seems at least plausible to contend that these costs would, from a pro-human rights perspective, have been worth it.

All that has been claimed here, in this brief section, is that armed intervention by the United States at the beginning of the Rwandan tragedy, to protect the Hutus from the internal aggression of the Tutsi-dominated Rwandan state mechanism, would have been morally permissible, according to the above norms of justified armed intervention. It has not been claimed that such was obligatory and that failure to have done so constituted moral callousness, though many have expressed those thoughts. The aim here was simply to illustrate the material applicability, relevance and importance of these general principles of the justified resort to armed force to a real world case, and one of clear contemporary importance.[40]

Conclusion

This extended chapter was focused on elucidating contemporary Kantian norms of *jus ad bellum*, namely, JAB 1-6. A state can resort to war justly in the international system if and only if: it has a just cause; it has the right intention; it declares its intentions publicly and commits itself to rights protection, at home and abroad; it does not go to war precipitately; and its resort to war has some probability of success and promises benefits at least proportional to its costs. The account in this chapter sought to advance beyond traditional just war theory through a wider and deeper explanation of the core principles, especially just cause (via principle NP), right intention, proper authority, probability of success and proportionality.

The elucidation of these proffered norms consisted of both substantive prescriptive grounding, in light of principles thus far developed, and illustrative application to several cases, whether real-world or thought experiments. These rules are manifestly relevant to contemporary conflicts, and of clear and pressing applicability.

An important subsidiary task of this chapter was to discern the substance of what current international law has to say about these matters. We witnessed, in this regard, a substantial convergence between current law and the claims of contemporary Kantian just war theory.[41] Kantian internationalism thus offers justification for the current *jus ad bellum* laws and, arguably, provides a deeper and more coherent justification of these principles than that offered in the laws themselves.

The question arises: if Kantian internationalism, by its own admission, does not improve radically on the current international laws on *jus ad bellum* (save in the sense of grounding them more satisfactorily), nor indeed—as was conceded in chapter 5—on the laws of *jus in bello*, what exactly does it have to offer the current body of law on warfare? How can it contribute to the improvement of international law in this regard? The answer resides in the next chapter's investigation of justice after war.

Notes

1. Offered in chapter 3 as part of KI 1-10, the core elements of Kantian internationalism.

2. These state rights and duties were constructed in chapter 4 as part of the general conception of international justice proffered by Kantian internationalism.

3. In chapter 2, where traditional norms of just war theory were sketched.

4. These are points cogently made by M. Walzer, in *Just and Unjust Wars* (New York: Basic, 1977), 21-50 and 287-324.

5. This point is absolutely critical to the very plausibility of just war theory, since many have objected to it precisely on the grounds that it is liable to self-applying abuse by nation-states. Robert Phillips seems to have the right response when he says: "It does seem to me, however, to be no very severe criticism of a moral position that it can be misused." (From his *War and Justice* [Norman, OK: University of Oklahoma Press, 1984], p. 4) We might add that we should scarcely be left with any moral theories if we had to reject all those that have been twisted, abused and subjectively applied throughout history. Excellent defences of the publicity of these criteria can be found in Walzer, *Wars*, 3-50 and G.E.M. Anscombe, "War and Murder," in R. Wasserstrom, ed., *War and Morality* (Belmont, CA: Wadsworth, 1970), 42-60. For almost hysterical examples of the rejection of just war theory based on this inaccurate charge of subjectivism, see J. Ladd, "The Idea of Collective Violence," in J. Brady and N. Garver, eds., *Justice, Law and Violence* (Philadelphia, PA: Temple University Press, 1991), 24-25; and especially R.J. Myers, "Notes on the Just War Theory: Whose Justice, Which Wars?" *Ethics and International Affairs* (1996): 116-30.

6. F.M. Kamm, "Making War (and Its Cousins) Unjustified," (forthcoming paper).

7. That being said, there may be particular cases where military action will seem to verge on the morally necessary, especially in cases of self-defence against a particularly brutal aggressor and/or intervention in a non-aggressive country whose people are suffering unspeakable violence by a murderous regime. I find it both tempting and compelling, for instance, to assert that the overthrow of the Nazi regime in Germany, and even the regime of Imperial Japan, whether through war or intervention, was probably morally necessary. Neutrality or non-involvement during World War II, in my view, was not a morally defensible policy stance. On neutrality, see Walzer, *Wars*, 233-50.

8. This core *jus ad bellum* view of the armed defence of rights and the protection of rights-bearers is shared by no less a diverse grouping than: The U.S. Catholic Bishops, "Pastoral Letter: The Challenge of Peace," in J.B. Elshtain, ed., *Just War Theory* (Oxford: Basil Blackwell, 1992), 77-168; Walzer, in *Wars*, passim; D. Luban, in "Just War and Human Rights," *Philosophy and Public Affairs* (1980): 160-81; Kamm, "Making," passim; and Anscombe, "Murder," 42-60.

9. I say "especially as done through the use of armed force" because there are imaginable circumstances in which the relevant state rights get violated with-

out the actual use of armed force. As Kamm has contended, powerful country A might shut down the main supplies of energy and/or water running through it to small country B. Such would indeed seem tantamount to aggression by A against B, since it poses a serious and potentially lethal threat to the lives and rights of those living in B.

10. Walzer, *Wars*, 50-75; H. Bedau, "Punitive Violence and Its Alternatives," in J. Brady and N. Garver, *Justice, Law and Violence* (Philadelphia, PA: Temple University Press, 1991), 193-209; J. Narveson, "Violence and War," in T. Regan, ed., *Matters of Life and Death* (Philadelphia, PA: Temple University Press, 1980), 109-49; and J. Narveson, "Pacifism: A Philosophical Analysis," *Ethics* 75 (1965): 259-71.

11. Walzer, *Wars*, 62.

12. W. Reisman and C. Antoniou, eds. *The Laws of War* (New York: Vintage, 1994), 5-42.

13. The other criteria of *jus ad bellum* will follow in this chapter. In addition to just cause, they are: right intention; public authority; no precipitate force; probability of success and (macro-) proportionality. The criteria of *jus in bello*, sketched out in chapter 5, include: discrimination between combatants and non-combatants (with resulting non-combatant immunity from direct and intentional targeting); (micro-) proportionality; and the avoidance of intrinsically heinous means.

14. For more on the interpretation of the positive laws of war and armed conflict, see Reisman and Antoniou, eds., *Laws*; S. Bailey, *Prohibitions and Restraints in War* (Oxford: Oxford University Press, 1972); G. Best, *War and law since 1945* (Oxford: Clarendon, 1994); I. Brownlie, *International Law and the Use of Force by States* (Oxford: Clarendon, 1963); I. Detter Delupis, *The Law of War* (Cambridge: Cambridge University Press, 1987); Y. Dinstein, *War, Aggression and Self-Defence* (Cambridge: Cambridge University Press, 1995); M. Howard, *The Laws of War: Constraints on Warfare in the Western World* (New Haven, CT: Yale University Press, 1994); H. Lauterpacht, *International Law*, Vols. 3 and 4: *The Law of War and Peace* (Cambridge: Cambridge University Press, 1977-78); R. Miller, ed., *The Law of War* (Lexington, MA: Lexington Books, 1975); and W.V. O'Brien, *The Law of Limited Armed Conflict* (Washington, DC: Georgetown University Press, 1965).

15. See R. Regan, *Just War: Principles and Cases* (Washington, DC: The Catholic University of America Press, 1996), 179-211, for more on these conflicts from a just war perspective. Relevant Security Council resolutions on Somalia include 751, 775, 794 and 814, whereas those for Bosnia include 713 and 743. For a detailed look at the positive international law regarding armed intervention, see L. Damrosch, ed., *Enforcing Restraint: Collective Intervention in Internal Conflicts* (New York: Council on Foreign Relations, 1993) and W. O'Brien, *U.S. Military Interventions: Law and Morality* (Beverly Hills, CA: Sage, 1979).

16. Walzer, *Wars*, 86-108.

17. For more on armed interventions, see Regan, *Cases*, 68-83; O'Brien, *Intervention*; Damrosch, ed., *Enforcing*; the symposium in the 1995 volume of *Ethics and International Affairs*; R. Regan, *The Moral Dimensions of Politics* (New York: Oxford University Press, 1986); J.N. Moore, ed., *Law and Civil War in the Modern World* (Baltimore, MD: John Hopkins University Press, 1974); and C. Beitz, "Nonintervention and Communal Integrity," *Philosophy and Public Affairs* (1979/80): 385-91.

18. In this I agree with Walzer, *Wars*, 50-75 and Rawls, in "Law," 41-82, and his untitled contribution to *Dissent*'s Summer 1995 symposium on the fiftieth anniversary of the bombing of Hiroshima.

19. Then again, maybe not. The 1961 case of the Bay of Pigs invasion might seem relevant in this regard as a case of a largely private group (i.e., a self-selected group of Cuban Americans) of its own accord mounting an armed invasion attempt against another state. But the support and linkages between this private group and such public institutions as the CIA clouds over this example and renders pronouncement difficult. An interesting footnote to this case occurred recently in August 1998, when an American grand jury indicted some Cuban Americans for the crime of plotting—still, after all these years—to assassinate Fidel Castro.

20. See Regan, *Cases*, 20-47, for more on legitimate authority, especially as applied to the United States. Also relevant is L. Fisher, *Presidential War Power* (Lawrence, KS: University of Kansas Press, 1995) and Reisman and Antoniou, *Laws*. The case of the Vietnam War is also highly relevant for a consideration of the cogency and contemporary relevance of the proper authority criterion. Many critics of President Lyndon Johnson blasted him, at the time and since, for escalating the war through a series of executive orders, as opposed to submitting the matter for more representative debate in Congress. Infuriated by what it saw as an abuse, with devastating consequences, of the short-term presidential war-power, the U.S. Congress passed the War Powers Resolution in 1973. For more on this Resolution, see Regan, *Cases*.

21. On "emergency regimes" and rights-protection on the domestic front, see J. Nickel, *Making Sense of Human Rights* (Berkeley, CA: University of California Press, 1987), 131-46; A. Rosas, "Emergency Regimes: A Comparison," in D. Gomien, ed. *Broadening the Frontiers of Human Rights* (Oslo, Norway: Scandinavian University Press, 1992), 162-200; The International Commission of Jurists, *States of Emergency: Their Impact on Human Rights* (New York: ICJ, 1983); J. Fitzpatrick, "Protection against Abuse of the Concept of Emergency," in L. Henkin and J.L. Hargrove, eds., *Human Rights: An Agenda for the Next Century* (Washington, DC: The American Society for International Law, 1994), 203-28; and J.F. Hartman, "Derogation from Human Rights Treaties in Public Emergencies," *Harvard International Law Review* (1981): 1-52.

In terms of positive international law, lists of so-called "non-derogable" human rights exist in both the International Covenant on Civil and Political Rights and the European Convention on Human Rights. The most famous and complete of such lists is in the 1977 Second Amendment to the Geneva

Convention, which says that the following human rights can never be sacrificed during a public emergency such as war: non-discrimination; to life; not to be tortured; not to be enslaved; not to be taken hostage; to "minimal judicial guarantees"; not to be subject to medical experiment; not to be subject to retroactive laws; to be recognized as a legal person; to freedom of thought, conscience and religion; to a fair trial; to a subsistence level of food and water; and special protections for children. It is becoming a matter of consensus that all, or nearly all, of the UDHR human rights are non-derogable: there is an increasing sense in which, to be at all plausible and defensible, human rights have to form an interlocking and inviolable whole.

22. On conscription, see Walzer, *Wars*, 34-40 and 138-43 and M. Walzer, *Obligations: Essays on Citizenship, War and Disobedience* (Cambridge, MA: Harvard University Press, 1970), passim. Consult Walzer, *Wars*, for more on the very controversial issue of "supreme emergencies" and what they may ground in response.

23. Walzer, *Wars*, xiv.

24. See, for example, Regan, *Cases,* and L. Freedman and E. Karsh, eds., *The Gulf Conflict (1990-91): Diplomacy and War in the New World Order* (Princeton, NJ: Princeton University Press, 1993).

25. See Regan, *Cases,* for more on the Persian Gulf war conflict. In terms of economic sanctions, see Walzer, *Wars*, xxv-xxxii; A. Pierce, "Just War Principles and Economic Sanctions," *Ethics and International Affairs* (1996): 99-113; and L.F. Damrosch, "The Collective Enforcement of International Norms Through Economic Sanctions," *Ethics and International Affairs* (1994): 60-80; and D. Cortright and G. Lopez, *Economic Sanctions: Panacea or Peacebuilding in a Post-Cold War World?* (Boulder, CO: Westview, 1995).

26. For some examples, see Walzer, *Wars*, 67-73, and Dyer, *War.* One, from ancient history, would be the victory of Alexander the Great over Darius of Persia at Issus in 333 BC.

27. Reisman and Antoniou, eds., *Laws*, 47.

28. Just cause and proportionality are really the most important, and difficult, of the just war criteria.

29. For Kant's case, see Part 1; for Walzer's, see *Wars*, xxv-xxxii.

30. Regan, *Cases*, 63-64.

31. In Kamm, "Making"; F. Kamm, *Creation and Abortion: A Study in Moral and Legal Philosophy* (New York: Oxford University Press, 1992), 5; and F. Kamm, "Harming Some to Save Others," *Philosophical Studies* 57 (1989): 232.

32. Thus, this account does not fall victim to the criticism levelled at pacifism in chapter 5, namely, that it fails to provide for such an accounting.

33. For insightful contemporary sources on *jus ad bellum* in general, see Walzer, *Wars*, 3-33 and 51-125; O'Brien, *Conduct*, 13-37; Regan, *Cases*, 3-86; Phillips, *Justice*, 14-27; Christopher, *Ethics*, 87-100; Johnson, *Modern*, 11-66; J.T. Johnson, "Towards Reconstructing the *Jus ad Bellum*," *Monist* 57 (1973): 461-88; Childress, "Theories," 427-45; Ramsey, *Just*, passim; Wasserstrom, *Morality*, passim; and Elshtain, *Theory*, passim.

34. For a more contemporary application of *jus ad bellum* to the 1991 Persian Gulf War, see chapter 5's section on the refutation of the CP element of pacifism.

35. As opposed to, say, the actual 1992-93 international armed intervention in Somalia.

36. Material about World War II fills entire sections of libraries. One of the most relevant sources for the issues here discussed (and one of the most famous and cited books about the war) is A.J.P. Taylor, *The Origins of the Second World War* (New York: Atheneum, 1962). On the application of *jus ad bellum* norms to World War II, see Walzer, *Wars*, passim; M. Walzer, "World War II: Why Was This War Different?," *Philosophy and Public Affairs* (1971/72): 3-21; and O'Brien, *Conduct*, passim.

37. The only international assistance came in the form of: 1) an observer force, which soon was forced to retreat; and 2) humanitarian aid to temporary refugee camps that were established along the Zairean border in 1995.

38. Such as the notorious My Lai massacre.

39. Indeed, it seems cogent to contend that the perceived failure of the U.S. mission to Somalia may have had much to do with the causal explanation of its refusal to get involved in Rwanda in any substantive way.

40. For more on the Rwanda crisis/genocide, see African Rights Watch, *Rwanda: Death, Despair and Defiance* (London: African Rights Watch, 1995); G. Prunier, *The Rwanda Crisis: History of a Genocide* (New York: Columbia University Press, 1995); and C. Braeckman, *Rwanda, histoire d'un genocide* (Paris: Fayard, 1994). I deal with these and related issues in my "Armed Intervention: Principles and Cases," *Flinders Journal of History and Politics* (March 1998): 5–32.

41. In particular, we saw that norms JAB 1, 3, 4 and 6 are explicitly codified in international law. JAB 2 and 5, while lacking explicit endorsement, can indeed be teased out of several articles. For example, probability of success has clear affinities with proportionality and thus might well be "read into" the proportionality articles. Ditto for right intention in terms of just cause.

CHAPTER 7

Jus post Bellum

We have stressed in previous chapters how it is that Kant really deserves the main credit for being the first prominent thinker to insist on this separate, third category of just war theory.[1] Where members of the Just War Tradition have always contented themselves with the stock and time-honoured distinction between the justice *of* war and the justice *in* war, Kant cogently insists that a complete theory in this regard must also consider justice *after* war. And the reasoning grounding this insistence is identical to, and thus equally strong with, that reasoning grounding the distinction between the two traditional just war categories: just as we can imagine a war justly begun being fought unjustly, so too we can imagine a war justly begun, and justly fought, but ending with a set of unjust settlement terms. Thus, a complete just war theory—and emphatically a just war theory that purports to be Kantian in nature, as per KI 10[2]—must consider the topic of what constitutes justice towards the end, and after, war.

This chapter proposes to contribute to the issue by constructing a comprehensive theory of *jus post bellum*. The inquiry will proceed first by examining the actual status quo with regard to

Notes to chapter 7 are on pp. 256–263

war termination, and undertaking an examination of its few strengths and many weaknesses. Then, the account will seek to fashion a more satisfactory set of norms and laws to regulate state conduct during the immediate aftermath of a particular war. These abstract norms, once constructed and grounded, will be applied to a recent and concrete case, namely, that of the lengthy termination process of the Persian Gulf War of 1991.[3] The theory will next shift its attention from short-term principles, regulating the endings of particular wars, to longer-term norms, rules and institutional reforms required to transform the international system itself into one in which the incidence and destructiveness of war, with all the attending war termination problems, are reliably and realistically reduced.[4]

The Status Quo of War Termination and Its Deficiencies

War termination is a serious problem in the current international system in at least three senses: legally; prudentially; and morally. War termination is a legal problem inasmuch as there is next to no substantive law regulating the war-ending process. The sum total of international law regulating war termination (with the important exception of war crimes trials, to be dealt with below) is contained in Articles 32-41 of The Hague Convention (IV). The Articles are worth quoting in their entirety:

"Article 32. A person is regarded as bearing a flag of truce who has been authorized by one of the belligerents to enter into communication with the other, and who advances bearing a white flag. He has a right to inviolability, as well as the trumpeter, bugler or drummer, the flag-bearer and interpreter who may accompany him.

"Article 33. The commander to whom a flag of truce is sent is not in all cases obliged to receive it. He may take all necessary steps to prevent the envoy taking advantage of his mission to obtain information.

"Article 34. The envoy loses his rights of inviolability if it is proved in a clear and incontestable manner that he has taken advantage of his privileged position to provoke or commit an act of treachery.

"Article 35. Capitulations agreed upon between the contracting parties must take into account the rules of military honour. Once settled, they must be scrupulously observed by both parties.

"Article 36. An armistice suspends military operations by mutual agreement between the belligerent parties. If its duration is not defined, the belligerent parties may resume operations at any time, provided always that the enemy is warned within the time agreed upon, in accordance with the terms of the armistice.

"Article 37. An armistice may be general or local. The first suspends the military operations of the belligerent States everywhere; the second only between certain fractions of the belligerent armies and within a fixed radius.

"Article 38. An armistice must be notified officially and in good time to the competent authorities and to the troops. Hostilities are suspended immediately after the notification, or on the date fixed.

"Article 39. It rests with the contracting parties to settle, in the terms of the armistice, what communications may be held in the theatre of war with the inhabitants of one belligerent State and those of the other.

"Article 40. Any serious violation of the armistice by one of the parties gives the other party the right of denouncing it, and even, in cases of urgency, of recommencing hostilities immediately.

"Article 41. A violation of the terms of the armistice by private persons acting on their own initiative only entitles the injured party to demand the punishment of the offenders or, if necessary, compensation for the losses sustained."[5]

These articles were ratified in 1907, and sound like it. Their quaint references to white flags and buglers, their vague commitments to military honour, their pedantic distinctions between general and local armistices, and the overwhelming emptiness of their nature renders these articles all but irrelevant in the current context. One of the most shocking and unfortunate facts about international law is that, in the century since ratification of Hague IV, no other rules regarding war termination have been codified into the laws of armed conflict.[6]

Compare and contrast the formality, generality and sheer vacuity of the above articles on war termination with the relative substance and content of the following *jus ad bellum* law, related to just cause. It is Article 51 of the Charter of the United Nations (UN), which was ratified in 1945:

Nothing in the present Charter shall impair the inherent right of individual or collective self-defence if an armed attack occurs against a Member of the United Nations, until the Security Council has taken the measures necessary to maintain international peace and security. Measures taken by Members in the exercise of this right of self-defence shall be immediately reported to the Security Council and shall not in any way affect the authority and responsibility of the Security Council under the present Charter to take at any time such action as it deems necessary to maintain or restore international peace and security.[7]

Consider also the impressive specificity and real-world dimension of just one of the very large number of international laws governing state conduct during wartime, or *jus in bello*:

1. Without prejudice to the rules of international law applicable in armed conflict relating to treachery and perfidy, it is prohibited in all circumstances to use:

(a) Any booby-trap in the form of an apparently harmless portable object which is specifically designed and constructed to contain explosive material and to detonate when it is disturbed or approached, or

(b) Booby-traps which are in any way attached to or associated with:

(i) Internationally recognized protective emblems, signs or signals;

(ii) Sick, wounded or dead persons;

(iii) Burial or cremation sites or graves;

(iv) Medical facilities, medical equipment, medical supplies or medical transportation;

(v) Children's toys or other portable objects or products specially designed for the feeding, health, hygiene, clothing or education of children;

(vi) Food or drink;

(vii) Kitchen utensils or appliances except in military establishments, military locations or military supply depots;

(viii) Objects clearly of a religious nature;

(ix) Historic monuments, works of art or places of worship which constitute the cultural or spiritual heritage of peoples;

(x) Animals or carcasses.

2. It is prohibited in all circumstances to use any booby-trap which is designed to cause superfluous injury or unnecessary suffering.[8]

One does not have to point to the incredible detail and sophistication of the Hague and Geneva Conventions on the Treatment of Prisoners of War[9] to realize that there is a gross imbalance in the international laws of armed conflict. And it is war termination that gets the short end of the stick. Traditional just war theory suffers from this blindness, and so the international laws of armed conflict—which have been derived from it—reflect this sad state of affairs. In light of this situation, one might reasonably conclude that, currently, de facto victors in war enjoy a permissive de jure right to set whatever settlement terms they desire. To the winners go the spoils of war.

The global community ought to be very concerned to fill in this glaring gap in the laws of war. Why? First, there is the just-mentioned problem of the current lack of law effectively providing the victor with license to set any terms of the peace it desires. This is a problem because the raw fact of military strength, or good fortune in battle, does not logically entail anything in terms of political or legal entitlements. This was something Kant insisted on. Even if it is possible to speak meaningfully of entitlements at the end of war, it certainly does not follow that these entitlements ought to be unlimited, and all on the side of the victor.

The second reason to be concerned about the status quo on war termination is that the lack of international law means that there are no settled expectations of state behaviour during this very fragile time. This causes serious insecurities in the affected communities and thus the current situation militates against prudence. Indeed, one could argue plausibly that the current situation contributes to prolonged fighting on the ground, as the belligerents keep jockeying for position, since they have little idea what to expect at the bargaining table.

The lack of law on war termination further means that, not only are there no standards of aspiration codified in law, there are not even minimal standards of conduct. There is an absence of ground rules surrounding the activity. This vacuum, it seems, can only encourage extremism and arbitrariness on the part of the victor during the settlement process, and evasiveness, resentment and plans for future revenge on the part of the vanquished. The lack of law causes enormous interpretative problems regarding what constitutes a reasonable peace settlement, since there are not even general guidelines in place from which to launch a fair dialogue and negotiation process.

Finally, the lack of established norms with regard to war termination has led to ad hoc, patchwork "solutions" to very serious outbreaks of violence. These "solutions" tend to be randomly and uncertainly administered, sometimes at the insistence of intervening foreign powers, themselves unclear about their mandate, their tour of duty, and when and how they might be able to extricate themselves and not have the local belligerents erupt into warfare once more.

One need only reflect on the termination process of the recent civil war in Bosnia—a process which some contend in still underway[10]—to witness these grim and destabilizing realities. And these points of law and political security are separate issues from the standard claims of justice that:

1) wrongdoers in wartime should, as part of war termination, face punishment for their criminal activity;

2) victims of crimes in wartime are owed restitution and rehabilitation;

3) war termination processes ought to minimize suffering and maximize amelioration, with the aim being the restoration of a functioning set of relations between the former belligerents;

4) in war termination, as with war inauguration and wartime conduct, there ought to be firm and principled side-constraints regulating state conduct, so that the great dangers of unlimited escalation are avoided; and

5) moral consistency demands that the endings of war be examined and evaluated as readily as the beginnings of war and conduct within war.

Thus, the lack of rules regulating postwar conduct on the part of states creates serious problems of legal vacuum, political insecurity and profound injustice. The situation requires rectification, ideally through the establishment of international laws of war termination which are codified and effectively observed. Such a set of laws would provide the community of nations with the following beneficial functions:

1. At their most narrow, these laws would specify the content of minimally acceptable behaviour during war termination.

2. At their most broad, these laws would serve as shared standards of commitment and aspiration with regard to healing the wounds of war.

3. These laws would establish guidelines, or a kind of procedure, whereby belligerents could communicate to their opponents their intentions for action during postwar negotiations.

4. These laws would thereby help to stabilize and ground expectations of state behaviour during a very uncertain and delicate period, leading to shared modes of interpreting and evaluat-

ing peace treaties and mitigating reliance on prolonged fighting to strengthen position at the bargaining table.

5. In many instances, the laws will, if properly framed, express morally worthy aims, such as the protection of human rights, the minimization of postwar deprivation and suffering, the directing of punitive measures away from innocent non-combatants and the gradual transformation of the international system itself into one in which war is resorted to less frequently, with diminished rates of death and destruction.

Given that the case has been made with regard to how war termination is a serious problem in contemporary international law and interstate relations, and given that the benefits of having an updated and substantive set of laws regulating war termination has been established, the task that remains is the rather large one of actually constructing these *jus post bellum* principles.

Particular Wars, Immediate Aftermaths

Consideration of the justice of the end of a particular war can only begin from a firm grasp of the just aims of a just war. The focus here will be on what a just state (i.e., one that fulfils all of MJ 1-4),[11] justly prosecuting a war, may permissibly do—in this case, with regard to the termination phase of a war. We are, after all, considered with discovering those principles of morality and justice which a just state ought to take as its normative guide with regard to its wartime conduct. These principles ought to be enshrined in a reconstituted body of international laws on armed conflict. The key question, then, becomes: what should a just state aim at with regard to a just war?

Before responding to this query, it needs to be noted that the important, further assumption shall be made that the just state in question has been, or is about to be, victorious in the pursuit of its just aims. (Please see the note for more on the vexed and intriguing question of what a just state, prosecuting a just war, should aim at if it looks like it is about to lose the war to the aggressor.)[12] Finally, prior to a consideration of what constitutes the just end of a just war, it needs to be asserted, alongside Kant, that the raw fact of victory does not of itself confer rights upon the victor, nor duties upon the vanquished. Might does not equal right. It is only when the victorious regime has fought a just and lawful war that we can speak meaningfully of rights and duties of victor and vanquished at the conclusion of an armed conflict.[13]

It is often contended, to return to our main concern, that the just goal of a just war is the proverbial *status quo ante bellum*: the victorious just regime ought simply to reestablish the previously existing ground rules, and/or state of affairs, which obtained before the war broke out. However, as Walzer has contended, such an assertion makes no sense at all: one ought not to want the literal restoration of the *status quo ante bellum* because that situation was precisely what led to armed conflict and war in the first place.[14] One might add that, given the sheer destructiveness of war, and the way in which wars designed to roll back aggression are fought, any such literal restoration is empirically impossible. War simply changes too much. Perhaps it might then be contended, by way of improvement, that the just goal of a just war, once won, is a more secure and more just state of affairs than existed prior to the war. This Walzerian formulation seems undeniable, as does Kamm's contention that the appropriate goal for a justified war is a justified peace, defined as "a condition one could not justifiably alter by war."[15] What might such a condition be?

The general answer, given previous argumentation, seems to be a more secure possession of our rights. More precisely, the answer to the question, "What should a just state aim at with regard to the ends of a just war?" is one we have already encountered, in the form of the just cause criterion JAB 1: a just state may permissibly aim at the vindication of its rights, and/or those principles of international justice and law, which have been violated by an aggressor regime. The aim of a just and lawful war is the vindication of the fundamental rights of political communities, SRs 1-9,[16] ultimately on behalf of the human rights of their citizens. It is, in the gripping words of Walzer, "to reaffirm our own deepest values" with regard to justice, both domestic and international.[17] And it has been contended that, from a contemporary Kantian point of view, no deeper political values exist than those human rights that justify a reasonable political life and set of social institutions as such.

From this general contention, that the proper aim of a just war is the vindication of those rights whose violation grounded the resort to war in the first place, more detailed commentary needs to be offered. For what does such "vindication" of rights amount to: what does it include, what does it permit and what does it forbid? The last aspect of the question seems the easiest to answer, at least in abstract terms: the principle of rights vindication forbids the continuation of the war after the relevant rights have, in fact, been vindicated. To go beyond that limit, as Walzer points out, would itself be aggression: men and women in both belligerents would die for no just cause. This bedrock limit to the justified continuance of a just war seems required in order to prevent a just war from spilling over into something like a Crusade, which demands the utter destruction of the demonized enemy. We see here once more that, according to this conception, the very essence of a Kantian conception of the justice of, in, and after war is about there being firm moral limits, or side-constraints, upon its aims and conduct.

This emphasis upon the maintenance of limits in wartime has the important consequence that, in Walzer's words, there can be no such thing as a (morally mandated) unconditional surrender, since moral conditions, along with those of justice, always inhere in relations between rational beings entitled to rights and responsive to correlative duties. It is far too dangerous, and at odds with proportionality, for a justified victor to insist on the unconditional surrender of the defeated aggressor. The moral and legal principles vindicated successfully by the victim themselves impose outside constraints on what can be done to an aggressor following its defeat.[18] If it did not verge on the tautological, it would be apposite at this juncture to point out that justice demands that the just war in question end at the right point: neither too early, such that the violated rights fail to be vindicated; nor too late, such that continuance of the war itself constitutes the violation of other rights.[19]

What does the just aim of a just war—namely, rights vindication—precisely include or mandate? The following seems to be a plausible list of propositions (P) regarding what would be at least permissible with regard to a just settlement of a just war:

P1) The aggression needs, where possible and proportional, to be rolled back, which is to say that the unjust gains from aggression must be eliminated. If, for example, the aggression has involved invasion and the unjust taking of land L, then justice requires that the invader be driven out of L and secure borders reestablished. The corollary to this principle is that the victim of the aggression is to be reestablished as a political community with all the objects of the state rights, SRs 1-9, to which it is entitled. For example, if the victim's legitimate government was forcibly overthrown by the aggressor, it requires to be reinstated, and so on.

P2) The raw commission of aggression, as a serious international crime, requires punishment, in two forms: 1) compensation to the victim for (at least some of) the costs incurred during the fight for its rights; and 2) war crimes trials for the initiators of aggression (for the crime of violating *jus ad bellum*).

P3) The aggressor state might also require some demilitarization and political rehabilitation, depending on the nature and severity of the aggression it committed and the threat it would continue to pose in the absence of such measures.[20]

As propositions P1-3 make clear, the general aims of a just ending to a particular war are: 1) rolling back aggression and reestablishing the integrity of the victim of aggression *as* a rights-bearing political community; 2) punishing the aggressor; and 3) in some sense deterring future aggression, notably with regard to the actual aggressor but perhaps also, to some extent, other, would-be aggressors. Metaphorically, one might say that a just war, justly prosecuted, is something like radical surgery—an extreme yet necessary measure to be taken in defence of life and fundamental values (like human rights) against serious, lethal threats. And if just war, justly prosecuted, is like radical surgery, then the justified conclusion to such a war can only be akin to the rehabilitation and therapy required after the surgery, in order to ensure that the original intent (defence of life and rights, and defeat of the threat) is effectively consolidated and secured, and that the patient is materially better off than prior to the exercise. And the "patient," from a contemporary Kantian point of view, can only be the entire international system, composed of each and every person.[21]

General comment has already been offered on what proposition P1 requires and why: aggression, as a crime that justifies war, needs to be rolled back and have its gains eliminated as far as possible and/or proportional; and the victim of aggression needs to have the objects of its state rights, SRs 1-9, restored to itself. This principle seems to be quite straightforward as one of justice as rectification. But what of P2 and P3? What of compensation, "political rehabilitation" and war crimes trials?

Consider first the issue of compensation. Because aggression is a crime that violates critically important rights and causes much damage, it seems reasonable to contend that the aggressor nation, "Aggressor," owes some duty of compensation to the victim of the aggression, "Victim." This is the case because, in the absence of the aggression, Victim would not have to reconstruct itself following the war, nor would it have had to fight for its rights and their objects in the first place, with all the death and destruction that implies. To put the matter bluntly, Aggressor has cost Victim a considerable amount, and so at least some compensation for that cost seems due. The critical question seems to be: *how much*, and *from whom* in Aggressor is the compensation to be paid out?

The "how much" question, obviously, will be relative to the nature and severity of the act of aggression itself, alongside considerations of what Aggressor can reasonably be expected to pay. Care needs to be taken not to bankrupt or seriously cripple Aggressor's resources, if only for the reason that the people of Aggressor still, as always, retain their claims to law and order and human rights fulfilment, and the objects of such rights require that resources be devoted to them. There needs, in short, to be an application of the principle of proportionality at this point, as elsewhere in just war theory. The compensation required may not be draconian in nature: indeed, perhaps it need only be a token amount of purely symbolic significance, should Victim feel that would suffice for respect of the principle.

This reference to the needs of the civilians in Aggressor gives rise, furthermore, to considerations of discrimination with regard to answering the "from whom" question: when it comes to exacting or establishing terms of compensation, care needs to be taken by the victorious Victim (and/or any third-party Vindicators on behalf of Victim) not to penalize unduly the civilian population of Aggressor for the aggression carried out by their regime. This would seem to entail, for example, that any monetary compensation due to Victim (say, to help it rebuild its infrastructure) ought to come, first and foremost, from the personal wealth of those political and military elites in Aggressor who were most responsible for the crime of aggression. Historically, such personal assets (of dictators and their ilk) have often been enormous and thus could go some considerable way towards meeting the just compensation claims of Victim. But, in the absence of such personal assets, some modest claims of compensation by Victim may well be made upon the entire civilian population of Aggressor, for instance through a moderate, universal tax of some kind, for a pre-set period, designed to raise only the agreed-upon amount for just compensation.

In terms of demilitarization and political rehabilitation, the notion here seems to be that the Aggressor nation may reasonably be required to demilitarize, at least to the extent that it will not pose a serious threat to Victim, and/or other members of the international community, in the foreseeable future. The appropriate elements of such demilitarization will, obviously, vary with the nature and severity of the act of aggression and with the extent of Aggressor's residual military capabilities, following its defeat. But they may involve: the creation of a demilitarized "buffer zone" between Aggressor and Victim, whether on land, sea or air; the capping of certain aspects of Aggressor's military capability; and especially the destruction of Aggressor's weapons of mass destruction. But, once more, proportionality must be brought to bear upon this general principle: Aggressor may not be so demilitarized as to jeopardize its ability to fulfil its function of maintaining law and order within its own borders, and of protecting its people from other countries who might be tempted to invade (for whatever reason) if they perceive serious weakness in Aggressor.[22] Here, as elsewhere, we see that the requirements of just war theory are (perhaps surprisingly) stringent and exacting: the notion is to invoke the appropriate principles of justice and law at the appropriate time and for the right reason, but not so much so that they become counter-productive from a prudential point of view, nor (moreover) indefensible from a moral point of view. Justice at the end of, and after war, must not be draconian: *rights are to be vindicated but not, so to speak, in a vindictive fashion.*

The imposition of some substantial requirement of political rehabilitation is perhaps the most serious and invasive measure permitted a just regime, following its justified victory over Aggressor. As both Kant and Walzer assert, the "outer limit" of any surrender by Aggressor to Victim is the construction and maintenance of a new kind of domestic political regime, one more peaceable, orderly and pro-human rights in nature, within Aggressor. It is probably correct to agree with Walzer, however, when he cautions that, as a matter of proportionality, such measures are in order only in the most extreme cases, such as Nazi Germany and Imperial Japan at the close of World War II.[23] If the actions of Aggressor during the war were truly atrocious, and/or if the nature of the regime in Aggressor at the end of the war is still so heinous or threatening that its continued existence still poses a serious and credible threat to international law and human rights, then—and only then—may such a regime be forcibly dismantled and a new, more defensible regime established in its stead. But we should be quick to note, and emphasize, that such construction would seem to necessitate an additional commitment *on the part of Victim and/or its Vindicators* to assist the new regime in Aggressor with this enormous task of political restructuring. This assistance would be composed of seeing such "political therapy" through to a reasonably successful conclusion—for instance, until the new regime can stand on its own, as it were, and fulfil its core MJ 1-4 functions of domestic law and order, human rights fulfilment, protection vis-à-vis other states and adhering to the basic norms of international justice. The rehabilitation of the governing structures of both West Germany and Japan following World War II, largely by the United States, seem quite stellar and instructive examples in this regard. They also illustrate the profound and costly commitments that must be borne by any Victim seeking to impose such far-reaching and consequential terms on the relevant Aggressor following defeat.[24]

This leaves the vexed topic of war crimes trials, which unfortunately cannot be discussed here as fully as it ought to be. But the core principles seem reasonably clear. The first aspect to note is that the normative need for such trials follows from Walzer's dictum that: "There can be no justice in war if there are not, ultimately, responsible men and women."[25] Individuals who play a prominent role during wartime must be held responsible and accountable for their actions and what they bring about.

We can recall that *jus ad bellum* war crimes have to do with the initiation of aggression, and that responsibility for the commission of such a crime falls on the shoulders of the political leader(s) of the aggressor regime. In the novel language of the Nuremberg war crimes prosecutors, such aggressive leaders commit "crimes against peace." What this principle entails, then, is that—once more subject to proportionality[26]—the leaders of Aggressor are to be brought to trial before an impartial and fairly composed international tribunal and accorded full due process rights in their defence. Should they be found guilty, through a public and fair proceeding, then the court is at liberty to determine a reasonable punishment, which will obviously depend upon the details of the relevant case. Perhaps the punishment will only consist of penalizing the leaders financially for the amount of compensation owed to Victim, as previously discussed. Or perhaps, should the need for political rehabilitation be invoked, such leaders will need to be stripped of power and barred from political participation, or perhaps even jailed. It is clear that it is not possible, a priori, to stipulate what exactly is required or permitted with regard to such personal punishments. The point here is simply that the principle itself, of calling those most responsible for the aggression to task for their crimes, must be respected as an essential aspect of justice after war. It may also be relevant to add that the actual enforcement of this principle might constitute a non-trivial deterrent to future acts of aggression on the part of ambitious heads of state. If such figures have good reason to believe that they will themselves, personally, pay a price for the aggression they instigate and order, then perhaps they will be less likely to undertake such adventures in the first place.[27]

It will no doubt come to mind, following previous reasoning, that *jus ad bellum* war crimes trials are not the only ones that seem mandated by the appropriate set of just war values and principles: attention must also, in the aftermath of conflict, be paid to punishing those who commit *jus in bello* war crimes. Such crimes include: the deliberate use of indiscriminate and/or disproportionate force; failing to take due care to protect civilian populations; the employment of weapons (for instance, those of mass destruction) that are intrinsically indiscriminate and/or disproportionate; employing intrinsically heinous means (such as mass rape campaigns); and treating prisoners of war in an inhumane manner, which violates the Hague and Geneva Conventions on Prisoners of War. We also saw that primary responsibility for these war crimes must fall on the shoulders of those soldiers, officers and military commanders who were most actively involved in their commission.[28]

A critical thing to note here is that, unlike *jus ad bellum* war crimes, the war crimes of *jus in bello* can be, and usually are, committed by both (or all) sides in the conflict. So, care needs to be taken that Victim, and/or its Vindicators, avoid the very tempting position of punishing only *jus ad bellum* war crimes. In order to avoid charges of asymmetry—or "double standard"—and revenge punishment, Victim (and/or its Vindicators), despite the justice of its cause in fighting, must also be willing to submit members of its military for the commission of *jus in bello* war crimes to an international tribunal, impartially constructed, should that tribunal decide that sufficient evidence exists that such crimes were committed. Indeed, this matter brings up, and ties into, one aspect of the longer-term prescriptions of *jus post bellum* that will be dealt with shortly: the need for the construction and maintenance of a permanent, competent and impartially constituted international court for war crimes trials, perhaps to be located at The Hague as part of a revamped International Court of Justice (ICJ).[29] All war crimes, in all wars, ought to be seriously investigated and tried according to a set of fair procedures. And all sides to such conflicts ought to fall under scrutiny in this regard, and not simply those who happened to be on the losing side (even if such were the aggressors). Finally, the having of a permanent international court for war crimes trials (and not merely those ad hoc courts currently in existence) would seem needed to build up the kind of consistent, coherent and morally defensible jurisprudence surrounding war crimes that seems essential to add further legitimacy and effectiveness to war crimes prosecution.

The exact kind of punishment of *jus in bello* war crimes, obviously, cannot be specified philosophically in advance of considering the concrete details of the case in question. It may involve such things as disciplinary action within the service, expulsion from the armed forces, jail time, perhaps the paying of personal restitution, and so on.

Summary of **Jus post Bellum** *Principles*

Perhaps it would be convenient and helpful, on the basis of the foregoing contentions, to list a coherent set of substantive principles for *jus post bellum* (JPB), in a manner similar to that for the two other just war categories. A just state, seeking to successfully terminate its just war, ought to be guided by all of the following rules:

JPB 1. Just cause for termination. A state has just cause to seek termination of the just war in question if there has been a reasonable vindication of those rights whose violation grounded the resort to war in the first place. Not only have most, if not all, unjust gains from aggression been eliminated and the objects of Victim's rights been reasonably restored, but Aggressor is now willing to accept terms of surrender which include not only the cessation of hostilities and its renouncing the gains of its aggression but also its submission to reasonable principles of punishment, including compensation, *jus ad bellum* and *jus in bello* war crimes trials, and perhaps rehabilitation.

JPB 2. Right intention. A state must intend to carry out the process of war termination only in terms of those principles contained in the other *jus post bellum* rules. Revenge is strictly ruled out as an animating force. Furthermore, the just state in question must commit itself to symmetry and equal application with regard to the investigation and prosecution of any *jus in bello* war crimes.

JPB 3. Public declaration, legitimate authority and domestic rights-protection. The terms of the peace must be publicly proclaimed by a legitimate authority—i.e., the national level of government that fulfils MJ 1-4—and domestic rights must be fulfilled just as readily as external rights.

JPB 4. Discrimination. In setting the terms of the peace, the just and victorious state is to differentiate between the political and military leaders, the soldiers and the civilian population within Aggressor. Undue and unfair hardship is not to be brought upon the civilian population in particular: punitive measures are to be focused upon those elites most responsible for the aggression.

JPB 5. Proportionality. Any terms of peace must be proportional to the end of reasonable rights vindication. Absolutist crusades against, and/or draconian punishments for, aggression are especially to be avoided. The people of the defeated Aggressor never forfeit their human rights, and so are entitled not to be "blotted out" from the community of nations. There is thus no such thing as a morally mandated unconditional surrender.

Any serious defection from these principles of *jus post bellum*, after they have been agreed to in good faith, on the part either of Victim/Vindicators or Aggressor, is a violation of the rules of just and legitimate war and, as such, ought to be rectified and/or punished. At the very least, such violation of *jus post bellum* mandates a new round of good-faith diplomatic negotiations—perhaps even binding international arbitration—between the relevant parties to the dispute. At the very most, such violation gives the aggrieved party a just cause—*but no more than a just cause*—for resuming hostilities. (After all, full recourse to the resumption of armed hostilities may be made only if all the other criteria of *jus ad bellum*, JAB 2-6, are satisfied in addition to just cause.)

Thus, the contention is that these *jus post bellum* principles, JPB 1-5, ought to be codified in the positive international laws of armed conflict. Now that progress has been achieved on banning land mines and on founding a permanent international court for crimes against humanity, perhaps the attention of international legal reformers could next turn to the pressing problem of war termination.

The above norms, JPB 1-5, are quite plausible candidates for inclusion in any such international legal reform for the following powerful reasons:

1. They are direct outgrowths of, and thus are fundamentally consistent with, existing moral thought and legal norms regulating the resort to war and conduct within it.

2. They are clear and readily understandable, yet of obvious substance. They would constitute a great improvement over the current legal vacuum with regard to war termination.

3. They express principles that are not merely clear and consistent with established legal and political norms but are also of compelling moral character, focused as they are on successful war termination, human rights protection, and the strengthening of a

well-functioning international system composed of states that satisfy the requirements of minimal justice, MJ 1-4.

One Real-World Application of Jus post Bellum: The Persian Gulf War

Perhaps it would be fitting and illustrative to apply these principles of short-term, particular *jus post bellum*, JPB 1-5, to a real, recent and concrete case. Looking in detail at such a case can reveal how these principles can assist us in evaluating actual peace settlements, thereby assisting over the longer term in the production of more adequate and successful peace treaties. One accessible case, in this regard, would be the end of the Persian Gulf War of 1991. How does the (rather drawn-out)[30] termination process of that conflict fare when measured against the above norms of *jus post bellum?*

The first thing that needs to be considered is whether or not the norms of just war really apply to this conflict. After all, it might be said that Kuwait itself was not, by the previous criteria of MJ 1-4, a reasonable or well-ordered state entitled to the full panoply of state rights, such as nonintervention. And this would be the case because, while (at the time just prior to Iraq's August 2, 1990 invasion) Kuwait did provide law and order to its people, and had managed to protect them until the invasion, and did fulfil most of its obligations to the international community, it did not satisfy the human rights of its people to a reasonable degree. This is especially clear with regard to standard political rights, such as those to vote, to participate in governance, to free political speech and criticism, and so on. The Kuwaiti regime, at the time, did indeed seem to be, in the words of Walzer, "a semifeudal despotism of the al-Sabah family."[31]

These reflections seem undeniable and they elicit the following response. Even if we grant that Kuwait was not a reasonable or well-ordered regime at the time of the invasion—and so perhaps the raw fact of Iraq crossing into its borders was not morally or legally offensive—the subsequent actions of Iraq, once in Kuwait, did clearly constitute aggression against the Kuwaiti people, which would then have grounded the armed response of the Allies. As the Amnesty International report of December 1990 made clear at the time, the Iraqi regime was, between August and December of that year, engaged in a systematic campaign of atrocities against the Kuwaiti people, including widespread destruction and looting of property, random attacks and severe beatings, torture, countless rapes and even murders. So, even if it is problematic, according to previous considerations, to say that Iraq aggressed against Kuwait the minute it crossed the latter's borders, it is unproblematic to say that the minute Iraq's invading force began its campaign of deprivations against the Kuwaiti people, it committed aggression against that polity. Iraq thus forfeited its rights not to be attacked by the Allied forces, as led by the United States.

Let us, to facilitate analysis, assume that the war on the part of the Allies managed to meet the other criteria of *jus ad bellum*. And let us bracket for the meantime the question of how well *jus in bello* was fulfilled on both sides. Given these assumptions, how just and lawful was the termination phase of this otherwise justified war?

Consider first JPB 1, just cause for termination. When did the Allies terminate the war? The de facto end to the war came on February 27, 1991, when American President George Bush ordered the Allied forces to adhere to a ceasefire, following the rout and flee of Iraqi forces from Kuwait. The de jure end to the war came on April 3, 1991, when UN Security Council Resolution 687 proclaimed its end. Did the Allies have just cause to terminate the war when they did? It seems that the answer to this question is probably yes. It appears that the rights of the Kuwaiti people were reasonably vindicated, first and foremost by having the Allies cease the Iraqi aggression and, indeed, drive the Iraqi aggressors out of Kuwait entirely. Many people at the time complained that the war was ended too soon, and several generals publicly grumbled about not being able to drive into Baghdad and forcibly depose the Saddam Hussein regime. While that argument might have had some strategic rationale, its rationale according to just war criteria was significantly weaker: the aggression against the Kuwaiti people, which had grounded the Allied attack, had been halted and repulsed, indeed in resounding fashion. It is deeply unclear whether driving on into Baghdad and deposing the regime could plausibly have been seen as a part of *that* just cause; my own view is that such action would have inaugurated an importantly different, second phase of the war wherein the moral and legal justification on the part of the Allies would have been in serious question. So perhaps Bush, at least from a just war point of view, actually should have been commended for restraining the armed force in that conflict to the defence and defeat of aggression against Kuwait.

Between March and April 1991, terms of the ceasefire were hammered out under the auspices of the UN Security Council. Those terms included the following requirements of Iraq: 1) it had to both actually cease hostilities and declare a formal end to them; 2) it had to rescind its claim to Kuwait and return looted property; 3) it had to release immediately all prisoners of war; 4) it had to accept liability for loss, injury and damage in Kuwait which resulted from its invasion; and 5) it had to provide to the UN total disclosure of its program for making weapons of mass destruction and commit itself to that program's destruction, subject to verification by on-site UN inspectors.

Items 1-3 of these terms of the Gulf War peace agreement are the essential elements of agreeing to end a war: to stop fighting; to accept responsibility for aggression; to renounce unjust claims; and to release POWs. Article 4 provides for the kind of compensation for aggression that was defended above. The compensation was paid out in the following way. Following the war, the UN established a compensation fund that was financed by a gradual lifting of the oil embargo that was levelled on Iraq after its initial invasion of Kuwait. Under the terms of the lifting, 30 percent of the oil export sales of Iraq were allowed to be kept by its government, with the stipulation that such monies be employed to provide for the humanitarian needs (foodstuffs and medicine) of its people. The remaining 70 percent was split between: 1) the compensation fund; 2) a special fund designed to pay for the expenses of the on-site UN weapons inspectors; and 3) an escrow account, which was to be handed over to Iraq once full compliance with the terms of settlement was achieved. Such an account seems to have been an enlightened actualization of the compensation principle.

Article 5 of the ceasefire provided for that partial disarmament and demilitarization of the aggressor, defended above as part of the goal of achieving a more secure and peaceful international order than was the case prior to the war. In addition to the verifiable dismantling of Iraq's mass weapons program, the Security Council also established demilitarized zones within Iraq, north of the thirty-sixth parallel (to greater protect Israel, Turkey and the Kurdish minority within Iraq) and south of the thirty-second parallel (to greater protect Kuwait, Saudi Arabia and the Shiite minority within Iraq). Iraq pledged neither to fly nor to occupy those areas for an indeterminate amount of time. It also acquiesced to Allied air patrols of the no-fly zones (NFZ), for enforcement purposes. It seems that such terms were also entirely in line with the criteria of *jus post bellum* defended above: Iraq was to be demilitarized not to the point of collapse but at least to the point where it would not pose either a short- or medium-term threat to international peace and security within the region.

One criticism which might be levelled at this specific arrangement was that it was indefinite and open-ended, and thus a flare-up was bound to occur, as it has several times. The first time was in January 1993, when Iraq tested the Allies by flying into both NFZs, firing some surface-to-air missiles, and quickly crossing the border into Kuwait to retrieve some weaponry it had abandoned during the retreat back into Iraq during February 1991. The U.S. retaliated with three air attacks and missile strikes on military targets, albeit with at least one errant missile striking a residential section within Baghdad. Military fire was exchanged several times in 1996. Then, starting in late 1997 and moving into the summer of 1998, Iraq refused to comply with the UN weapons inspectors. By December 1998 American President Bill Clinton ordered Operation Desert Fox.[32] British and American forces combined to bombard military targets in Iraq for four days. The operation attempted to enforce compliance with the inspections regime and, in any event, to set back that part of Iraq's weapons program that had eluded inspection. The latter aim may have succeeded, but not the former: Iraq has refused to let any UN weapons inspectors back into its territory. Furthermore, in early 1999, Iraq's military took potshots once more at American forces. As of the time of writing, the tug of war continues.[33]

Consider now the second criterion of *jus post bellum*, right intention. Did the Allies have the right intention during the termination and peace-settlement phase of the Persian Gulf War? On the one hand, the terms of the peace settlement would indeed seem to indicate that they were focused above all on repealing and punishing the aggression displayed by Iraq in Kuwait, on mandating that Iraq provide at least some compensation for having committed aggression, and on demilitarizing Iraq to an extent that it could not pose such a stark threat to neighbouring political communities. It seems that this criterion was clearly met on the whole: for instance, exceptional, vindictive measures were not meted out on the Iraqi people, the oil supplies of Iraq were not appropriated and so on. Indeed, the Allies refrained from trying to force extensive domestic retooling of the political situation in Iraq. But, on the other hand, it could be contended that America, at least, might have had some ulterior motives with regard to consolidating its favoured (strategic) conception of the "new world order," which was then taking shape during the winding down of the broader Cold War struggle between the U.S. and the U.S.S.R. And there can be no doubt that, central to the thinking of the Allies during the termination phase—perhaps almost equal in weight to rights-vindication—was ensuring the security, integrity and openness of the region's oil supply. One aspect of JPB 2 which clearly was not met was the failure to commit to holding any war crimes trials at all, on either side. There was nothing credible in the ceasefire agreement to this effect, nor was there any public commitment on the part of the Allies, particularly the United States. Perhaps this was understandable in terms of *jus ad bellum*, given the serious instability that would have resulted in Iraq from an attempt to bring its leaders to justice. But *jus in bello* seems another question entirely. Whatever the explanation in this regard, it clearly cannot have been because there were no such crimes committed.

In terms of JPB 3—i.e., public declaration and legitimate authority—it seems that the Allies fulfilled these requirements straightaway. The terms of the ceasefire were publicly proclaimed, both in general and to the Iraqis in particular, by the legitimate authorities for doing so: the UN and the major Allied powers.

It seems that, if there is a serious question to be raised with regard to *jus post bellum* on the part of the Allies in this war, it resides in consideration of JPB 4, discrimination. The relevant focus here concerns the substantial maintenance of the sweeping economic sanctions after the ceasefire and for a considerable duration after that. Indeed, as of the time of writing, not all of the sanctions have been dismantled. As noted before, soon after the war, the Allies partially eased the previous economic embargo on Iraqi oil exports, stipulating that the 30 percent Iraqi take from such new sales be devoted to meeting the humanitarian needs of its people (foodstuffs, medicine, infrastructure repairs). However, perhaps it could be argued that this was too strict and indiscriminate a policy on the part of the Allies. After all, everything that everyone knew about the Saddam Hussein regime indicated that the funds would be used for its own buttressing and benefit, and there were no effective enforcement mechanisms built in to the terms of Iraq's receiving this money. So perhaps it was disingenuous for the Allies simply to leave the matter at that, particularly with regard to the damage that their bombing had inflicted on part of the water treatment supply system in Iraq. Perhaps effective enforcement mechanisms could have been built into the receipt of that cash and/or perhaps more could have been made available, from the oil fund, to non-governmental aid and relief agencies. In the absence of such measures, the Allies might have been guilty of some callousness with regard to the postwar sufferings of the Iraqi people. Of course, this is not at all to exonerate the Saddam Hussein regime, whose truculence and indifference to the well-being of its own people must loom large in any fairminded account of why the Iraqi populace seemed to suffer such deprivations during and after the war.

Perhaps it might be said that the fact that the Allies created so-called "safe havens"—protected by military force and liberally supplied with humanitarian aid—within both demilitarized zones for the Kurdish and Shiite minorities does, in fact, indicate substantial adherence to the norm of discriminating between the people of a given aggressor and the aggressive regime itself. And so it does. However, the account cannot be left to end at this point. After all, during the war Bush himself explicitly, and publicly, called on the Iraqi people to overthrow Saddam Hussein. And the Kurds and Shiites heeded that call, but were crushed in the immediate postwar period by the remnant of Saddam Hussein's armed forces. It is arguably true that such a call, and such a response, created an obligation independent of the norm of discrimination on the part of the Allies, especially the United States, to create safe havens for those persecuted people in the wake of war.

Despite these difficulties, it needs to be admitted and reiterated that the vast majority of the postwar measures were directly targeted at the aggressor regime: forcing it to abandon its claims, reducing its military capacity, limiting its resources and regional sway, and so on. So, the judgment with regard to discrimination seems quite difficult and conflictual. It seems that, on the whole, the Allies did indeed focus on punishing the regime, but the extent and depth of Iraqi civilian deprivation in the aftermath leaves one wondering whether the Allies could have done more to ease their suffering, without providing any comfort or succour to their aggressor regime. We come at last to JPB 5, proportionality. It seems that, perhaps with the exception of the maintenance of the sanctions, and the inefficiently lengthy process of weapons inspections, the measures taken by the Allies were truly proportional to the end they sought to achieve. Despite temptations, the Allies resisted calls to make this war into a crusade against Saddam Hussein and did not overthrow him and subject the Iraqi people to years of complicated, costly and questionable political tutelage. The Allies, by and large, contented themselves with a set of measures designed to secure Iraq's withdrawal from Kuwait, its providing reasonable compensation for its aggression and substantially curtailing its destructive capacity. The aim, and the means to achieve it during the postwar period, seem to have been to achieve a reasonable degree of rights vindication.

We can see from this section that the JPB norms previously constructed from just war theory and the existing international laws governing armed conflict are well-suited to real-world application. Their codification would assist greatly in determining the legitimacy and adequacy of peace treaties and various processes of war termination.[34]

War in General: Long-term Structural Reform

Whenever one contemplates the construction of new rules of international law and justice—such as JPB 1-5—one is always faced with the serious problem of ensuring state compliance. Some suggestion has already been made as to how compliance can be brought about with regard to JPB 1-5: violation of any one of JPB 1-5 constitutes just cause for the resumption of hostilities. Force, and the threat of force, can be employed to incline states to adhere to the terms. And this is leaving unsaid the fact that ratification of JPB 1-5 would, like other elements of the international laws of war, come to exert over time the pressures of custom and diplomatic expectation and propriety.

But is this really sufficient? Is there nothing more that can be done to ensure that states wrap up their wars in a satisfactory fashion, or—better still—increasingly resolve their disputes through judicial processes instead of resorting to armed force? In short, attention must now be paid to what Kant insisted, long ago, was the logical second part of the pressing problem of armed conflict: considering what, if anything, might be done through global institutional reform to reduce dramatically the long-term incidence and destructiveness of war.

Perhaps it hardly requires mention that this section will be the most abstract, sketchy and speculative, peering as it does into our distant future and what we will require in terms of just political arrangements if we are to live worthwhile lives, secure in the possession of the objects of our human rights. The account offered below will be utterly normative—I do not feel competent to talk about the exact empirical pre-conditions for a secure world system, or what sweeping institutional reforms would have the greatest practical chances for acceptance and why, and so on. I will merely offer what seems to be a compelling normative account of long-term *jus post bellum*, along with a general, common-sense account of what kinds of institutional reforms seem possible and supportive with regard to its central ends.

It is important to mention the linkage between these forthcoming principles of long-term institutional reform and the previous Kantian principles of international justice, international law and just war. The forthcoming principles of global institutional reform seek to help actually realize the general principles of international justice, SRs 1-9 and SDs 1-9, whose violation currently grounds the resort to war, in accordance with our Kantian just war principles. In other words, the forthcoming reforms are aimed at eventually undermining the grounds for resorting to war and to the laws of armed conflict, namely, by reducing significantly the likelihood that states will have need to resort to armed conflict at all. The core notion is that, provided we can securely supply minimally just states with the objects of their state rights, SRs 1-9, and that they in turn perform their state duties, SDs 1-9, and that human rights can thus be fulfilled much more adequately, the reasons for resorting to war will be lessened dramatically, though perhaps never eliminated entirely.

Why should we want to constrain the outbreak and resort to war at all, in such fashion? There seem to be at least two cogent responses in this regard. The first is that recent history demonstrates that war, even in its just and lawful forms, is becoming increasingly destructive and can only continue to become more so in the future, given the advances in military technology, the increase in weapons proliferation and increased global population and interdependence. We ought, rationally, to be extremely concerned with placing severe constraints upon the outbreak of war in the future in order to avoid such incredible devastation, especially with regard to weapons of mass destruction. The second reason why we should concern ourselves with seriously reducing the incidence and destructiveness of war is that *we should not have to fight for our rights at all.* We should, rather, have the objects of our rights provided to all of us as a matter of rational conduct and just political and social arrangements. Over the long term, as Kant reminds us, war is not the way in which rational agents like us should pursue their rights.[35] It is, so to speak, beneath our rational dignity to keep being forced to stoop to warfare in order to secure the objects of our rights on the international plane. The only practical alternative thus seems to be some kind of gradual, long-term structural reform of the international status quo.

Suggestions have already been made as to how some defensible improvements in the current international structure might be forged. The first of these concerned the denial of recognition to a state which fails to fulfil any of its four proper MJ functions of domestic law and order, domestic human-rights fulfilment, protection and representation vis-à-vis the world community, and adherence to the basic norms of international justice.[36] Such denial of recognition might involve refusal to acknowledge such states diplomatically, the withdrawal of ambassadors and diplomatic corps from them, perhaps even expulsion from the UN, or (more plausibly) some kind of second-rate status at the UN and the various relevant global governance regimes. The point is to provide meaningful incentives for pro-human rights fulfilment within these outlaw states.

The second long-term reform already advocated in the international structure was in terms of providing sufficient resources to destitute states, such that they can make sustained efforts at human rights fulfilment, as SR 3 and SD 5 elucidated in chapter 4. Economic factors, especially stark disparities and the perception of exploitation, frequently play into the causal mix which produces armed conflict. Such need to be mitigated, for the sake of strengthening the long-term functioning of the international system. Various proposals on how to provide such resources were aired previously.

The third suggestion previously made in favour of longer-term institutional reform at the global level was for the establishment of a permanent global court for war crimes trials at the ICJ, which is in The Hague in Holland. On July 17, 1998, the society of states passed a treaty in Rome, initiating the process for the creation of just such a court. Sixty countries must still ratify the treaty before the court will exist as a legitimate branch of the international legal landscape.

The proposed world court has its critics, not the least of which is the government of the United States. But their arguments seem dubious. Their critical observations on the court's existence boil down to two propositions: 1) the existing, ad hoc process for trying war criminals is adequate; and 2) the proposed world court represents an excessive and unconscionable infringement of national sovereignty.

The current international legal regime on war crimes, which allows for the establishment only of ad hoc war crimes tribunals, allows many war crimes in many wars to go unpunished. Consider that from 1945 until today, there have been only four international war crimes tribunals: the two tribunals in Nuremberg and Tokyo following World War II; and the two tribunals now sitting in judgment on the Bosnian civil war of 1992-95 and the

Rwandan ethnic massacres of 1994-95. Yet many wars occurred during the same period. A partial list of them includes Korea, Vietnam, Afghanistan, Iran-Iraq and the Persian Gulf War. Are the critics of the permanent court implying that war crimes were not committed in all these other conflicts? Or, more implausibly, that crimes against humanity ought not to be punished at all? The critics of the world court are here faced with an ugly dilemma: either to deny that war crimes should be punished at all, or to assert that, of all the war crimes that have been committed in all these conflicts, only those of the four conflicts first mentioned deserve trial and punishment. The very ad hoc nature of the current judicial regime indicates its fundamental inadequacy: it is an *arbitrary* regime, fuelled largely by super-power guilt over having failed to intervene in a timely manner in the conflicts just mentioned. And arbitrariness is at odds with the orderly and rational pursuit of a just society under law. Thus, the demand is for a permanent world court, set at arm's length from the flights of fancy on the part of those big powers that dominate the international system.

The critics' most visceral argument against a permanent world court is that it would infringe national sovereignty. But which specific aspect of national sovereignty would a world court infringe? The freedom to let one's own war criminals go unpunished? Perhaps the critics are referring to the more general point that a world court would require a nation to defer to the court's judgment with regard to certain war crimes. This complaint has been stated vehemently by some recent American commentators and politicians, who demand only "American justice for American war criminals." But this complaint gets it wrong in at least two ways. First, the international court will not be the tool of some rogue nation with an axe to grind. It will, rather, be composed of eighteen distinguished international jurists operating at arm's length from global politicking. Second, the critics' argument has distasteful implications and analogies. The implication is that American jurists are somehow better judges of their fellow nationals than are international jurists. This, however, is false: the distribution of legal talent respects no national borders. More ominous is the dark analogy behind this reasoning. The reasoning indicates that only those who share a certain (largely unchosen) property— i.e., citizenship—are fit to sit in judgment over others who also possess that same property. But this is somewhat like saying that only white males are fit to sit in judgment over other white males. Modern democracies, sensibly, have moved beyond such a biased and inaccurate assessment of impartiality and competence.

Most crucially, it is not as though any U.S. soldier appearing before the permanent world court would be prosecuted according to a scale of values radically at odds with those of his own political community. America, after all, has exhibited abhorrence at past war crimes, assisted in their prosecution and is a founding and leading member of the UN. This fact commits America—indeed, all UN members—to the core values of the UN, which are peace, security and human rights protection. Any war crimes trial held by the permanent world court would be in accord with these fundamental values, which the community of nations has already endorsed by taking out UN membership. In a sense, the world court is something to which the people of the world have already committed themselves. Now, it is a matter of fulfilling that commitment.

There is no denying that a well-constructed world court[37] will curtail national sovereignty: it will require that nations offer up to the world court for a fair and public trial any of their citizens who face war crimes charges. This trial will be followed by a verdict, which nations will be duty-bound to respect. But there can be great benefits to be had from agreements and institutions that curtail national sovereignty to some extent. Consider NATO during the Cold War, or the free trade agreements currently in place around the globe. A rational agent realizes that it is possible to benefit oneself in the long term by sacrificing some short-term benefits. And the long-term benefits of a permanent world court are numerous and weighty. The include the following:

1. The moral benefit of ending arbitrariness and the double standard of "victor's justice" by having a consistent international judicial system enabling the prosecution of all war crimes in all wars.

2. The deterrence benefit. If all war crimes, in all wars, are prosecuted and punished by an impartial world court, then it stands to reason that future, would-be war criminals might well be deterred from committing their ghastly actions if they know that they will themselves pay a personal price for their crimes.

3. The war-termination benefit. The having of a permanent and non-partisan world court can assist nations in wrapping up their armed conflict, punishing acts that need punishment in an impartial manner which applies to all of them equally.

4. The systematic benefit. The global community has already witnessed the huge benefits of having an international system based on rules of law that are reasonable, impartial and applicable to all. The trade sector is the clearest and most recent example of this. The construction of a permanent world court would help complete the international landscape, thereby adding to the existence of a global system that runs smoothly on a consistent and comprehensive set of shared values.

5. The commitment benefit. The construction of a permanent war crimes court would allow the world community to keep its commitments to the core values of the UN: peace; security; and human rights. A world court would enhance peace by punishing deeds which, if left unpunished, could sow the seeds of future wars. This would augment global security more broadly. Finally, the existence of a world court for war crimes and crimes against humanity would be another much needed advance in the compelling cause of human rights protection around the world.

Thus, it seems that, provided that the court is well-constructed, the critics of the forthcoming permanent court for war crimes are incorrect: the current international judicial regime is not adequate and the proposed court does not represent an excessive infringement of national sovereignty. There are compelling reasons for the international community to proceed with ratifying the treaty passed in Rome in the summer of 1998, authorizing the construction of such a court.

The final, and most radical and substantive suggestion for long-term institutional reform at the international level, concerns Kant's storied proposal for some kind of cosmopolitan federation.[38]

Kant, we have seen,[39] believed that a full-blown world government, modelled after a national government, is both factually impossible and morally impermissible. It is factually impossible because history teaches us that overstretched political regimes cannot sustain their hold over all their territories. Effective state mechanisms face size constraints. Not even despotic control can be sustained over vast territories, to say nothing about the far-flung nations of the world. Furthermore, Kant pointed out that there is only so much overarching governance that peoples of different cultures, languages, religions, histories and beliefs can support. And he locates the limits of that tolerance threshold well below that required to support a world government.

A full-blown world government is morally impermissible, according to Kant, because it is at odds with the right of freedom that peoples have to consent to their governing structures. And Kant felt it obvious that the peoples of the world would, owing to their diversity, never willingly endorse a full-blown world government.

Kant suggested that we must move towards something like, but not quite, a full-blown world state. We must get as close to a world state as is practically and morally feasible. International federalism, and not a world republic, is Kant's solution to the problem of war and the guarantor of a secure global peace. What exactly is the nature of this posited federation? Kant speaks of a group of like-minded states voluntarily agreeing to form a pacific federation, renouncing war as a means of conflict resolution among themselves, and in doing so this federation "will provide a focal point for federal association among other states...and the whole will spread further and further by a series of alliances of this kind." In fact, Kant confidently predicts that such a federation will extend "gradually to encompass all states, thus leading to perpetual peace."⁴⁰

So, Kant's idea is of a voluntary and renewable social contract among states to renounce war, to perform their state duties and to respect each other's state rights. The "federalism" part is not readily apparent—at least if we think of federalism as implying some kind of actual division of power between state and sub-state levels, with the sub-state levels enjoying considerable autonomy over a certain specified list of powers. The idea is more in the vein of a very familiar Kantian move: states are to act *as if* there were a real, effective federal system operative at the global level. They are, voluntarily, to constrain their own behaviour in such a way that the result—namely, peace and the secure enjoyment of rights, both state and human—is the same as if there were an actual federal system between states, based on an actual division of power and authority between the global authority and the nation-state sub-units.[41]

As intriguing and progressive as Kant's conception of a cosmopolitan federation might be, many have diagnosed fatal flaws in its specifics. Foremost among these is the realization that the historical evidence casts a long, skeptical shadow over the tenability of a purely voluntary interstate organization, not backed by force or an institutional structure. States are simply subject to too many pressures and possible insecurities in the current global system to be assured by a merely voluntary organization. But the idea of some kind of cosmopolitan federation retains some strength.

The principal strength relevant to our concern with war termination is that, if effective in design and implementation, a cosmopolitan federation of states really could lessen substantially the assurance problem at the heart of the current international system—a problem that frequently leads to war. It stands to reason that a supra-state association, backed by force and with institutional embodiment, could well contain a reliable dispute-resolution mechanism for resolving lawfully those kinds of disputes that can lead to ruptures in peaceful co-existence among states. An effective federation could lessen the security dilemmas states face by providing a further institutional context designed to resolve such dilemmas lawfully. Simply put, it would lessen greatly the many strains of self-help currently foisted on states by the set-up of the international arena, so accurately described by weak descriptive realism.[42] But what would be the structure and nature of this posited long-term reform to the international land-scape—this cosmopolitan federation?

The cosmopolitan federation would be a worldwide political alliance uniting regional, state and sub-state governments within a supra-state association. Its cosmopolitan nature would come not only from its raw extent and domain but, moreover, from its grounding in the core notion that all individual persons, as freely united into political communities of their own choosing, are the ultimate units of moral, legal and political concern. What would be the core values of this cosmopolitan federation? First, there would be the desire for international peace and security. Second, there would be the desire for the objects of state rights, SRs 1-9, for all political communities. And third, there would be the desire for the objects of all human rights. It needs to be stressed that such a listing is not a priority ranking; it is simply a move from international to domestic to individual planes: in fact, human rights, as has been contended repeatedly, take the foremost priority in terms of claim on our attention and effort. Indeed, it is precisely because secure enjoyment of all our human rights, for each and every one of us, seems to require a cosmopolitan federation that we are duty bound to attempt to construct it. Reflection on what we need as human beings leads us, domestically, to the construction of a state mechanism which can provide us with law and order and reasonable fulfilment of human rights. But then reflection on the precarious nature of the interstate environment, notably with its threat of war, leads us inexorably to the conclusion that we require a more secure international institutional context if our freely chosen state mechanism is to fulfil properly its own role in human rights fulfilment.

The federal nature of the cosmopolitan structure would come from the *actual and enforceable* division of powers between the supra-state, state and sub-state levels, based on the principle of subsidiarity: power should be kept close to the people over whom it is exercised, consistent with its ability to fulfil its intended function (which will be based on the core cosmopolitan values just listed). The grounds for this principle are respectably Kantian in that they highlight individual autonomy: in Pogge's words, each person must have as great an opportunity as feasible "to influence the social conditions that shape her life."[43] The sizable question that remains is: what precise powers should the cosmopolitan federation have? What exactly would it look like? After we have answered this question reasonably, we can then leave the matter with the further observation that all residual powers (which will be very considerable) are to rest at the state and sub-state levels.

It seems that the cosmopolitan federation should be something of a revamped and empowered United Nations. This conception also has the advantage of being rooted in familiar institutional starting points from which gradualist reform can be carried out. The UN is the most obvious and compelling site for any greater push towards cosmopolitan federation. Not only is it the most prominent international organization, its Universal Declaration of Human Rights (UDHR), we have contended in chapter 4, serves as an excellent model and list of a contemporary conception of human rights, whose satisfaction is to be the basis of the cosmopolitan federation.

Such a federation, logically, will need to have (only) those powers required to provide a secure and just context within which state rights SRs 1-9 and SDs 1-9 can be fulfilled, just as the national state needs (only) those powers required for its individual citizens to enjoy their human rights on the domestic front. What might such international powers be, and over what? To answer the latter question first, these powers will need, centrally, to be over questions of international conflict, peace and security, as well as grievous human rights violations, the international resource transfers required for human rights fulfilment, and anything else that the community of states wishes it to look after: for instance, those international issues that affect the well-being of our species and world as a whole, such as the regulation of pollution, population (flows), the eradication of certain diseases and tending to common areas such as the oceans, the atmosphere and outer space.

To respond to the former question, with regard to the nature of such needed international powers, it seems cogent to contend that the cosmopolitan federation will need to have some legislative, executive and judicial capacities if it is to be effective in its role of providing a more orderly and just context within which states and peoples can enjoy the objects of their rights.

In terms of its legislative functions, it is clear that something like a reformed and empowered UN General Assembly would be a promising candidate in this regard. The first thing to be stressed here is that, as in the European Union, fully fledged membership ought to be denied to those states who are seriously deficient with regard to performing any one of their four core MJ functions. It should be noted, in this regard, that Article 6 of the UN Charter already gives the General Assembly the authority to strip countries of their membership, should they behave in a manner that "persistently violates" the purposes of the UN Charter. So, the first proposition is that outlaw states be denied membership (or, at least, *fully fledged membership*) in the reformed UN which is to serve as the base for the eventual growth of a cosmopolitan federation. The point is to deny human rights violators the fruits of membership, recognition and legitimation and thus provide them with needed incentives to respect human rights, to the extent possible, within their own borders.[44]

The empowered General Assembly (GA) shall need to have legislative, and not merely deliberative, powers with regard to those matters listed above. It ought to be able to declare authoritatively the substantive content of international law with regard to war and peace, human rights fulfilment and the other agreed-upon global subject matters. Since the GA is composed of states, there seems no devastating objection to this proposal on the grounds that it would ride roughshod over communal self-determination. Indeed, as has been contended repeatedly throughout this work, such an organization is required precisely to facilitate and render more secure self-determination and the human rights fulfilment which is its logical end and aim. One interesting proposal, with regard to GA reform, might be the following: the GA ought to be composed solely of (minimally just) states and each state should only have one vote. But the results of the vote are to be counted in two ways: 1) the raw result of one country, one vote; and 2) the result of the vote as weighted by the population of the countries (such that countries with more of the world's population count proportionately for more). Only when the results of 1 and 2 line up together is the proposed legislation to be passed and considered world law.[45]

In terms of the judicial functions of the cosmopolitan federation, the sensible site here for reform is the UN's International Court of Justice (ICJ). It has already been contended that a permanent court for war crimes ought to be set up under the auspices of the ICJ. More generally, the ICJ ought to be seen as the authoritative interpreter and court of last resort with regard to the nature of international law and the fair and peaceable solution of international disputes.[46]

In terms of the executive functions, one plausible option for the future is an empowered UN Security Council (SC). Such a Council would, however, need to be more relevant in its structure (for instance, by including as permanent members at least one country from continents not already represented, such as South

America and Africa). Plus, all SC members would need to fulfil MJ 1-4. The member countries of the UN also need to make good on their pledges, in Articles 43-47 of the Charter, to found a Permanent Military Force (PMF) for use and disposal by the SC, in accord with the principles of the Charter, which feature both peace and security and human rights. Such a PMF, which would initially need to be of considerable size and strength, would be the ultimate enforcement tool behind the pronouncements of the GA, the SC and the decisions of the ICJ. Of course, it needs to be stressed that the PMF need not be the only tool of such enforcement: we can imagine the threat of the denial of membership, for instance, constituting a powerful enforcement mechanism within the cosmopolitan federation. Furthermore, we can imagine scenarios in which the federation will need to have the power to raise revenues directly, perhaps in conjunction with its authority over the resource transfers required to realize human rights in poorer countries. This way, the UN could not be held so easily in the sway of the most powerful and wealthy nation-states. And this kind of economic power could also be brought to bear upon the behaviour of outlaw states, through the levying of additional fines upon them, or some such mechanism.[47]

The PMF would seem to enhance greatly the security of the global community. Its existence would mean that states would no longer need to feel that, in the face of aggression from outlaw states, it is either a matter of self-help or capitulation. The promise of an effective international response to rights violations would seem, thereby, to promote cross-border confidence and perhaps even sizable incentives for greater national disarmament, especially with regard to weapons of mass destruction.[48] Furthermore, with the actual enforcement of international law and judicial decisions, and with them both emanating from more adequately constituted bodies to begin with, much greater confidence could be placed in international law, with regard to its fairness and effectiveness. Reasonable states would, as a result, be more likely to submit even serious disputes to the processes of international law rather than resort to war and all its risks. In short, there would be much less of a need to resort unilaterally to armed force, even in defence of a just cause. Obviously, the PMF would itself need to be guided by the principles of just war theory, and the laws of armed conflict, at least until that posited day, far in the future, when the success of the cosmopolitan federation would overwhelmingly incline different political communities to submit their disputes to adjudication, reasoned argument and principled judgment rather than to the many vicissitudes and brutalities of war.[49]

Perhaps it requires reiteration that all powers not explicitly mentioned here would remain the preserve of state and sub-state levels of government. As a result, this conception of a cosmopolitan federation leaves a very considerable role for the nation-state and more local political communities. Now, it is true that the conception defended here, following Pogge,[50] does disperse governmental authority and power away from the state in two directions: 1) up to the global level; and 2) down to more local levels, such as provinces. But this dispersal need not and would not entail the death of the state. Indeed, as scholars as diverse as Walzer, Rawls and Henry Shue have contended, some such reforms seem required to balance the interstate system and to civilize the state—perhaps even to save the institution of the state from itself, given the inherent instability of an anarchical society composed solely of such entities.[51] The aim of a cosmopolitan federation is not to become some kind of monolithic world government: it is, rather, to constrain and civilize the nation-state in an analogous fashion to the way in which a reasonable nation-state can constrain and civilize individual persons. A cosmopolitan federation is required, so to speak, to neutralize the corrosive acids in the current international system—and the attendant competition, rivalry, insecurity, fear and fighting they can produce.[52]

A related notion is that, because the powers of the cosmopolitan federation would not be enormous, and in fact would leave a considerable role for the state and sub-state levels of government, this would leave some large measure of space for value pluralism as well as national and regional differentiation. Above and beyond the core, bedrock cosmopolitan principles of international law and order and human rights for all, national communities would be free to shape their characters, policies and destinies free from coercive interference from the rest of the global community.[53]

Speaking of freedom, perhaps it should be noted how this

cosmopolitan federation would contribute to that most Kantian of values: first, it would contribute by helping to secure our freedom from devastating wars and violence, and the continuing insecurities of the international arena; second, it would help to free peoples currently trapped in oppressive and unjust states by putting serious pressure on the sustainability of such regimes; and finally, by constituting a further and final level of governance, it would add another layer of checks and balances onto existing structures and thus only strengthen what Kant saw as being a prime component of political freedom: the effective constraining, and checking and balancing, at multiple points, of the exercise of political power.

Human rights, the core of the posited federation, not only seem to be the most defensible and potent of basic moral and political norms in the contemporary world, they also seem to make the best candidate by far in terms of securing actual cross-cultural agreement on their normative adequacy. They stand the best chance of actually becoming what Pogge has called those "non-negotiable shared moral values" on which international institutions ought to be grounded. Indeed, one might be inclined to claim that it is precisely *because* of their overwhelming normative importance to the kinds of creatures we are that human rights have, in fact, become the object of such widespread concurrence.[54]

In summary, there are good reasons to believe that the long-term structural reforms advocated here in this section could go a long way towards reducing the incidence and destructiveness of war, which must be the logical end and ultimate aim of any complete and forward-looking just war theory. The economic reforms dealing with the transfer of resources would greatly reduce the launching of war out of economic desperation or resentment. They would provide hitherto poorer nations with the resources with which to fulfil their citizens' human rights claims. The constraints placed upon the state by the overarching cosmopolitan federation would also make the conquest of other states seem much less palatable, given the dispersion of power, authority and resources. The federation, being enforced by actual, effective coercive powers (notably through membership/recognition, taxation and military force) would greatly reduce the strains that come with thinking in terms of self-help and the likelihood that war will result from such thinking. By having an enforced and still developing international law, states would be more inclined to submit their competing claims to adjudication and not to the force of arms. Finally, by helping all levels of government fulfil their collective function of providing us with law and order and the objects of our human rights, a reconstituted global order would be much more peaceful, in that the realizing of human rights—i.e., the meeting of vital needs, the living of minimally good lives—would provide us with one less powerful reason for resorting to means and methods as brutal as those of war.

Perhaps it needs to be stressed that this conception is offered as a necessarily schematic and utterly normative—indeed, speculative—conception of cosmopolitan federation. No pretence is made of knowing how exactly we might move from here to there. But the important thing to note is that the overall picture seems not implausible, and certainly defensible from a Kantian point of view of morality and justice. This is quite a separate issue from whether or not we will, in fact, be able to live up to these prescriptions, despite their appeal. I myself have grave doubts about this: there is no historical reason, for example, to believe that we will improve ourselves considerably with regard to such critically important matters. In the absence of a truly revolutionary shift in moral consciousness and political will, or in the absence of some catastrophic series of events which materially endanger us all, it seems far more likely that we shall continue to do as we have always done, and that is to continue in the sombre cycle of alternating rounds of progress, hope and reform, on the one hand, and then, on the other, suspicion, distrust, indignity and ultimately struggle and death.

But such melancholy speculations do not in any way detract from the moral, legal and political cogency of the claims that have been advanced in this chapter. All we need to be convinced of, in this regard, is the moral compellingness of the cause and the non-impossibility of its ever coming to pass. It is clear that, however difficult and unlikely it seems, the founding of a cosmopolitan federation based on human rights—the realization of a more secure, safe and just world—is not demonstrably impossible. It is not beyond the grasp of creatures such as us. And so our reason to work towards it remains firm and unyielding.

Conclusion

This chapter sought to complete the set of contemporary Kantian just war rules by constructing a comprehensive and defensible theory of what the war termination process should be. The inquiry opened by diagnosing the many deficiencies of the status quo with regard to war termination. The account then sought to fashion a more satisfactory set of *jus post bellum* norms to regulate state conduct during the immediate aftermath of a particular war, JPB 1-5. These norms were then applied to a recent, real-world case—that of the Persian Gulf War—as a demonstration of their usefulness and cogency. The theory proceeded to shift its attention from short-term principles, regulating the endings of particular wars, to longer-term institutional reforms required to transform the international system itself into one in which the incidence and destructiveness of war, with all the attending war termination problems, are reliably and realistically reduced. It was contended that some kind of cosmopolitan federation may well represent our best and most effective chance in this regard, as we continue on our fitful journey towards a more peaceful and humane world order.

Notes

1. I owe this emphasis, and the term, to Thomas Pogge. Perhaps it should be stressed how it is not as though members of the Just War Tradition who preceded Kant were utterly ignorant of this phenomenon. But, in terms of emphasis, no one conceived the issue separately, and rigorously, until Kant. See chapter 2 for more.
2. Proposition KI 10, one of the ten principles of contemporary Kantian internationalism, outlined at the end of chapter 3, requires attention to processes of war termination.
3. A process which arguably, indeed, continues to this day.
4. This follows Kant's own distinction, described in chapter 2, between short-term and long-term *jus post bellum*.
5. These articles can be gleaned from many sources, including W. Reisman and C. Antoniou, eds., *The Laws of War: A Comprehensive Collection of Primary Documents on International Laws Governing Armed Conflict* (New York: Vintage, 1994), 130-33.
6. It might be suggested that, while there have been no new positive laws regulating war termination, there have been other recent developments in international law that can be interpreted in such a way as to apply to war

termination. The passage of the various international human rights declarations and conventions might be offered as examples. This suggestion seems compelling; it is consistent with what will follow. But it does not detract from the cogency of the present claim. For the suggestion is like saying that the March 1999 passing into law of the International Convention Banning Land Mines is legally superfluous, in light of the previous passage of the various human rights covenants and the Geneva Conventions. But there is great merit—especially in terms of legal clarity and political momentum—to getting states to consent formally to explicit and positive principles regulating their own conduct. We have such content and positivity for the beginnings of wars and for conduct during wars, but not for war termination, except for the rather empty proclamations of Hague IV.

7. Reisman and Antoniou, eds., *Laws*, 8.

8. Convention II, Article 6, of the Convention on Prohibitions or Restrictions on the Use of Certain Conventional Weapons Which May Be Deemed to Be Excessively Injurious or to Have Indiscriminate Effects. This Convention was ratified in 1980. From Reisman and Antoniou, eds., *Laws*, 53.

9. See Reisman and Antoniou, eds., *Laws*, 150-230.

10. And the 1998-99 outbreak of violence in the nearby province of Kosovo is cogent evidence of this claim.

11. The four criteria a state must meet if it is to count as a minimally just state entitled to the full panoply of state rights, SRs 1-9. The four criteria are: the state can rule its people effectively; it is doing a reasonable job, on the domestic front, ensuring human rights satisfaction for its citizens; it can protect its citizens from outside attack; and it obeys basic rules of international law, notably non-aggression and non-interference. For more on SRs 1-9, refer back to chapter 4.

12. When it looks as though a just state is about to lose a war to an aggressor, the core recommendation to the just state, as Frances Kamm points out, is essentially to try and cut its losses, both prudential and moral. A just and rational state will, where possible (an important qualification), attempt to spare its people from the full wrath of the aggressor nation by offering it enough to satisfy its unjust desires and make it desist from its criminal activity. But, obviously, if the aggressor desires something like the annihilation of the people of the just state, followed by the conquest and takeover of its territory, then the recommendation would be to fight on, clearly while imploring the international community to intervene on its behalf and turn the tide against the aggressor. Indeed, it might be argued that a just state on the verge of such a defeat to an aggressor has a *fully fledged right to claim* such international intervention. On this issue of a just state losing to an aggressor, see F.M. Kamm, "Making War (and Its Cousins) Unjustified" (forthcoming paper). The issue also arises, in a purely prudential context, in E. Kecskemeti, *Strategic Surrender: The Politics of Victory and Defeat* (Stanford, CA: Stanford University Press, 1964).

In my view, a just state, losing a just war against an aggressor country, should, while seeking to end the war, be animated by the following principles:

1. Just cause for seeking termination. A state has just cause to seek termination of a war it is losing to an aggressor regime if it can foresee that continuing the war shall result in even greater losses for its people. Essentially, a state has just cause to terminate a losing war in order to cut its losses.

2. Right intention. A state losing a just war against an aggressor should seek peace only with the intention of cutting its losses and protecting its citizens from further, grievous harm.

3. Public declaration and proper authority. The terms of the peace the just state is seeking from the aggressor must be publicly proclaimed by a legitimate authority, defined as that highest level of government, representative of the entire state, which fulfils the criteria of a minimally just state, MJ 1-4.

4. No precipitate surrender. A just state, seeking to terminate its losing war against an aggressor regime, must take care not to surrender too readily, owing to the serious and unfortunate consequences of surrendering to an unjust, aggressor regime. The just state must take reasonable steps to ensure that suing for peace is the last and most reasonable resort for its people.

5. Probability of success. A just state suing for peace against an aggressor should have reasonable grounds to believe that the preferred terms may succeed not only in securing the aggressor's agreement but also in protecting the fundamental interests and rights of its citizens.

6. Proportionality. The terms of the peace—the sacrifices that the just state makes in order to placate the aggressor—must be in some sense proportional to a defensible scale of values. In particular, a just state may never permissibly trade off its capacity to fulfil the MJ 1-4 criteria of minimal justice in exchange for peace. Should the aggressor state insist on just such concessions, a just state should fight on and claim its due in armed assistance from third party vindicators of its rights. This last issue points out the need for more broad solutions to the problem of war termination, such as the cosmopolitan federation proposed later on in this chapter.

13. I. Kant, *The Metaphysics of Morals, Part I: The Doctrine of Right,* in H. Reiss, ed., *Kant: Political Writings* trans. H. Nisbet (Cambridge: Cambridge University Press, 1995), 169-71.

14. M. Walzer, *Just and Unjust Wars* (New York: Basic Books, 1977), 119.

15. Kamm, "Making."

16. See chapter 4 for more on these rights. They include political sovereignty and territorial integrity.

17. Walzer, *Wars,* 110 and 123.

18. This line of reasoning has sparked some resistance from those who view favourably the Allied insistence on unconditional surrender during the closing days of World War II. But we need to distinguish between rhetoric and reality here. The policy of unconditional surrender followed by the Allies at the end of World War II was not truly unconditional; there was never any

insistence on the Allies being able to do whatever they wanted with the Axis powers and their people. There was a clear, albeit general, vision of rehabilitation that the Allies had in mind and that was commonly understood at the time. At the very most, the policy that the Allies pursued was genuinely unconditional only vis-à-vis the governing regimes of the Axis powers—but not vis-à-vis the civilian populations in those nations. Such a more discriminating policy on surrender may be defensible in extreme cases, involving abhorrent regimes, but is generally impermissible. For insistence on unconditional surrender is disproportionate and will reliably prolong fighting as the defeated aggressor refuses to cave in, fearing the consequences of doing so. The prevention of needless and gratuitous killing and suffering is one thing that just war theory prides itself on. Presumably this holds true for the corpus of international law as well. It is thus the undeniable responsibility of the victor to communicate clearly to the losing aggressor its intentions for postwar settlement—intentions which must be consistent with those principles enumerated below in this section.

19. Walzer, *Wars,* 109-24.
20. Walzer, *Wars,* 109-24.
21. This image of just war as radical surgery and just settlement as the subsequent therapy came to mind while reading N. Oren, "Prudence in Victory," in N. Oren, ed., *Termination of War: Processes, Procedures and Aftermaths* (Jerusalem: Hebrew University Press, 1982): 147-64.
22. Another way this requirement could be fulfilled would be for the victors to provide reliable security guarantees to the people of Aggressor.
23. Walzer, *Wars,* 109-24.
24. For a relevant empirical/historical account of these and other war-endings and reconstructions, see A.J.P. Taylor, How Wars End (London: Hamilton, 1985).
25. Walzer, Wars, 288.
26. How does proportionality affect the principle of trying the political leaders in Aggressor? The answer is that, sometimes, such leaders, in spite of their moral decrepitude, retain considerable popular legitimacy in Aggressor and that bringing them to trial could seriously destabilize and/or rupture the polity within Aggressor. The international community has recently faced this situation: 1) in Somalia in 1992-93, when an attempt was made to arrest Mohammed Farah Aidid for war crimes—with the result being a serious escalation in the conflict, which ultimately led to the withdrawal of international forces; and 2) in Bosnia in 1994-95, when charges against Bosnian Serb leaders Ratko Mladic and Radovan Karadzic seriously increased tensions and delayed the onset of a not unreasonable peace agreement. Obviously, care needs to be taken, as always, that appeal to proportionality does not amount to rewarding aggressors, or to letting them run free and unscathed despite their grievous crimes. And yet this care does not vitiate the need to consider the destruction and suffering that may result from adhering totally to what the requirements of justice as retribution demand. One interesting and not

unprincipled compromise position, with regard to Bosnia, has been not to move directly into Bosnian Serb lands to arrest Mladic and Karadzic (due to the serious instability and conflict that would probably produce) but, rather, to pen the two of them into their narrow territory for the rest of their lives, by stipulating that, should they ever cross an international border, they will immediately be arrested and brought to The Hague for war crimes trials. For brief summaries of both of these conflicts, and for more detailed sources about them, see Regan, *Cases*, 172-212.

27. For more on (positive international law regarding) war crimes trials, especially those at Nuremberg, see Reisman and Antoniou, eds., *Laws*, 317-405. Also relevant is the citation of the Nuremberg decision at 102-14 in R. Wasserstrom, ed., *War and Morality* (Belmont, CA: Wadsworth, 1970); and S.L. Paulson, "Classical Legal Positivism at Nuremberg," *Philosophy and Public Affairs* (174/75): 132-58. All these sources contain references to further sources as well. A related moral account of *jus ad bellum* war crimes trials can be found at Walzer, *Wars*, 287-303.

28. Walzer, *Wars*, 304-28; and P. Christopher, *The Ethics of War and Peace* (Englewood Cliffs, NJ: Prentice Hall, 1994), 139-64. See also G. Lewy, "Superior Orders, Nuclear Warfare and the Dictates of Conscience" in R. Wasserstrom, ed. *War and Morality* (Belmont, CA: Wadsworth, 1970), 115-34; R. Wasserstrom, "The Relevance of Nuremberg," *Philosophy and Public Affairs* (1971/72): 22-46; S. Levinson, "Responsibility for Crimes of War," *Philosophy and Public Affairs* (1972-73): 244-73; and D.A. Peppers, "War Crimes and Induction: A Case for Selective Nonconscientious Objection," *Philosophy and Public Affairs* (1973-74): 129-66.

29. As will be discussed in greater detail below in the section on long-term *jus post bellum,* the members of the international community on July 17, 1998, voted in favour of a treaty, at Rome, establishing such a permanent court at The Hague. The treaty requires the ratification of sixty countries, though, before the court will be legitimate and functioning.

30. Indeed, the lengthy termination process arguably continues to this day, at least eight years after the end of the war.

31. M. Walzer, "Justice and Injustice in the Gulf War," in D. Decosse, ed., *But Was It Just? Reflections on the morality of the Persian Gulf War* (New York: Doubleday, 1992), 10.

32. Some were scandalized that Clinton ordered the operation on the night before the first scheduled vote on his impeachment in the U.S. House of Representatives. Others noted the unhappy title of the operation, since "Desert Fox" was Nazi General Erwin Rommel's nickname during World War II.

33. Perhaps this interminable problem is indicative of some flaws in the peace agreement, to be discussed in greater detail below. Of particular concern is the continuance of the sanctions on Iraq and the inability to complete the program of weapons inspections, which has drawn out far beyond anyone's estimate. The fact that the U.S. seems now to have linked the two (such that

the sanctions will only be lifted after the weapons inspections are done) may make the termination phase drag on indefinitely.

34. Information for this section on the Persian Gulf War has been drawn from the following sources: Regan, *Cases,* supra n. 23, 172-79; L. Freedman and E. Karsh, *The Gulf Conflict: Diplomacy and War in the New World Order* (London: Farber and Farber, 1991); W. Danspeckgruber and C. Tripp, eds., *The Iraqi Aggression Against Kuwait* (Boulder, CO: Westview, 1996); U.S. News and World Report, *Triumph without Victory* (New York: Random House, 1992); James Turner Johnson and G. Weigel, eds., *Just War and Gulf War* (Washington, DC: University Press of America, 1991); and A. Beyer and B. Green, eds. *Lines in the Sand: Justice and the Gulf War* (Louisville, KY: John Knox, 1992). I also deal with these issues in my "Jus Post Bellum," forthcoming (summer 2000) in *The Journal of Social Philosophy.*

35. Kant, *Right,* 174,

36. This reform was outlined in chapter 4.

37. And it needs to be conceded that, at the time of writing, not all the details on the nature of the world court and how it will operate have been decided. There is thus some room for principled disagreement as to its exact functioning and powers. Those American court critics who focus their opposition on these structural issues are thus on more solid ground than their nationalist colleagues.

38. One fascinating aspect of the history of ideas concerns the concurrence of both Bentham and Kant on this point. It is both curious and arguably important that the two foremost exponents of such opposed moral, political and jurisprudential doctrines as classical utilitarianism and Kantian deontology should, of all things, agree on the wisdom of constructing some kind of cosmopolitan federation. It would make for an interesting study.

39. In chapters 1 and 2.

40. Kant, *Perpetual Peace,* in H. Reiss, ed., Kant: Political Writings, trans. H. Nisbit (Cambridge: Cambridge University Press, 1970): 104-105.

41. Kant, *Right,* 174-75.

42. Weak descriptive realism was described in detail in chapter 5.

43. T. Pogge, "Cosmopolitanism and Sovereignty," *Ethics* (1992): 64-65.

44. This suggestion can also be found in F. Teson, "The Kantian Theory of International Law," *Columbia Law Review* (1992): 100; A. Beyefsky, "Making the Human Rights Treaties Work," in L. Henkin and J.L. Hargrove, eds., *Human Rights: An Agenda for the Next Century* (Washington, DC: The American Society of International Law, 1994): 229-96; and C. Beitz, "Nonintervention and Communal Integrity," 385-391, D. Luban, "The Romance of the Nation-State," 392-97 and G. Doppelt, "Statism without Foundations," 398-403, all three in *Philosophy and Public Affairs* (1979-80).

45. See also G. Clark and L. Sohn, *World Peace Through World Law* (Cambridge, MA: Harvard University Press, 1966) and, in what is arguably the most wide-ranging and detailed program for eliminating war as such since Kant himself,

R.J. Glossop, *Confronting War: An Examination of Humanity's Most Pressing Problem* (London: McFarland, 3rd ed., 1994).

46. See also R.B. Bilder, "Possibilities for Development of New International Judicial Mechanisms," 317-46; M.C. Bassiouni, "Enforcing Human Rights through International Criminal Law and through an International Criminal Tribunal," 347-82; and D.F. Orentlicher, "Addressing Gross Human Rights Abuses: Punishment and Victim Compensation," 425-76, all in L. Henkin and J.L. Hargrove, eds., *Human Rights: An Agenda for the Next Century* (Washington, DC: The American Society of International Law, 1994).

47. Glossop, *Confronting,* passim; and T. Buergenthal and H.G. Maier, *Public International Law* (St. Paul, MN: West, 1990), passim.

48. It would also assist greatly the serious and sad problem of what to do when just states are about to lose wars to aggressors, which was mentioned above. See also Pogge, "Cosmopolitanism," 61-62.

49. See also Pogge, *Rawls,* 240-80; T. Pogge, "Creating Supra-National Institutions Democratically," *Journal of Political Philosophy* (1997): 163-82; D. Archibrigi and D. Helds, eds., *Cosmopolitan Democracy* (Cambridge, MA: Polity Press, 1995); D. Held, *Democracy and The Global Order: From the Modern State to Cosmopolitan Governance* (Stanford, CA: Stanford University Press, 1995); R.J. Glossop, *World Federation? A Critical Analysis of Federal World Government* (London: McFarland, 1993); E. Haas, *Beyond the Nation-State: Functionalism and International Organization* (Stanford, CA: Stanford University Press, 1964); and H. Newcombe, *Design for a Better World* (Lanham, MD: University Press of America, 1983). Some publications of the UN are also relevant, especially recent editions of the annual *Human Development Report* (particularly 1994), along with B. Boutros-Ghali, *An Agenda for Peace* (New York: UN, 1992).

50. Pogge, "Cosmopolitanism," 48-75 and *Rawls,* 240-80.

51. M. Walzer, "The Reform of the International System," in O. Osterud, ed., *Studies of War and Peace* (Oslo, Norway: Norwegian University Press, 1986), 227-50; Rawls, "Law," 41-82, but especially 73-74 and also endnotes 35 and 52 on pp. 227-29; and Shue, *Rights,* 173-80 in the new Afterword.

52. See Pogge, Rawls, 211-80 and T. Pogge, "Moral Progress," in S. Luper-Foy, ed., *Problems of International Justice* (Boulder, CO: Westview, 1988), 283-304.

53. This point is stressed by Rawls, in "Law," 41-82.

54. It should be reiterated here that nearly every nation-state in the world today is party to the UN, via ratification of its Charter. It is very important to note that in the Charter (Articles 1-6) it says that becoming a member of the UN implies a commitment to adhering to its core norms, notably international peace and security and the fulfilment of human rights. So there is a powerful argument that, whether or not they see themselves as doing so, all state parties to the UN have *committed themselves* legally to the fulfilment of human rights. Furthermore, a great number of state parties have individually ratified the particular human rights conventions, such as those listed in *Twenty-Five Human Rights Documents* (New York: Columbia University

Center for the Study of Human Rights, 1995). No other moral norm or concept has even come remotely close to the success and promise that the idea of human rights enjoys as the prime candidate for the basis of a truly global conception of law and justice. It is, accordingly, on this conceptual and moral site that we must develop the ideas and policies required to make this unstable, sub-optimal and occasionally wretched world a morally more adequate place. I deal with these, and related, issues in my "Terminating War and Establishing Global Governance," *Canadian Journal of Law and Jurisprudence.* (July 1999), 253-95.

Conclusion

Conclusion

This book has been devoted to demonstrating two complementary propositions. The first is that Immanuel Kant himself, contrary to most interpretations, developed a plausible and principled just war theory that broke important new ground. The second is that Kant's theory can be used as the foundation for a contemporary Kantian account that contributes substantially to the ethics of war and peace. The Kantian tradition has something original and significant to add to the Just War Tradition, and to the international laws of armed conflict which have been derived from it. This contribution includes the following elements:

1. A well-grounded conception of human rights and the need to protect those who have such rights;
2. A compelling vision of the ideals of international law in general;
3. A much more refined and sustained confrontation with realism and pacifism, the two main rivals to just war theory;
4. A deeper understanding of the nature of aggression and the grounds of self- and other-defence, through principle NP;
5. Several refinements of standard just war principles, such as right intention, proper authority, probability of success; and proportionality; and, above all,
6. The new and increasingly important category of *jus post bellum,* over both the short- and long-term.

Contemporary Kantian internationalism offers the following norms of just war theory as a reasonable, unified and comprehensive view of the ethics of war and peace. These general rules, which ought to guide state conduct as a matter of international law, mark the culmination of contemporary Kantian just war theory:

Jus ad bellum (The justice of the resort to war.)

JAB 1. Just cause. A state may resort to armed force against another state if and only if it is required to vindicate universal principles of justice. These principles include human rights and those state rights and duties (SRs 1-9 and SDs 1-9) that are compatible with, and/or necessary for, their realization. The key principle here is the defence and vindication of fundamental rights, and the protection of those who have them from serious harm. From these general considerations, three just causes, in particular, can be deduced: 1) self-defence from aggression; 2) the defence of others from aggression; and 3) armed intervention in a non-aggressive country wherein grievous human rights violations are occurring.

JAB 2. Right intention. There are two relevant aspects of the right intention criterion, from a Kantian point of view:

1) A state resorting to war must do so only for the sake of vindicating those rights whose violation grounds its just cause in fighting. A state may not employ the cloak of a just cause to prosecute a war for the sake of ethnic hatred or national glory, for example. The vindication of SRs 1-9 and SDs 1-9, and human rights in general, remains the sole just cause grounding resort to warfare.

2) A state resorting to war must, in advance, commit itself to upholding, to the best of its ability, the norms of *jus in bello* and *jus post bellum.*

JAB 3. Proper authority, public declaration and domestic rights-protection during war. War must be declared, in the appropriate public fashion, by the legitimate political authority within the state in question. This authority is that national level of government which fulfils the MJ 1-4 criteria of minimal justice. Commitment must also be made to preserving domestic human rights satisfaction in the midst of war.

JAB 4. No precipitate resort to force. Some reasonable attempt at peaceful conflict resolution must be tried and exhausted prior to resorting to war.

JAB 5. Probability of success. A state may not resort to war if it can foresee that doing so will have no measurable impact upon the situation. While there is a presumption in favour of permitting an armed response to aggression, states owe it to their own citizens to consider soberly the probability of success in doing so.

JAB 6. (Macro-) proportionality. A state must, prior to initiating a war, weigh the expected universal good to accrue from its prosecuting the (otherwise just) war against the universal evils expected to result. Only if the benefits, such as rights vindication, seem reasonably proportional to the costs, such as casualties, may the war action proceed.

Jus in bello (The justice of conduct within war.)

JIB 1. Discrimination and non-combatant immunity. Belligerents shall at all times distinguish between the civilian population and combatants, and between civilian objects and military objectives, and accordingly shall direct their operations only against military objectives, subject to the Doctrine of Double Effect.

JIB 2. (Micro-) proportionality. States and their military systems are, when in the midst of war, to weigh the expected universal goods of each significant military tactic employed within the war against its reasonably expected universal evils. Only if the benefits of the proposed tactic seem reasonably proportional to the costs may a state and its armed forces employ it.

JIB 3. No intrinsically heinous means may be employed. Such include: the use of indiscriminate force (especially the use of weapons of mass destruction); the deliberate targeting of civilians; the use of mass rape campaigns; and treating captured soldiers in a manner that violates the Hague and Geneva Conventions.

Jus post bellum (The justice of the termination phase of war.)

JPB 1. Just cause for termination. A state has just cause to seek termination of the just war in question if there has been a reasonable vindication of those rights whose violation grounded the resort to war in the first place. Not only have most, if not all, unjust gains from aggression been eliminated and the objects of the victim's rights been reasonably restored, but the aggressor is now willing to accept terms of surrender that include not only the cessation of hostilities and its renouncing the gains of aggression but also its submission to reasonable principles of punishment, including compensation, *jus ad bellum* and *jus in bello* war crimes trials, and perhaps rehabilitation.

JPB 2. Right intention. A state must intend to carry out the process of war termination only in terms of those principles contained in the other *jus post bellum* rules. Revenge is strictly ruled out as an animating force. Furthermore, the just state in question must commit itself to symmetry and equal application with regard to the investigation and prosecution of any *jus in bello* war crimes.

JPB 3. Public declaration and legitimate authority. The terms of the peace must be publicly proclaimed by a legitimate authority.

JPB 4. Discrimination. In setting the terms of the peace, the just and victorious state is to differentiate between the political and military leaders, the soldiers and the civilian population within the aggressor regime. Undue and unfair hardship is not to be brought upon the civilian population in particular: punitive measures are to be focused upon those elites most responsible for the aggression.

JPB 5. Proportionality. Any terms of peace must be proportional to the end of reasonable rights vindication. Absolutist crusades against, and/or draconian punishments for, aggression are especially to be avoided. The people of the defeated aggressor regime never forfeit their human rights and so are entitled not to be blotted out from the community of nations. There is thus no such thing as an unconditional surrender.

How are such norms of just war theory "Kantian"? They are Kantian, first, by being direct and recognizable outgrowths of Kant's own just war theory, which was summarized in chapter 2 in propositions KJWT 1-10. They are Kantian, secondly, by being situated within a contemporary Kantian conception of international justice in general, as distinguished by the principles KI 1-10 laid out in chapter 3. Most generally, they are Kantian in being based on the norm of human rights protection and the preservation and enhancement of each and every rational agent. They establish a firm and comprehensive set of universal rules, or side-constraints, designed to secure respect for rational agency and to prevent people from suffering serious harm as beings capable of living their own lives. They are norms constructed, above all, to constrain war, to limit it to very narrow, rights-vindicating purposes and, in so doing, to establish a framework within which a more enduring solution to the problem might be found.

It was noted how the core function of such Kantian norms is to protect human rights as best they can be protected during war. They are to guide just, rights-respecting states with regard to how they ought to act before, during and after a war and, as such, ought to guide our evaluation of the current international laws of war. Some needed reforms were suggested in this regard, especially concerning processes of war termination. Admission was made, however, that such a set of comprehensive wartime principles cannot be the resting point of any relevant and forward-looking just war theory. For such an account will note that war, even in its just forms, is becoming increasingly destructive in our era. Furthermore, as rational agents possessing inherently dignified status, it is ultimately beneath our nature to have to fight for our rights. Just war theory, in essence, tries to make the best, morally, out of a precarious and undesirable situation. Thus, the logical conclusion of Kantian just war theory must be an account of how to structure our international conduct and institutions over the long term so that resort to war is increasingly diminished. Some kind of cosmopolitan federation may well represent our best chance in this regard.

Finally, we should note that this work opened with two quotes. One was from Kant, the other from Rousseau—but both offered a ringing endorsement of the value of human freedom. In terms relevant to the problem of war, this principle stipulates that we need to be *free from* political violence, with all its indignities and sufferings, and we need to be *free to* live our own lives, in a minimally just and peaceful fashion, as we best see fit. The most central role of contemporary Kantian just war theory is to contribute to that task by seriously constraining political violence between states—in terms of its beginning, middle and end—until that day, too far afield to yet glimpse, when we shall have managed to deliver ourselves from the dangerous extremities of war to the secure comforts of a rights-respecting peace.

Bibliography

Bibliography

Anscombe, G.E.M. "War and Murder." In *War and Morality,* edited by R. Wasserstrom, 41-53. Belmont, CA: Wadsworth, 1970.

Archibrigi, D. and D. Held, editors. *Cosmopolitan Democracy.* Cambridge, MA: Polity Press, 1995.

Arendt, H. *Lectures on Kant's Political Philosophy.* Chicago: University of Chicago Press, 1982.

————. *On Violence.* New York: Harcourt Brace Jovanovich, 1970.

Atkinson, R.F. "Kant's Moral and Political Rigorism." In *Essays on Kant's Political Philosophy,* edited by H. Williams, 228-48. Cardiff: University of Wales Press, 1992.

Aune, B. *Kant's Theory of Morals.* Princeton, NJ: Princeton University Press, 1979.

Axinn, S. *A Moral Military.* Philadelphia, PA: Temple University Press, 1989.

Bailey, S. *Prohibitions and Restraints in War.* Oxford: Oxford University Press, 1972.

Baron, M. *Kantian Ethics Almost Without Apology.* Ithaca, NY: Cornell University Press, 1995.

Barry, J. *The Sword of Justice: Ethics and Coercion in International Politics.* London: Praeger, 1998.

Baynes, K. *The Normative Grounds of Social Criticism: Kant, Rawls and Habermas.* Albany, NY: SUNY Press, 1992.

Beck, L.W. "Kant's Two Conceptions of The Will in Their Political Context." In *Kant and Political Philosophy: The Contemporary Legacy,* edited by R. Beiner and W. Booth, 38-49. New Haven, CT: Yale University Press, 1993.

Beiner, R. and W. Booth, editors. *Kant and Political Philosophy: The Contemporary Legacy.* New Haven, CT: Yale University Press, 1993.

Beitz, C. *Political Theory and International Relations.* Princeton, NJ: Princeton University Press, 1979.

————."Cosmopolitan Ideals and National Sentiment." *The Journal of Philosophy* (1983): 591-600.

————. "Nonintervention and Communal Integrity." *Philosophy and Public Affairs* (1979/80): 385-91.

Beitz, C., et al., editors. *International Ethics*. Princeton, NJ: Princeton University Press, 1985.

Benson, P. "External Freedom According to Kant." *Columbia Law Review* (1987): 559-79.

Best, G. *Humanity in Warfare*. New York: Columbia University Press, 1980.

————. *War and Law since 1945*. Oxford: Clarendon, 1994.

Booth, W.J. "The Limits of Autonomy: Karl Marx's Kant Critique." In *Kant and Political Philosophy: The Contemporary Legacy,* edited by R. Beiner and W. Booth, 245-75. New Haven, CT: Yale University Press, 1993.

Bourke, J. "Kant's Doctrine of Perpetual Peace." *Philosophy* (1942): 324-33.

Boutros-Ghali, B. *An Agenda for Peace*. New York: United Nations, 1992.

Boyle, J. "Just War Thinking in Catholic Natural Law." In *The Ethics of War and Peace: Religious and Secular Perspectives,* edited by T. Nardin, 40-53. Princeton, NJ: Princeton University Press, 1996.

————. "Natural Law and International Ethics." In *Traditions of International Ethics,* edited by T. Nardin and D. Mapel, 112-35. Cambridge: Cambridge University Press, 1992.

Brady, J. and N. Garver, editors. *Justice, Law and Violence*. Philadelphia, PA: Temple University Press, 1991.

Brandt, R.B. "Utilitarianism and the Rules of War." *Philosophy and Public Affairs* (1971/72): 145-65.

Brierly, J.L. *The Law of Nations*. New York: Waldock, 6th ed., 1963.

Brilmayer, L. Justifying International Acts. Ithaca, NY: Cornell University Press, 1989.

Brown, M., et al., editors. *Debating the Democratic Peace*. Cambridge, MA: MIT Press, 1996.

Brown, P. and H. Shue, editors. *Boundaries: National Autonomy and Its Limits*. Totowa, NJ: Rowman Littlefield, 1981.

Brownlie, I. *International Law and The Use of Force by States*. Oxford: Clarendon Press, 1963.

————. *System of The Law of Nations*. Oxford: Oxford University Press, 1983.

Bull, H. *The Anarchical Society: A Study of Order in World Politics*. New York: Columbia University Press, 1977.

Buergenthal, T. and H. Maier. *Public International Law*. St. Paul, MN: West Press, 1990.

Burns, J.P. *War and Its Discontents: Pacifism and Quietism in The Abrahamic Traditions.* Washington, DC: Georgetown University Press, 1996.

Byrd, S. "The State as a 'Moral Person'." In *Proceedings of The Eighth International Kant Congress,* edited by H. Robinson, 171-90. Milwaukee, WI: Marquette University Press, 1995.

Cady, D. *From Warism to Pacifism: A Moral Continuum.* Philadelphia, PA: Temple University Press, 1989.

Cady, D. and R. Werner, editors. *Just War, Nonviolence and Nuclear Deterrence.* Wakefield, NH: Longwood Academic, 1991.

Cahill, L.S. *Love Your Enemies: Discipleship, Pacifism and Just War Theory.* Minneapolis, MN: Fortress, 1994.

Campbell, D. and M. Dillon, editors. *The Political Subject of Violence.* Manchester: Manchester University Press, 1993.

Carson, T. "Perpetual Peace: What Kant Should Have Said." *Social Theory and Practice* (1988): 173-214.

Cartwright, M.C. "Conflicting Interpretations of Christian Pacifism." In *The Ethics of War and Peace: Religious and Secular Perspectives,* edited by T. Nardin, 197-213. Princeton, NJ: Princeton University Press, 1996.

Cavallar, G. "Kant's Society of Nations: Free Federation or World Republic?." *Journal of the History of Philosophy* (1994): 461-82.

—————. *Pax Kantiana: Systematisch-Historische Untersuchung des Entwurfs "Zum ewigen Frieden" (1975) von Immanuel Kant.* Vienna: Boehlau Verlag, 1992.

Ceadel, M. *Thinking about Peace and War.* Oxford: Oxford University Press, 1987.

Chanteur, J. *From War to Peace,* translated by S. Weisz. Boulder, CO: Westview, 1992.

Childress, J. "Just-War Theories." *Theological Studies* (1978): 427-45.

Christopher, P. *The Ethics of War and Peace: An Introduction to Legal and Moral Issues.* Englewood Cliffs, NJ: Prentice Hall, 1994.

Cimbala, S. and K. Dunn, editors. *Conflict Termination and Military Strategy: Coercion, Persuasion and War.* Boulder, CO: Westview, 1987.

Clark, G. and L. Sohn. *World Peace Through World Law.* Cambridge, MA: Harvard University Press, 1966.

Clausewitz, Carl von. *On War.* Translated by A. Rapoport. Harmondsworth, UK: Penguin, 1995.

Coates, A.J. *The Ethics of War.* Manchester, UK: University of Manchester Press, 1997.

Cochran, D.C. "War-Pacifism." *Social Theory and Practice* (1996): 162-80.

Cohen, M. "Moral Skepticism and International Relations." In *International Ethics,* edited by C. Beitz, et al., 3-50. Princeton, NJ: Princeton University Press, 1985.

Cranston, M. *What Are Human Rights?* New York: Basic Books, 1973.

Cummiskey, D. *Kantian Consequentialism.* New York: Oxford University Press, 1996.

Damrosch, L. "The Collective Enforcement of International Norms Through Economic Sanctions." *Ethics and International Affairs* (1994): 60-80.

Damrosch, L., editor. *Enforcing Restraint: Collective Intervention in Internal Conflicts.* New York: Council on Foreign Relations, 1993.

Davis, G. *Warcraft and the Fragility of Virtue.* Lincoln, NE: University of Nebraska Press, 1992.

Davis, G.S. *Religion and Justice in the War over Bosnia.* New York: Routledge, 1996.

Detter Delupis, I. *The Law of War.* Cambridge: Cambridge University Press, 1987.

Dinstein, Y. *War, Aggression and Self-defence.* Cambridge: Cambridge University Press, 1995.

Dombrowski, D. *Christian Pacifism.* Philadelphia, PA: Temple University Press, 1991.

Donaldson, T. "Kant's Global Rationalism." In *Traditions of International Ethics,* edited by T. Nardin and D. Mapel, 136-57. Cambridge: Cambridge University Press, 1992.

Donnelly, J. *International Human Rights.* Boulder, CO: Westview, 1987.

――――――. "Twentieth Century Realism." In *Traditions of International Ethics,* edited by T. Nardin and D. Mapel, 85-111. Cambridge: Cambridge University Press, 1992.

Doppelt, G. "Statism Without Foundations." *Philosophy and Public Affairs* (1979-80): 398-403.

――――――. "Walzer's Theory of Morality in International Relations." *Philosophy and Public Affairs* (1978/79): 3-26.

Doyle, M. "Liberalism and Internationalism." In *Kant and Political Philosophy: The Contemporary Legacy,* edited by R. Beiner and W. Booth, 173-204. New Haven, CT: Yale University Press, 1993.

――――――. "Kant, Liberal Legacies and Foreign Affairs." *Philosophy and Public Affairs* (1984): 204-35 and 323-53.

Dubik, J. "Human Rights, Command Responsibility and Walzer's Just War Theory." *Philosophy and Public Affairs* (1982): 354-71.

Dworkin, R. *Taking Rights Seriously.* Cambridge, MA: Harvard University Press, 1977.

Dyer, G. *War.* New York: Crown, 1985.

Ellis, A., editor. *Ethics and International Relations.* Manchester: Manchester University Press, 1986.

Ellis, A. "Utilitarianism and International Ethics." In *Traditions of International Ethics,* edited by T. Nardin and D. Mapel, 158-79. Cambridge: Cambridge University Press, 1992.

Elshtain, J.B., editor. *Just War Theory.* Oxford: Basil Blackwell, 1992.

Elshtain, J.B., et al., editors. *But Was It Just? Reflections on the Morality of the Persian Gulf War.* New York: Doubleday, 1992.

Feinberg, J. *Rights, Justice and the Bounds of Liberty.* Princeton, NJ: Princeton University Press, 1980.

──────. *Social Philosophy.* Englewood Cliffs, NJ: Prentice Hall, 1973.

──────. "The Nature and Value of Rights." *Journal of Value Inquiry* (1970/71): 243-57.

Filice, C. "Pacifism: A Philosophical Exploration." *Journal of Philosophical Research* (1992): 119-53.

Finnis, J. "The Ethics of War and Peace in the Catholic Natural Law Tradition." In *The Ethics of War and Peace: Religious and Secular Perspectives,* edited by T. Nardin, 15-39. Princeton, NJ: Princeton University Press, 1996.

Fisher, Louis. *Presidential War Power.* Lawrence, KS: University of Kansas Press, 1995.

Fitzpatrick, J. "Protection against Abuse of the Concept of 'Emergency'." In *Human Rights: An Agenda for the Next Century,* edited by L. Henkin and J. Hargrove, 203-28. Washington, DC: American Society of International Law, 1994.

Fleischacker, S. "Kant's Theory of Punishment." In *Essays on Kant's Political Philosophy,* edited by H. Williams, 191-212. Cardiff: University of Wales Press, 1992.

Fletcher, G. "Defensive Force as an Act of Rescue." *Social Philosophy and Policy* (1990): 42-59.

──────. "Law and Morality: A Kantian Perspective." *Columbia Law Review* (1987): 533-58.

──────. "The Right to Life." *Georgia Law Review* (1979): 1380-83.

──────. "Proportionality and the Psychotic Aggressor." *Israel Law Review* (1973): 367-90.

Forde, S. "Classical Realism." In *Traditions of International Ethics,* edited by T. Nardin and D. Mapel, 62-84. Cambridge: Cambridge University Press, 1992.

Forsyth, M. "The Tradition of International Law." In *Traditions of International Ethics,* edited by T. Nardin and D. Mapel, 23-41. Cambridge: Cambridge University Press, 1992.

Forsythe, D. *Human Rights and Peace.* Lincoln, NE: University of Nebraska Press, 1993.

Franck, T. *The Power of Legitimacy among Nations.* Princeton, NJ: Princeton University Press, 1990.

Freedman, L. and E. Karsh, editors. *The Gulf Conflict* (1990-91): Diplomacy and War in the New World Order. Princeton, NJ: Princeton University Press, 1993.

Frey, R.G. and C.W. Morris, editors. *Violence, Terrorism, and Justice.* Cambridge: Cambridge University Press, 1991.

Fullinwinder, R. "War and Innocence." *Philosophy and Public Affairs* (1975): 90-97.

Gallie, W.B. *Philosophers of War and Peace.* Cambridge: Cambridge University Press, 1979.

—————. "Kant's View of Reason in Politics." *Philosophy* 54 (1979): 19-33.

Galston, W.A. "What Is Living and What Is Dead in Kant's Practical Philosophy?" In *Kant and Political Philosophy: The Contemporary Legacy,* edited by R. Beiner and W. Booth, 207-23. New Haven, CT: Yale University Press, 1993.

Geismann, G. "World Peace: Rational Idea and Reality. On the Principles of Kant's Political Philosophy." In *Kant: Analysen, Probleme, Kritik,* edited by H. Oberer, 265-319. Konisberg: Konighausen & Neumann, 1996.

Gelven, M. *War and Existence.* Philadelphia, PA: Pennsylvania State University Press, 1994.

Gewirth, A. *Human Rights: Essays on Justification and Application.* Chicago: University of Chicago Press, 1982.

Geyer, A. *Lines in The Sand: Justice and the Gulf War.* Louisville, KY: John Knox Press, 1992.

Glossop, R.J. *Confronting War: An Examination of Humanity's Most Pressing Problem.* London: McFarland, 3rd ed., 1994.

—————. *World Federation? A Critical Analysis of Federal World Government.* London: McFarland, 1993.

Gowa, J. *Ballots and Bullets: The Elusive Democratic Peace.* Princeton, NJ: Princeton University Press, 1999.

Gray, J.G. *The Warriors: Reflections of Men in Battle.* New York: Harper and Row, 1970.

Gregor, M. "Kant on 'Natural' Rights." In *Kant and Political Philosophy: The Contemporary Legacy,* edited by R. Beiner and W. Booth, 50-75. New Haven, CT: Yale University Press, 1993.

—————. "Kant on Property Rights." *Review of Metaphysics* (1988): 566-90.

Grotius, H. *The Law of War and Peace.* Translated by F.W. Kelsey. Indianapolis, IN: Bobbs-Merrill, 1962.

Guyer, P., editor. *The Cambridge Companion to Kant.* Cambridge: Cambridge University Press, 1992.

Haas, E. *Beyond The Nation-State: Functionalism and International Organization.* Stanford, CA: Stanford University Press, 1964.

Haber, J., editor. *Absolutism and Its Consequentialist Critics.* Lanham, MD: Rowman Littlefield, 1994.

Haggenmacher, P. *Grotius et la doctrine de la guerre juste.* Paris: Presses Universitaires de France, 1983.

Hallett, B., editor. *Engulfed in War: Just War and The Persian Gulf.* Honolulu: University of Hawaii Press, 1991.

Hare, R.M. "Rules of War and Moral Reasoning." *Philosophy and Public Affairs* (1971/72): 166-81.

Hart, H.L.A. "Are There Any Natural Rights?" *Philosophical Review* (1957): 54-66.

Hartman, J. "Derogation from Human Rights Treaties in Public Emergencies." *Harvard International Law Review* (1981): 1-52.

Hauerwas, S. *Should War Be Eliminated? Philosophical and Theological Investigations.* Milwaukee, WI: Marquette University Press, 1984.

Hehir, J.B. "Intervention: From Theories to Cases." *Ethics and International Affairs* 9 (1995): 1-13.

Held, D. *Democracy and the Global Order: From the Modern State to Cosmopolitan Governance.* Stanford, CA: Stanford University Press, 1995.

Held, V. "Terrorism, Rights and Political Goals." In *Justice, Law and Violence,* edited by J. Brady and N. Garver, 223-40. Philadelphia, PA: Temple University Press, 1991.

Held, V., et al., editors. *Philosophy, Morality and International Affairs.* New York: Oxford University Press, 1974.

Henkin, L. *How Nations Behave: Law and Foreign Policy.* New York: Columbia University Press, 2nd ed., 1979.

Henkin, L. and J.L. Hargrove, editors. *Human Rights: An Agenda for the Next Century.* Washington, DC: American Society of International Law, 1994.

Herman, B. "Murder and Mayhem: Violence and Kantian Casuistry." *Monist* (1989): 103-26.

Hill, Jr., T. *Dignity and Practical Reason in Kant's Moral Theory.* Ithaca, NY: Cornell University Press, 1993.

——————. "Making Exceptions Without Abandoning The Principle: Or How a Kantian Might Think about Terrorism." In *Violence, Terrorism, and Justice,* edited by R. Frey and C. Morris, 196-229. Cambridge: Cambridge University Press, 1991.

Hinsley, F.H. *Power and the Pursuit of Peace: Theory and Practice in the History of Relations between States.* Cambridge: Cambridge University Press, 1963.

Hoffe, O. "'Even a Nation of Devils Needs the State': The Dilemma of Natural Justice." In *Essays on Kant's Political Philosophy,* edited by H. Williams, 120-42. Cardiff: University of Wales Press, 1992.

——————. *Immanuel Kant.* Munich: Beck, 1983.

Hoffe, O., editor. *Grundlegung zur Metaphysik der Sitten.* Frankfurt: Vittori Klostermann, 1989.

Hoffman, S. *Duties beyond Borders.* Syracuse, NY: Syracuse University Press, 1981.

Hohfeld, W. *Fundamental Legal Conceptions as Applied to Judicial Reasoning.* New Haven, CT: Yale University Press, 1919.

Holmes, R. *On War and Morality.* Princeton, NJ: Princeton University Press, 1988.

Howard, M. *The Laws of War: Constraints on Warfare in the Western World.* New Haven, CT: Yale University Press, 1994.

Huntington, S. *The Soldier and the State.* Cambridge, MA: Harvard University Press, 1957.

Huntley, W.L. "Kant's Third Image: Systemic Sources of the Liberal Peace." *International Studies Quarterly* (1996): 45-76.

International Commission of Jurists. *States of Emergency: Their Impact on Human Rights.* New York: The International Commission of Jurists, 1983.

Johnson, J. T. *Can Modern War Be Just?* New Haven, CT: Yale University Press, 1984.

——————. *Ideology, Reason and Limitation of War: Religious and Secular Concepts, 1200-1740.* Princeton, NJ: Princeton University Press, 1981.

——————. *The Just War Tradition and the Restraint of War.* Princeton, NJ: Princeton University Press, 1981.

——————. *The Quest for Peace.* Princeton, NJ: Princeton University Press, 1987.

——————. "Towards Reconstructing the Jus ad Bellum." *Monist* (1973): 461-88.

Johnson, J.T. and G. Weigel, editors. *Just War and Gulf War.* Washington, DC: Ethics and Public Policy Center, 1991.

Jones, D. "The Declaratory Tradition in Modern International Law." In *Traditions of International Ethics,* edited by T. Nardin and D. Mapel, 42-61. Cambridge: Cambridge University Press, 1992.

Jones, P. *Rights.* New York: St. Martin's Press, 1994.

Kamm, F.M. *Morality/Mortality.* New York: Oxford University Press, 1993.

——————. "Making War (and Its Cousins) Unjustified." Forthcoming paper.

——————. "Non-Consequentialism, The Person as an End-in-Itself and The Significance of Status." *Philosophy and Public Affairs* (1991): 354-89.

——————. "Harming Some to Save Others." *Philosophical Studies* 57 (1989): 227-60.

——————. "Why Is Death Bad and Worse than Pre-natal Non-Existence?" *Pacific Philosophical Quarterly* (1988): 161-64.

——————. "Harming, Not Aiding and Positive Rights." *Philosophy and Public Affairs* (1987): 3-32.

Kane, B. *Just War and the Common Good: Jus ad Bellum Principles in 20th Century Papal Thought.* San Francisco: Catholic Scholars Press, 1997.

Kant, I. *Critique of Practical Reason,* translated by L.W. Beck. New York: Macmillan, 1993.

———— *Critique of Pure Reason,* translated by N. Kemp-Smith. New York: St. Martin's, 1963.

———— *Groundwork for the Metaphysics of Morals,* translated by J. Ellington, in *Kant's Ethical Philosophy.* Indianapolis, IN: Hackett, 1983.

———— *Perpetual Peace and Other Essays,* translated by T. Humphrey. Indianapolis, IN: Hackett, 1983.

———— *Political Writings,* edited by Hans Reiss and translated by H.B. Nisbet. Cambridge: Cambridge University Press, 1995.

———— *Religion within the Limits of Reason Alone,* translated by T. Greene and H. Hudson. New York: Harper, 1969.

———— *The Metaphysical Elements of Justice,* edited and translated by J. Ladd. New York: Bobbs Merrill, 1965.

———— *The Metaphysics of Morals,* edited and translated by Mary Gregor. Cambridge: Cambridge University Press, 1995.

Kelsay, J. *Islam and War: A Study in Comparative Ethics.* Louisville, KY: Knox, 1992.

Kelsay, J. and J.T. Johnson, editors. *Just War and Jihad.* New York: Greenwood, 1991.

Kelsen, H. *Principles of International Law.* New York: Holt, Rinehart and Winston, 1966.

Kennan, G. *Realities of American Foreign Policy.* Princeton, NJ: Princeton University Press, 1954.

Keohane, R., editor. *Neorealism and Its Critics.* New York: Columbia University Press, 1986.

Kersting, W. "Kant's Concept of the State." In *Essays on Kant's Political Philosophy,* edited by H. Williams, 143-65. Cardiff: University of Wales Press, 1992.

————. "Politics, Freedom and Order: Kant's Political Philosophy." In *The Cambridge Companion to Kant,* edited by P. Guyer, 342-67. Cambridge: Cambridge University Press, 1992.

————. *Wohlgeordnete Freiheit: Immanuel Kants Rechts- und Staatsphilosophie.* Berlin: De Gruyter, 1984.

Knippenberg, J. "Moving beyond Fear: Rousseau and Kant on Cosmopolitan Education." *Journal of Politics* (1989): 809-27.

Koontz, T.J. "Christian Nonviolence: An Interpretation." In *The Ethics of War and Peace: Religious and Secular Perspectives,* edited by T. Nardin, 169-96. Princeton, NJ: Princeton University Press, 1996.

Korsgaard, C. *Creating the Kingdom of Ends.* Cambridge, MA: Harvard University Press, 1996.

————. "Kant's Formula of Humanity." *Kant-Studien* (1986): 183-202.

————————. "Kant's Formula of Universal Law." *Pacific Philosophical Quarterly* (1985): 24-47.

Kratochwil, F.V. *Rules, Norms and Decisions*. Cambridge: Cambridge University Press, 1991.

Laberge, P. "Humanitarian Intervention: Three Ethical Positions." *Ethics and International Affairs* (1995): 15-35.

Laberge, P., editor. *Actes du Congres d'Ottawa sur Kant*. Ottawa: Université d'Ottawa, 1976.

Lackey, D. *The Ethics of War and Peace*. Englewood Cliffs, NJ: Prentice Hall, 1989.

Ladd, J. "The Idea of Collective Violence." In *Justice, Law and Violence,* edited by J. Brady and N. Garver, 19-47. Philadelphia, PA: Temple University Press, 1991.

Larman, E. *Nuclear Pacifism: "Just War" Thinking Today*. New York: Lang, 1984.

Latham, N. "Causally Irrelevant Reasons and Action Solely from the Motive of Duty." *The Journal of Philosophy* (1994): 599-618.

Lauterpacht, H. *International Law*. Cambridge: Cambridge University Press, 1977-78.

————————. *International Law and Human Rights*. New York: Archon Books, 1968.

Levinson, S. "Responsibility for the Crimes of War." *Philosophy and Public Affairs* (1972-73): 244-73.

Little, D. "The "Just War" Doctrine and U.S. Policy in Vietnam." In *On the Endings of Wars,* edited by S. Albert and E. Luck, 157-71. London: Kennikat Press, 1980.

Luban, D. "Just War and Human Rights." *Philosophy and Public Affairs* (1979/80): 160-81.

————————. "The Romance of The Nation-State." *Philosophy and Public Affairs* (1979-80): 392-97.

Ludwig, B. "'The Right of a State' in Immanuel Kant's Doctrine of Right." *Journal of the History of Philosophy* (1990): 403-15.

Luper-Foy, S., editor. *Problems of International Justice*. Boulder, CO: Westview, 1988.

Lynch, C. "Kant, the Republican Peace, and Moral Guidance in International Law." *Ethics and International Affairs* (1994): 39-58.

Lyons, D. "Human Rights and the General Welfare." *Philosophy and Public Affairs* (1976/77): 113-29.

MacKinnon, C. "Crimes of War, Crimes of Peace." In *On Human Rights,* edited by S. Shute and S. Hurley, 83-110. New York: Basic Books, 1993.

Malvrodes, G. "Conventions and The Laws of War." *Philosophy and Public Affairs* (1975): 117-31.

Mapel, D. "Realism and The Ethics of War and Peace." In *The Ethics of War and Peace: Religious and Secular Perspectives,* edited by T. Nardin, 54-77. Princeton, NJ: Princeton University Press, 1996.

————. "The Contractarian Tradition and International Ethics." In *Traditions of International Ethics,* edited by T. Nardin and D. Mapel, 180-200. Cambridge: Cambridge University Press, 1992.

McCall, M. and O. Ramsbotham, editors. *Just Deterrence: Morality and Deterrence into the Twenty-First Century.* London: Brassey's Press, 1990.

McMahan, J. "Realism, Morality and War." In *The Ethics of War and Peace: Religious and Secular Perspectives,* edited by T. Nardin, 78-92. Princeton, NJ: Princeton University Press, 1996.

————. "Self-Defence and The Problem of The Innocent Attacker." *Ethics* (1994): 252-90.

Mertens, T. "War and International Order in Kant's Legal Thought." *Ratio Juris* (1995): 296-314.

Miller, R., editor. *The Law of War.* Lexington, MA: Lexington Books, 1975.

Miller, R.B. *Interpretations of Conflict: Ethics, Pacifism and the Just War Tradition.* Chicago: University of Chicago Press, 1991.

Miller, S. "Killing in Self-Defence." *Public Affairs Quarterly* (1993): 325-39.

Montague, P. "Self-Defence and Choosing between Lives." *Philosophical Studies* (1981): 207-20.

Moore, J.N. *Crisis in the Gulf: Enforcing the Rule of Law.* Dobbs Ferry, NY: Oceana, 1992.

Moore, J.N. editor. *Law and Civil War in the Modern World.* Baltimore, MD: Johns Hopkins University Press, 1974.

Morgenthau, H. *Politics among Nations.* New York: Knopf, 5th ed., 1973.

Mulholland, L. *Kant's System of Rights.* New York: Columbia University Press, 1994.

————. "Kant on War and International Justice." *Kant-Studien* (1987): 25-41.

Murphy, J. *Kant: The Philosophy of Right.* London: Macmillan, 1970.

Meyers, D. "Kant's Liberal Alliance: A Permanent Peace?" In *Political Realism and International Morality,* edited by K. Kipnis and D. Meyers, 212-19. Boulder, CO: Westview, 1987.

Myers, R.J. "Notes on the Just War Theory: Whose Justice, Which Wars?" *Ethics and International Affairs* (1996): 116-30.

Nagel, T. "Ruthlessness in Public Life." In *Mortal Questions,* written by T. Nagel, 75-90. Cambridge: Cambridge University Press, 1979.

————. "War and Massacre." *Philosophy and Public Affairs* (1971/72): 123-43.

Nardin, T. *Law, Morality and the Relations of States.* Princeton, NJ: Princeton University Press, 1983.

Nardin, T., editor. *The Ethics of War and Peace: Religious and Secular Perspectives*. Princeton, NJ: Princeton University Press, 1996.

Nardin, T. and D. Mapel, editors. *Traditions of International Ethics*. Cambridge: Cambridge University Press, 1992.

Narveson, J. "Force, Violence and Law." In *Justice, Law and Violence*, edited by J. Brady and N. Garver, 149-69. Philadelphia, PA: Temple University Press, 1991.

——————. "Pacifism: A Philosophical Analysis." In *War and Morality*, edited by R. Wasserstrom, 63-78. Belmont, CA: Wadsworth, 1970.

——————. "Terrorism and Morality." In *Violence, Terrorism, and Justice*, edited by R. Frey and C. Morris, 116-69. Cambridge: Cambridge University Press, 1991.

——————. "Violence and War." In *Matters of Life and Death*, edited by T. Regan, 109-47. Philadelphia, PA: Temple University Press, 1980.

Newcombe, H. *Design for a Better World*. Lanham, MD: University Press of America, 1983.

Nickel, J. *Making Sense of Human Rights*. Berkeley, CA: University of California Press, 1985.

Niebuhr, R. *Christianity and Power Politics*. New York: Charles Scribner's Sons, 1940.

Norman, R. *Ethics, Killing and War*. Cambridge: Cambridge University Press, 1995.

Nozick, R. *Anarchy, State and Utopia*. New York: Basic Books, 1974.

Nussbaum, M. "Human Functioning and Social Justice." *Political Theory* (1992): 202-46.

Nussbaum, M., et al., *For Love of Country: Debating the Limits of Patriotism*. Boston: Beacon, 1996.

Oberer, H, editor. *Kant: Analysen, Probleme, Kritik*. Konisberg: Konighausen & Neumann, 1996.

O'Brien, W. *The Conduct of Just and Limited War*. New York: Praeger, 1981.

——————. *The Law of Limited Armed Conflict*. Washington, DC: Georgetown University Press, 1965.

——————. *U.S. Military Intervention: Law and Morality*. Beverly Hills, CA: Sage, 1979.

O'Brien, W. and J. Langan, editors. *The Nuclear Dilemma and the Just War Tradition*. Lexington, MA: Lexington Books, 1986.

O'Connell, R. *Of Arms and Men: A History of War, Weapons, and Aggression*. Oxford: Oxford University Press, 1989.

O'Neill, O. *Constructions of Reason: An Exploration of Kant's Practical Philosophy*. Cambridge: Cambridge University Press, 1989.

——————. "Hunger, Needs and Rights." In *Problems of International Justice*, edited by S. Luper-Foy, 67-83. Boulder, CO: Westview, 1988.

——————. "The Public Use of Reason." *Political Theory* (1986): 523-51.

—————. "Which Are the Offers You Can't Refuse?" In *Violence, Terrorism, and Justice,* edited by R. Frey and C. Morris, 170-95. Cambridge: Cambridge University Press, 1991.

Oren, N. *Termination of War: Processes, Procedures and Aftermaths.* Jerusalem: Hebrew University Press, 1982.

Orend, Brian. *Michael Walzer on Justice.* Cardiff: University of Wales Press (forthcoming, 2001).

—————. "Evaluating Pacifism." *Dialogue* (forthcoming, 2001).

—————. "Innocence and Emergency: Walzer's Theory of *Jus in Bello.*" *Law and Philosophy* (forthcoming, 2001).

—————. "*Jus Post Bellum.*" *Journal of Social Philosophy* (forthcoming, spring 2000).

—————. "A Just War Critique of Realism and Pacifism." *Journal of Philosophical Research* (forthcoming, winter 2000).

—————. "Kant's Just War Theory." *Journal of the History of Philosophy* (April 1999): 323-53.

—————. "Review" of H. Williams, et al., *Francis Fukuyama and the End of History,* in *Canadian Philosophical Reviews* (June 1999).

—————. "Terminating War and Establishing Global Governance." *Canadian Journal of Law and Jurisprudence* (July 1999): 253-95.

—————. "Armed Intervention: Principles and Cases." *Flinders Journal of History and Politics* (March 1998): 5-32.

—————. "Kant on International Law and Armed Conflict." *Canadian Journal of Law and Jurisprudence* (July 1998): 329-81.

—————. "Review" of R. Beiner and W.J. Booth, editors, *Kant and Political Philosophy,* in *Canadian Philosophical Reviews* (August 1996): 241-43.

Osgood, R. and R. Tucker, editors. *Force, Order and Justice.* Baltimore, MD: Johns Hopkins University Press, 1967.

Otsuka, M. "Killing the Innocent in Self-Defense." *Philosophy and Public Affairs* (1992): 74-94.

Paskins, B. and M. Dockrill, *The Ethics of War.* Minneapolis, MN: University of Minnesota Press, 1979.

Paton, H.J. *In Defense of Reason.* London: Hutchinson's Library, 1951.

—————. *The Categorical Imperative.* Philadelphia, PA: University of Pennsylvania Press, 1971.

Peffer, R. "A Defense of Rights to Well-Being." *Philosophy and Public Affairs* (1978/79): 65-87.

Peirce, A. "Just War Principles and Economic Sanctions." *Ethics and International Affairs* (1996): 99-113.

Pennock, J., editor. *Nomos, XXIII: Human Rights.* New York: New York University Press, 1981.

Phillips, R. *War and Justice.* Oklahoma City, OK: University of Oklahoma Press, 1984.

Pippin, R. "On the Moral Foundations of Kant's Rechtslehre." In *The Philosophy of Immanuel Kant,* edited by R. Kennington, 107-42. Washington, DC: Catholic University Press of America, 1985.

Pogge, T. *Realizing Rawls.* Ithaca, NY: Cornell University Press, 1989.

————. "A Global Resources Dividend." In *Ethics of Consumption,* edited by D.A. Crocker and T. Linden, 501-36. Lanham, MD: Rowman Littlefield, 1998.

————. "The Bounds of Nationalism." In *Rethinking Nationalism,* edited by J. Couture, et al., 463-504. Calgary, AB: University of Calgary Press, 1998.

————. "Group Rights and Ethnicity." In *Nomos: Group Rights,* edited by W. Kymlicka, 198-224. New York: New York University Press, 1997.

————. "Kant on Ends and the Meaning of Life." In *Reclaiming the History of Ethics: Essays for John Rawls,* edited by A. Reath, 361-87. Cambridge: Cambridge University Press, 1997.

————. "Coercion and Violence." In *Justice, Law and Violence,* edited by J. Brady and N. Garver, 65-69. Philadelphia, PA: Temple University Press, 1991.

————. "The Categorical Imperative." In *Grundlegung zur Metaphysik der Sitten,* edited by O. Hoffe, 172-93. Frankfurt: Vittori Klostermann, 1989.

————. "Moral Progress." In *Problems of International Justice,* edited by S. Luper-Foy, 283-304. Boulder, CO: Westview, 1988.

————. "Human Flourishing and Social Justice." *Social Philosophy and Policy* (1999): 333-61.

————. "Is Kant's Rechtslehre Comprehensive?" *Southern Journal of Philosophy* (1998): 161-87.

————. "Creating Supra-National Institutions Democratically." *Journal of Political Philosophy* (1997): 163-82.

————. "How Should Human Rights Be Conceived?" *Jahrbuch fur Recht und Ethik* (1995): 103-20.

————. "An Egalitarian Law of Peoples." *Philosophy and Public Affairs* (1994): 195-224.

————. "An Institutional Approach to Humanitarian Intervention." *Public Affairs Quarterly* (1992): 89-103.

————. "Cosmopolitanism and Sovereignty." *Ethics* (1992): 48-75.

————. "Kant's Theory of Justice." *Kant-Studien* (1988): 408-33.

————. "Rawls and Global Justice," *Canadian Journal of Philosophy* (1988).

————. "Liberalism and Global Justice: Hoffman and Nardin on Morality in International Affairs." *Philosophy and Public Affairs* (1987): 67-81.

Porter, B. *War and The Rise of The Modern State.* New York: Macmillan, 1994.

Ramsey, P. *The Just War: Force and Political Responsibility.* New York: Charles Scribner's Sons, 1968.

——————. *War and the Christian Conscience: How Shall Modern War Be Conducted Justly?* Durham, NC: Duke University Press, 1961.

Rawls, J. *A Theory of Justice.* Cambridge, MA: Harvard University Press, 1971.

——————. "The Law of Peoples." In *On Human Rights,* edited by S. Shute and S. Hurley, 41-82. New York: Basic Books, 1993.

——————. "Themes in Kant's Moral Philosophy." In *Kant and Political Philosophy: The Contemporary Legacy,* edited by R. Beiner and W. Booth, 291-319. New Haven, CT: Yale University Press, 1993.

——————. "The Basic Structure as Subject." In *Values and Morals,* edited by A. Goldman and J. Kim, 30-48. Dordrecht: Reidel, 1978.

——————. Untitled, in *Dissent's* Summer 1995 symposium on the bombing of Hiroshima.

Raz, J. "The Nature of Rights." *Mind* (1984): 35-52.

——————. "Rights and Individual Well-Being." *Ratio Juris* (July 1992): 79-94.

Regan, R. *The Moral Dimensions of Politics.* New York: Oxford University Press, 1986.

——————. *Just War: Principles and Cases.* Washington, DC: Catholic University of America Press, 1996.

Reisman, W.M. "International Law after the Cold War," *American Journal of International Law* (1990): 859-76.

Reisman, W.M. and C. Antoniou, editors. *The Laws of War.* New York: Vintage, 1994.

Reitan, E. "The Irreconcilability of Pacifism and Just War Theory: A Response to Sterba." *Social Theory and Practice* (1994): 117-34.

Riley, P. *Kant's Political Philosophy.* Totowa, NJ: Rowman Littlefield, 1983.

——————. "The Elements of Kant's Practical Philosophy." In *Kant and Political Philosophy: The Contemporary Legacy,* edited by R. Beiner and W. Booth, 9-37. New Haven, CT: Yale University Press, 1993.

Robinson, H., editor. *Proceedings of the Eighth International Kant Congress.* Milwaukee, WN: Marquette University Press, 1995.

Rosas, A. "Emergency Regimes: A Comparison." In *Broadening the Frontiers of Human Rights,* edited by D. Gomien, 165-200. Olso, Norway: Scandinavian University Press, 1993.

Rosen, A. *Kant's Theory of Justice.* Ithaca, NY: Cornell University Press, 1993.

Ryan, C. "Self-Defence, Pacifism and Killing." *Ethics* (1983): 50-74.

Santiago, C. *The Ethics of Human Rights.* Oxford: Clarendon, 1991.

Scanlon, T. "Human Rights as a Neutral Concern." In *Human Rights and U.S. Foreign Policy,* edited by P. Brown and D. MacLean, 83-92. Lexington, MA: Lexington Books, 1977.

Scheffler, S. *The Rejection of Consequentialism.* Oxford: Oxford University Press, 2nd ed., 1994.

Scheffler, S., editor. *Consequentialism and Its Critics.* Oxford: Oxford University Press, 1988.

Schneewind, J.B. "Autonomy, Obligation and Virtue: An Overview of Kant's Moral Philosophy." In *The Cambridge Companion to Kant,* edited by P. Guyer, 309-41. Cambridge: Cambridge University Press, 1992.

Scott, J. B., editor. *Classics of International Law.* Washington, DC: Carnegie Institute, 1917. (Contains relevant works by Grotius, Vattel, Vittoria and Suarez).

Sen, A. "Rights and Agency." *Philosophy and Public Affairs* (1982): 4-39.

Shell, S. *The Rights of Reason.* Toronto: University of Toronto Press, 1980.

————. "What Kant and Fichte Can Teach Us about Human Rights." In *The Philosophy of Immanuel Kant,* edited by R. Kennington, 143-58. Washington, DC: Catholic University Press of America, 1985.

Shue, H. *Basic Rights: Subsistence, Affluence and U.S. Foreign Policy.* Princeton, NJ: Princeton University Press, 2nd ed., 1996.

Shute, S. and S. Hurley, editors. *On Human Rights.* New York: Basic Books, 1993.

Smith, M. "Liberalism and International Reform." In *The Ethics of War and Peace: Religious and Secular Perspectives,* edited by T. Nardin, 201-24. Princeton, NJ: Princeton University Press, 1996.

Sterba, J. *The Ethics of War and Nuclear Deterrence.* Belmont, CA: Wadsworth, 1985.

————. "Reconciling Pacifists and Just War Theorists." *Social Philosophy and Practice* (1994): 21-38.

Suganami, H. *The Domestic Analogy and World Order Proposals.* Cambridge: Cambridge University Press, 1989.

Sullivan, R. *An Introduction to Kant's Ethics.* Cambridge: Cambridge University Press, 1994.

Symposium on the Future of State Sovereignty. *Harvard International Review* (Summer 1995).

Symposium on Gulf War and International Law. *American Journal of International Law,* July 1991.

Symposium on War, the UN Charter and the War Powers in the American Constitution. *American Journal of International Law,* January 1991.

Taylor, A.J.P. *How Wars End.* London: Hamilton, 1985.

Teichman, J. *Pacifism and the Just War.* Oxford: Basil Blackwell, 1986.

Teson, F. "The Kantian Theory of International Law." *Columbia Law Review* (1992): 50-101.

Thompson, K.W. *Political Realism and the Crisis of World Politics.* Princeton, NJ: Princeton University Press, 1960.

Thomson, J.J. *The Realm of Rights.* Cambridge, MA: Harvard University Press, 1992.

——————. *Rights, Risk and Restitution.* Cambridge, MA: Harvard University Press, 1986.

——————. "Self-Defense," *Philosophy and Public Affairs* (1991): 283-310.

Tucker, R. *The Just War: A Study in Contemporary American Doctrine.* Baltimore, MD: Johns Hopkins University Press, 1960.

Uniacke, S. *Permissible Killing: The Self-Defence Justification of Homicide.* Cambridge: Cambridge University Press, 1995.

United Nations. *The United Nations and Human Rights, 1945-95.* New York: United Nations, 1995.

U.S. Catholic Bishops. *The Challenge of Peace: God's Promise and Our Response.* Washington, DC: U.S. Catholic Conference, 1983.

Van der Linden, H. *Kantian Ethics and Socialism.* Cambridge: Cambridge University Press, 1988.

Van Glahen, G. *Law among Nations.* New York: Macmillan, 1986.

Vaux, K. *Ethics and the Gulf War.* Boulder, CO: Westview, 1992.

Waldron, J. "Kant's Legal Positivism." *Harvard Law Review* (1996): 135-80.

Waltz, K. *Man, the State and War.* Princeton, NJ: Princeton University Press, 1978.

——————. "Kant, Liberalism and War." *American Political Science Review* (1962): 842-50.

Walzer, M. *Thick and Thin: Moral Argument at Home and Abroad.* Notre Dame, IN: Notre Dame University Press, 1994.

——————. *Just and Unjust Wars: A Moral Argument with Historical Illustrations.* New York: Basic Books, 2nd ed., 1991.

——————. *Obligations: Citizenship, War and Disobedience.* Harvard: Harvard University Press, 1970.

——————. "The Reform of the International System." In *Studies of War and Peace,* edited by O. Osterud, 227-50. Oslo: Norwegian University Press, 1986.

——————. "Moral Judgment in Time of War." In *War and Morality,* edited by R. Wasserstrom, 54-62. Blemont, CA: Wadsworth, 1970

——————. "The Moral Standing of States: A Response to Four Critics." *Philosophy and Public Affairs* (1979/80): 209-29.

——————. "World War II: Why Was This War Different?" *Philosophy and Public Affairs* (1971/72): 3-21.

Ward, I. "Kant and the Transnational Order: Towards a European Community Jurisprudence." *Ratio Juris* (1995): 315-29.

Wasserman, D. "Justifying Self-Defense." *Philosophy and Public Affairs* (1987): 356-78.

Wasserstrom, R. "The Relevance of Nuremberg." *Philosophy and Public Affairs* (1971-72): 22-46.

Wasserstrom, R., editor. *War and Morality.* Belmont, CA: Wadsworth, 1970.

Weigel, G. and P. Langan, editors. *The American Search for Peace: Moral Reasoning, Religious Hope and National Security*. Washington, DC: Georgetown University Press, 1991.

Weinrib, E. "Law as a Kantian Idea of Reason." *Columbia Law Review* (1987): 472-508.

Wellman, C. "Violence, Law and Basic Rights." In *Justice, Law and Violence*, edited by J. Brady and N. Garver, 170-86. Philadelphia, PA: Temple University Press, 1991.

Wells, D.A. *An Encyclopedia of War and Ethics*. Westport, CT: Greenwood, 1996.

Wiggins, D. *Needs, Values and Truth*. Oxford: Basil Blackwell, 1986.

Williams, H. *International Relations and the Limits of Political Theory*. New York: St. Martin's, 1996.

————. *International Relations in Political Theory*. Philadelphia, PA: Open University Press, 1992.

————. *Kant's Political Philosophy*. Oxford: Oxford University Press, 1983.

————. "Judgments on War: A Response." In *Proceedings of The Eighth International Kant Congress*, edited by H. Robinson, 1393-96. Milwaukee, WI: Marquette University Press, 1995.

Williams, H., editor. *Essays on Kant's Political Philosophy*. Cardiff: University of Wales Press, 1992.

Yack, B. "The Problem with Kantian Liberalism." In *Kant and Political Philosophy: The Contemporary Legacy*, edited by R. Beiner and W. Booth, 224-44. New Haven, CT: Yale University Press, 1993.

Yoder, John. *When War Is Unjust: Being Honest in Just-War Thinking*. Minneapolis, MN: Augsburg Press, 1984.

Zohar, N. "Collective War and Individualistic Ethics: Against the Conscription of 'Self-Defence'." *Political Theory* 21 (1993): 606-22.

Index

Index